COLLECTOR'S ENCYCLOPEDIA OF

PORCELAIN

Third Edition

Mary Frank Gaston

COLLECTOR BOOKS
A Division of Schroeder Publishing Co., Inc.

The current values of this book should be used only as a guide. They are not intended to set prices, which vary from one section of the country to another. Auction prices as well as dealer prices vary and are affected by condition as well as demand. Neither the author nor the publisher assumes responsibility for any losses that might be incurred as a result of consulting this guide.

Cover design by Beth Summers

Book design by Joyce Cherry

OTHER BOOKS BY MARY FRANK GASTON

Searching for a Publisher?

We are always looking for knowledgeable people considered to be experts within their fields. If you feel there is a real need for a book on your collectible subject and have a large comprehensive collection, contact Collector Books.

Collector Books
P. O. Box 3009
Paducah, KY 42002-3009

www.collectorbooks.com

CONTENTS

ACKNOWLEDGMENTS

First I would like to thank Collector Books and the publishers, Bill and Billy Schroeder, for publishing this new edition on Limoges porcelain. In 1979, Bill Schroeder accepted the proposal for my first book which was the first edition on this subject. Since that time, I have written about a number of other types of china. This edition will be my twentieth title released by Collector Books. I appreciate their support throughout this period. I also thank Lisa C. Stroup, editor at Collector Books, and her hard-working staff. They work as a team to ensure that the result is a professionally produced product.

For this revised third edition, I am indebted to a large number of individuals who contributed photographs and information. I really would not have been able to illustrate so well the variety of pieces, decorations, and marks of Limoges porcelain without the help of these collectors.

I thank Quentin "Reed" Welty, and his wife Gloria, who also were contributors to the second edition. Mr. Welty has been of immeasurable help on this new edition. He is a long-time collector of Limoges, and he has generously shared his knowledge and photographs with me over the years. His extensive Limoges collection is a study in itself, encompassing a wide selection of pieces, marks, and decoration. In addition to photographing his own collection, he also took the time and effort to travel to antique shows and visit dealers in order to photograph other beautiful and unique examples to send to me. He and I both thank the following for their assistance and cooperation: Luis Castillo, Margaret-Ann Duchant, Janet Post, and Georgie Radick.

I thank Dr. William H. King who is also an avid Limoges collector. His collection presented not only a variety of pieces and marks, but also many signatures of Limoges artists. A large number of pieces in this edition are from his collection. He graciously allowed me to "pick and choose" from his meticulously arranged photograph albums of Limoges. The detailed information about each piece was extremely helpful for studying not only his pieces but others' examples as well.

I thank Mr. and Mrs. Robert B. Yerby and their daughter and son-in-law, Mr. and Mrs. Edward J. Stein. It is wonderful, and very beneficial to me, that the whole family enjoys collecting Limoges porcelain! I do appreciate the outstanding pictures of lovely pieces and some new decorations which have not appeared in any of my earlier books. A number of the new Limoges marks which have been added for this edition were also provided by the Yerbys and Steins.

I thank Debby DuBay. Ms. DuBay is not only a collector, but she is also a dealer in Limoges porcelain. Her antique shop, in fact, is called, "Limoges Antique Shop!" I am happy to see a retail specialization for Limoges porcelain. From the photos she sent showing displays at her business, a collector would consider it to be Limoges heaven! Ms. DuBay was very helpful in providing pictures of beautiful hand-painted Limoges porcelain from her shop and her private collection. She also advised me concerning current price trends and popularity of certain types of pieces, based on her retail experience.

I thank Mr. and Mrs. Howard Lebovitz. Mrs. Lebovitz sent me pictures just a few months before I knew I would be writing this third edition. I am certainly glad I heard from them and did not miss being able to include Limoges from their collection. Their vases were particularly interesting, portraying a number of different shapes and decorations made by several manufacturers.

I thank Mr. Gilbert W. Higgs who generously responded when I wrote him to see if he could contribute to this edition. A variety of sets of china compose part of his large collection. These sets are not limited to table ware patterns but include outstanding cherub, fish, and game decorations.

I thank Mrs. Pauline V. Stauffer. Her collection includes a number of different table ware patterns made by Tressemann & Vogt. Collectors may find some designs which they have not seen among those pieces. They may also be encouraged to specialize in a collection of one or more of these distinctive decorations.

I thank Raymonde Limoges. In addition to photographs, Ms. Limoges provided detailed information about the Pastaud Company. She also sent interesting materials about several other factories and marks. Some of these have been reprinted for the specific company.

I thank Nathalie and Robert Vogt. The Vogts have a direct connection to the Tressemann & Vogt Company. They were very helpful in furnishing me with additional background materials about the history of that firm. I know collectors will appreciate this information which adds another, more personal, dimension to the company.

I thank Mr. Mark W. Stuart with whom I have corresponded for several years. I appreciate the photographs he has sent over that time as well as his responding to my recent request for pictures from his collection. His pieces filled a variety of "slots" for this edition, adding information about marks as well as lovely examples of Limoges.

I thank Mr. and Mrs. Roy Barefield. Hand-painted

Limoges, decorated with fruit, particularly blackberries, is the particular focus of their collection. Such colorful pieces greatly enhance the photographs.

I thank Tim and Jeannie Coss, whose interest in different marks on Limoges has helped me very much in expanding the number of marks for this edition.

I thank Ms. Freda Van Winkle. Some years ago, Ms. Van Winkle wrote to me about her collection of Limoges miniatures. She sent me a video of her pieces which piqued my interest. She has been instrumental in encouraging me to include a chapter in this edition on "Limoges Miniatures." Ms. Van Winkle provided the pictures and information for most of the miniature polychrome plates. Of particular interest is the background information regarding the decoration themes on the miniature plates. Ms. Van Winkle lectures and presents programs on the subject of Limoges miniatures and other decorations on china.

I thank Mr. Clive Cramb who also contributed to the chapter on miniatures. His information about his collection helped me gain a broader perspective on the subject.

I thank Barb and Bob Nelson who collect cobalt blue and gold Limoges miniatures. Photographs, not only of pieces, but also of the marks on those examples, as well as specific information regarding each, added greatly to this chapter. Their contribution illustrates an additional category of Limoges miniatures.

I thank Barbara J. Eckstein. Pictures from her collection of miniature Limoges boxes permitted me to include a brief discussion on this currently popular category of Limoges porcelain collectible. Ms. Eckstein also sent photographs of marks on the boxes which will be of interest to collectors.

Although the above collectors contributed the majority of the photographs for this third edition, I also thank the following people whose contributions were vital. Their help, even if it was only one picture of an interesting piece or shape; a particular pattern or different decoration; or a new mark or a variation of a mark, greatly enlarged the scope of this book and provided information which will benefit all Limoges collectors. I thank each one of you very much.

HelenLu Anderson
Bill Atzenhoffer
Jeffrey S. Barker
Dorothy M. Barrow
Pat Beasley
Carla B. Benhardt
Priscilla and Ludy Benjamin
Mrs. Lyle L. Bilby
Carla Bittner
June A. and Ernest L. Brown
Lewis Brown
Rick Brown
Harriett Burnett
Betty E. Bryner
Lorraine Caffall
R. H. Capers
Kristie Chiron
Rae Choma
Sandra Claver
Robin and Dave Collett
Ann Cusack
Mr. and Mrs. James S. Daley
Muriel Davis
Jean P. Dolan
Vicki Douglas
Jeanne S. Elder
Dr. Stuart P. Embury
Audrey Fairchild

Phyllis Feder
Grace B. Franklin
Jean L. Friedman
Blake W. Fuller
Diane George
Larry Gollmer
Robin Guyer
Judy Habraken
Pam Haisty
Gloria and Michael Hamfeldt
Julie Harper
Lynne M. Harren
Diane Hart
Lois Hasel
Jeanne Haxton
Jon Hays
F. E. Helbig
Patrick J. Higgins
Claire Hohnstein
Bobby T. Hughes
Tim Hurkmans
Phyllis Jacobs
Richard R. Jeffrey
Donna Johnson
Iva Johnson
Amy Jones
A. Kaning
Trevor Kartarik

Claire Kaufman
Darby Kelly
Betty King
La Tours Antiques
Marena Lagerstrom
Jerry Litka
Mary and Lance Loring
Diane and Maurice McGee
Marcia Maerten
Barbara W. Manning
Heather Maze
Dorothy Megee
Mr. and Mrs. George Milam
Deborah Miles
Ryan Moe
Sharon Moret
Jeffrey and Tamar Myers
Susan S. Olsson
Garnet M. Palmer
Richard Paroutaud
Ernie Pauscher
Janet Peppers
Donald C. Pharris
Mary Phillips
Eleanor H. Pike
Anne and Steven Pinchen
Jacques Plainemaison
Richard and Pat Platzek

Harry Poulos
Terri Prusack
Suzanne L. Richard
River Oaks Antique Center
William and Beatrice Ross
Edward S. Rutkowski
J. Pat Samter
Jacqueline San Pedro
Diane Sargent
Ginger R. Schilling
Gerald Schultz
Audrey and Dan Shanahan
Timothy D. Sharnas
Howard Sheffield
Allison Sheldon

Sandy Sher
Ellen Simon
Charlene S. Smith
Lota Smith
Mrs. Raymond Snider
Doris and Lowell Sonderman
Peter P. Spirito
Barbara Stepp
Marie Stine
Helen Strong
Elsie M. Sullivan
Victoria J. Sweeney
Sara A. Taylor
Penny Temple
Sue and Glenn Tingley

Margaret F. Toler
In memory of Mr. and Mrs. Felix Tryka
Chris Vargo
Judy Verschell
Lisa Waldron
Carol Wasdin
Marceline White
Coralyn Whitney
Jan and Richard Wilson
Ann and Peter Wood
Sabra Woody
William Wynn
Sarah M. Zafra
Marian Zickefoose

Finally, I thank my husband, Jerry, for photographing our collection and for sharing my interest in Limoges porcelain which has made collecting and writing about Limoges so much more fun over the last two decades.

PREFACE

My interest in Limoges porcelain began over twenty-five years ago, when I opened a china shop specializing in porcelain dinner services made during the late 1800s through the 1930s. These sets were manufactured by various companies in America, England, France, Czechoslovakia, and Germany. In the course of acquiring those services, I found many with "Limoges" stamped on the back, combined with, or incorporated within marks and initials which I did not recognize. I knew, however, that they were not the marks of the well-known Haviland Company which had been established in Limoges, France, during the mid 1800s. I was familiar with the marks of the Haviland Company because good reference materials were available, not only for the marks of the company, but also for the history, prices, and even patterns of that firm. However, I had a difficult time documenting the other Limoges marks, and often I could not.

As time passed and I gained experience through attending and exhibiting at antique shows, I discovered many other objects that carried Limoges marks. Most of these pieces were beautifully decorated and often hand painted. Examples included both large and ornate objects, such as vases, jardinieres, and tankards, as well as small decorative pieces such as trinket boxes, inkwells, and chamber sticks. The beauty, craftsmanship, and artwork, in addition to the variety of objects, fascinated me. I soon discovered that I was not alone in my appreciation of this porcelain. Dealers and collectors considered Limoges porcelain a recognized category of antiques.

I began buying examples of hand-painted Limoges for resale, in addition to dinnerware patterns, and table china. I

was pleased to find that such objects sold well. As my interest in "Limoges" marked objects increased, I wanted to find out more about the individual items. Very little information was available either from books of marks, history sources, or general antiques reference books. The information that was available was widely scattered, and as I have learned since, much was incorrect. Some sources would have information about one company, but the same facts might be missing from another source which might have information about marks or companies not included in the first source. Sometimes the information was conflicting. In order to find marks, I often had to find "Limoges" in the index and then proceed to look up each page listed under that name. Price guides sometimes included a Limoges section, but the information rarely listed the name of the company of manufacture. Usually items were just described according to type, size, and style of decoration with no company name or mark attributed to them.

From other antique dealers, I discovered that even though they might have beautiful examples of Limoges porcelain for sale, they did not always know about the history of the articles, except that they were French. Knowledge was scant concerning marks on the pieces. Some might say, "This is D. and C. Limoges," or "This is T. and V. Limoges," but who or what was "D. and C." or "T. and V."? Did these initials stand for a specific company? Did one company use one or several combinations of initials? What did two or three different marks indicate on an object? How old was the piece? Such specific questions were often answered with, "Well, all I know is that this (object) is Limoges." It seemed that the name "Limoges" spoke for the porcelain. The eye can see the beauty and craftsmanship of the piece. Knowledgeable dealers and collectors can tell by the feel, shape, type, and decoration of an article that the object was not made yesterday, that it is indeed old enough to warrant being collectible. But whether we are collectors of antique china or merely buyers of an antique as a decorative accessory or a gift, we like to know as much as possible about what we are buying. We want to know where it came from, who made it, and what it was used for, if that is not obvious.

Thus, my purpose in writing my first edition on Limoges porcelain was to provide, all in one source, information on the history, marks, products, and current market prices for the china manufactured and exported by companies in Limoges, France, from about 1850 to World War II. I concentrated on that particular time period not only because it would be an impossible task to document the hundreds of names (factories, decorators, exporters) associated with the Limoges porcelain industry since its start in the late 1700s through today, but also because the chosen era represented the height of the Limoges porcelain industry's export trade to the United States. It also coincided with, or was responsible for, the popularity of china painting in America. This avocation and vocation relied heavily on blanks furnished by the Limoges factories, and examples were and continue to be prevalent on the collectible china market.

In my research, I was greatly aided by some American and European publications which supplied helpful information and enabled me to start piecing together the puzzle of Limoges porcelain. After the first edition had gone to press, a superb reference, in French, was released, *La Porcelaine de Limoges,* by Jean d'Albis and Céleste Romanet. If that book had been published earlier, many of the conflicting points about various companies would have been clarified. That book remains the definitive source on the history of the Limoges porcelain industry. It is footnoted here, as it was in my second edition, for information concerning a number of Limoges companies. Please see, too, all other entries in the Bibliography for further and more detailed study of the subject of Limoges porcelain.

I am very pleased to be able to write this third revised edition. Since the first edition was published in 1980, now 20 years ago, interest in Limoges porcelain has increased tremendously. This is evident from the amount of Limoges porcelain offered for sale at antique auctions, shops, and shows across the country and, of course, on the Internet. Mail from collectors has also greatly increased over this time span, and happily, sales of the book have also increased. Prices of Limoges pieces reflect the surging interest as well, which is great if you are selling, but costly if you are buying.

In the first edition, Limoges companies were listed alphabetically along with the marks of those companies in one section of the book. The examples of Limoges porcelain followed. They were shown by object and decoration rather than by specific factory or mark. No differentiation was made between French decorated Limoges and Limoges

blanks decorated by American china painters. In the second edition, I divided the examples by origin of decoration, separating the French decorated pieces from the American decorated pieces. The histories of the companies were presented at the end of the book, and the marks of the various factories were also shown in a separate section.

In this third edition, I decided to make a major change in format. Because collectors are much more knowledgeable today about Limoges factories and marks, I have arranged the book by company and/or mark. Examples are arranged by the overglaze mark of a particular company, that is the decorating or exporting mark. For instance, a piece may have a Redon underglaze mark but an Ahrenfeldt overglaze mark, thus the example is shown under Ahrenfeldt; or the item may have a Coiffe underglaze mark and an L.S. and S. (Straus) overglaze mark, and the example is shown under the L. S. & S. mark. I have grouped information about a company, the marks used by the company, and the examples made by the company. Another change in this edition is a great increase of photographs with over twice as many pieces shown. Some pictures have been reprinted from the first and second editions because they show a mark, decoration, or object of collector interest. Marks have been increased for several companies, and some other companies have been included which were not in the previous editions. A number of unidentified marks have also been added. Hopefully, information may be found about some of these in the future.

Please note that several major Limoges companies are listed as one entry because one company was the successor to the other such as Délinières and Bernardaud; Charles Field Haviland, Gérard, Dufraisseix, and Abbot, and Gérard, Duffraisseix and Morel; David Haviland and Theodore Haviland; Martial Redon and La Porcelaine Limousine; and Tressemann & Vogt and Raynaud. Because marks are similar, as well as patterns and molds, grouping these companies better illustrates the history and continuity of the factories. Specific marks on the examples are noted in the captions. Reference to particular color of mark is not included, because the number of the mark indicates the color and whether the mark is an underglaze factory mark or an overglaze decorating mark. In the photograph section for each company, the factory and French decorated pieces are shown first, followed by the Limoges blanks decorated by American china painters. Current values are included with the descriptions of each piece. I think this type of format will make it easier for the beginner as well as the advanced collector, dealer, and appraiser to identify, document, and price examples of Limoges porcelain.

The first chapter of this edition is devoted to the history of the Limoges porcelain industry and to identifying and evaluating Limoges porcelain. The second chapter includes the histories, marks, and examples of the major (or most representative of the American market) Limoges factories, from the mid 1800s through the 1930s, or the pre World War II era. The third chapter lists other Limoges companies and marks and their examples. The china made by these companies is generally found less frequently. The fourth chapter focuses on marks and examples of unidentified Limoges companies. Initials and various symbols as well as a number of ambiguous "Limoges, France" marks will be found in this chapter. Blanks, or undecorated Limoges porcelain, are shown in chapter five. Chapter six is devoted to blanks decorated by American professional art studios. In these two chapters, the examples were made by various factories.

Chapter seven is composed of names and marks of Limoges companies without examples. Some of these companies were mentioned in the first and/or second edition, and one might find them in other reference sources. Lack of many, if any, examples by those factories, however, indicates that their production was not geared to the American market, and thus no photographs are in this chapter.

Chapter eight addresses Limoges miniatures, an area of Limoges collecting which has not been included in either of

my other editions. Because of so many inquiries from collectors about the miniatures, I have added this subject, although these pieces are representative of Limoges made after my cut-off date of the 1930s. Most are no earlier than the 1940s to 1950s, and others are contemporary, from the 1980s and 1990s. This chapter is offered as a general introduction to the subject to help answer basic questions by collectors about the "minis."

The Index and Cross Reference to Limoges Companies, Initials, and Symbols has been maintained. This index is vital, especially for beginning collectors, to locate examples and information, if they are not familiar with company names or aware of what names are identified by various initials. An Index to Limoges Artists is also included.

Mary Frank Gaston
P. O. Box 342
Bryan, TX 77806

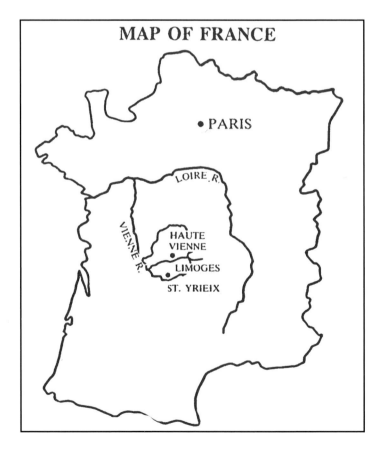

The Limousine region of France, an area of the country blessed with rich deposits of kaolin and feldspar.

Identifying and Collecting Limoges Porcelain

The Unique Quality of Porcelain

To fully understand and appreciate Limoges porcelain, a brief definition of porcelain, as well as a short discussion of how porcelain relates to other forms of pottery or china, is necessary.

Porcelain is pottery in its most exquisite form. The word "porcelain" comes from the Portuguese word *porcella,* the name for the shell made by a type of mollusk, the cowrie. This shell is translucent, and the Portuguese gave this name to the translucent pottery they were importing from China during the 1500s. To understand the unique quality of porcelain, translucency, it is necessary to understand the processes that each type of pottery requires for production. A brief summary here of these processes will give a basic understanding of the differences among the types of pottery. (Some references in the Bibliography give detailed descriptions.)

Pottery is any object made of clay and fired (or baked) at a high temperature. Clay is a form of earth. Earth, depending on its location, is composed of different natural ingredients. Thus the type of pottery which can be made in an area is determined by the presence and type of ingredients found in the earth in that area.

There are two types of pottery: earthenware and stoneware. Pottery is *earthenware* if it has a porosity of more than 5 percent. Earthenware articles may be waterproof if they are covered by a glaze, but the glaze and the body of the object are not fused together during the firing process. As a result, the glaze of earthenware can be penetrated. And, if the glaze is penetrated, crazing usually results. Crazing is tiny hairlines that develop under the glaze on the surface of the object. Crazing detracts from the appearance of the article and weakens it. Also if the glaze is penetrated, certain liquids which might come in contact with the surface of the object can cause staining or discoloration. Earthenware is not as durable as stoneware. Earthenware can be made from many different types of natural clays including kaolin, ball clay, and cornish stone. Earthenware is fired at temperatures below 1200 degrees centigrade which is lower than the temperature at which stoneware is fired. If a glaze is applied to the object, it is refired below 1100 degrees centigrade. Earthenware is opaque and may be glazed like majolica or remain unglazed like clay flower pots.

Pottery is *stoneware* if it has a porosity of less than 5 percent. Stoneware is fired at extremely high temperatures, 1200 to 1400 degrees centigrade. During the first firing, the body and glaze melt or fuse together and become vitrified, that is, like glass. This vitreous quality results in the low percentage of porosity. Stoneware can have but need not have additional glazes applied after the first firing, because the vitreous quality is achieved during the first firing. Stoneware is made from natural stoneware clays which are of a sedimentary type and fine grained. These clays are quite plastic, meaning that they can be worked with and shaped easily. Stoneware is opaque. Stoneware items are heavier than earthenware items. They are also harder and more durable. Basalt, ironstone, and certain types of crockery are examples of stoneware.

Technically, *porcelain* is considered to be a special type of stoneware. The reason for this is that porcelain, like stoneware, is fired to a state of vitrification. However stoneware is not fired to a state of translucency as porcelain is. Porcelain objects are first fired at a temperature of around 900 degrees centigrade. A glaze is then applied, and the article refired at from 1300 to 1500 degrees centigrade. Vitreosity is attained during this second firing. Although porcelain is vitreous, like stoneware, it is also translucent whereas other stoneware is opaque. Translucent means that light can pass through an object. Opaque means that light cannot pass through an object. Put your hand behind a plate, a cup, a bowl, or the bottom of a figurine and hold it up to the light. If it is porcelain, you will be able to see the shadow of your hand through the object. The better you can see the shadow, the thinner the porcelain. This translucent quality of porcelain is obtained from the type of ingredients used in the paste. Paste is the basic clay and other minerals which are mixed together to form a particular object.

After the object formed from the paste is fired for the first time, the resulting product is called bisque or biscuit, meaning unglazed. The bisque is translucent at this stage, but it is not vitreous. To achieve vitreosity, the object must be baked a second time with a glaze. It is during this second firing that the glaze and body melt together, resulting in a glass-like product. Articles can be decorated before or after the glaze is applied and the article baked the second time. More than one glaze and different colored glazes can be used.

Porcelain is whitish in color in its natural state before the glazes have been applied. If an object is not glazed and remains in the bisque form, it has a higher degree of porosity. Figurines are examples of porcelain which are often found in bisque. The base of some glazed wares may be left in bisque form to allow the object to grip a surface better. Glazed porcelain is slick like glass, so articles such as vases, dresser boxes, and trays are not as likely to slide on a surface if their base is unglazed. Some erroneously think that the object is not well made or not finished if the base is left as bisque.

The distinguishing characteristic of porcelain as compared to earthenware and other forms of stoneware is its translucency. Because of this difference, many prefer to divide pottery into three categories: earthenware, stoneware, and porcelain. The three classifications do seem more helpful for ease in identification.

Other differences between porcelain and earthenware and stoneware are that porcelain objects are not as heavy as stoneware and have a more delicate appearance. Earthenwares can be light in weight like porcelain, but they are not as strong. Porcelain will not craze as earthenware does. Porcelain objects may break or develop a crack if some force is applied. The break line will just appear where the force was applied, but the other parts of the surface will not develop lines or crazing. Porcelain is nonporous whereas earthenware is porous under the glaze. If the glaze of an earthenware object is penetrated, matter can become "trapped" under the glaze. Porcelain glazes cannot be penetrated. If some harmful substance comes into contact with the surface of porcelain, it can be washed off. The object will not be discolored or stained. Earthenware can be produced more cheaply than porcelain because it is fired at lower temperatures. The natural ingredients necessary to make both earthenware and stoneware exist in many areas throughout the world, but there are comparatively few areas in the world with deposits of the natural ingredients needed to make porcelain.

Porcelain is divided into three types: *bone paste, soft paste*, and *hard paste*. The paste type depends on the type and percentage of basic ingredients used as well as the process of manufacture. All three types are translucent in both the bisque and glazed states, they are light in weight but still strong, and they are vitreous if glazed.

Bone paste (or bone china) is so called because its principal ingredient is an ash made from calcined animal bone. This bone ash constitutes at least 50% of the paste with such materials as china clay and feldspar making up the rest of the formula. The paste is not as white in color as that of hard paste. Bone paste is stronger than soft paste porcelain, and the manufacturing process is cheaper than that of soft paste. Bone paste is fired at a lower temperature than hard paste. The product is first fired unglazed to a translucent state at a temperature of over 1200 degrees centigrade. It is fired a second time with the glaze at a lower temperature, below 1100 degrees centigrade. The Spode, Worcester, and Wedgwood factories introduced bone china in England during the latter part of the 1700s and early 1800s. England is still the

center for this type of porcelain production.

Soft paste porcelain is known as *pâte tendre* or *petit feu* in French. The latter term refers to the degree of temperature needed for the firing process which is lower than those required for bone paste and hard paste. The porcelain is not actually "soft." Objects are first fired at about 1100 degrees centigrade and at a lower temperature with the glaze at the second firing. Due to the lower firing temperatures, this type of porcelain is not as durable as bone paste or hard paste. The glazes can be scratched, and there is thus some degree of porosity under the glaze.

Europeans long admired the hard paste porcelain products of China, but they did not know the formula for this type of manufacture. During the 1600s, primarily in France, soft paste production was begun as an attempt to imitate the hard paste Chinese porcelain. Soft paste was actually an artificial type of porcelain in those days. Glass or glasslike materials were ground up and mixed with clay and other ingredients. This glass matter was known as the frit and was necessary to cause the other materials in the paste to melt together and achieve the translucent and vitreous qualities. Lead was also used in the glazes to enable easier fusing of the glaze and the body. In the early days of soft paste production, the clay and glassy materials were often not well mixed, and the firing process was not evenly controlled. As a result some parts of an object were more translucent than other parts. Chemical analysis was not very sophisticated so often the proportion of ingredients varied, resulting in uneven quality products. Sometimes the pieces became warped and developed cracks during the firing. Many pieces of soft paste were wasted due to the inexact manufacturing process. Although the soft paste process is still costly today, the formulas can be exact and the firing process controlled. Also the natural ingredient feldspar is used instead of bits of glass to achieve translucency and vitreosity. Lead, which is harmful for table china, does not have to be used in the glazes.

Hard paste porcelain is known as *pâte duré* or *grand feu* in French, meaning that such porcelain is fired at very high temperatures. Hard paste is considered to be a natural porcelain because its ingredients exist in the earth. This is not the case with bone china, or the seventeenth and eighteenth century soft paste mixtures. Kaolin and feldspar are the principal ingredients for hard paste porcelain. Kaolin which accounts for about 50% of the paste is a type of earth containing hydrated aluminum silicates. The word comes from the Chinese "Kao-ling," the name of the mountain region in China where this type of earth was found many centuries ago. Feldspar or petuntze (petuntse) is the other important natural ingredient. Feldspar comes from a rock, and it is necessary both in the paste and the glaze. Feldspar adds strength to the paste, allowing the object to be fired at a high temperature and to become translucent. The glaze and object are made of similar materials, but the glaze contains a larger percentage both of feldspar and quartz enabling the glaze and paste object to melt together and fuse into one entity. The object is then vitreous or like glass. Hard paste objects are first fired at around 900 degrees centigrade. The second firing with the glaze is from 1400 to 1600 degrees centigrade.

The secret of making hard paste was not known in Europe until circa 1708. Johann Friedrich Böttger, an alchemist of Meissen (Germany), is credited with this discovery which led a few years later to the establishment of a hard paste factory in Meissen (the Meissen factory) and thus the first of its kind in Europe. Once the formula for "true" or "natural" porcelain was known, many of the problems and guesswork connected with earlier soft paste production were eliminated. When the natural ingredients of kaolin and feldspar were discovered in other regions, the potters of those areas were eager to turn to making hard paste porcelain.

The Story of Limoges Porcelain

Limoges porcelain is hard paste porcelain. Limoges is the city where factories producing this type of porcelain have been located for more than 200 years. The name of the city has in fact become synonymous with the high quality porcelain products manufactured by those companies. Tilmans (page 217), a French writer, put it aptly:

Le Limousine semble prédestiné
á abriter les Arts du Feu.

That means literally that the Limousine region of France seemed predestined to be the home for the arts of fire (porcelain). Why? Because the soil of the area surrounding Limoges is rich in deposits of kaolin and feldspar, the essential ingredients for natural, or hard paste, porcelain. Equally important is the fact that pottery making, particularly faience, was carried on in the area prior to the discovery of kaolin. Thus the people with the special knowledge, skills, and equipment were available and ready to start hard paste production when the formula was known and the necessary ingredients were discovered in the area. Additionally of importance, when porcelain first began to be produced in Limoges during the late 1700s, the region had plentiful forests to supply the necessary fuel for the kilns, and the rivers provided easy transportation facilities for the wood.

The city of Limoges is located about 200 miles south of Paris in the region known as the Haute Vienne. The Vienne is the principal river flowing through the area. The town itself is located at the base of Mont Jovis. Kaolin was discovered near Limoges at the village of Saint Yrieix in 1768. The discovery of this essential ingredient for hard paste porcelain is attributed to Mme. Darnet, the wife of a local doctor. Tests made of the white earth she found proved it in fact to be a pure and superior form of kaolin.

The discovery of this clay near Limoges did not occur, however, until about 60 years after the formula for making hard paste porcelain had been discovered by Böttger of Meissen. Although the Meissen company had tried to keep the formula a secret, the knowledge eventually spread to other areas in Europe as workers left the company and took the knowledge of the process with them. Of course the knowledge was useless if the necessary ingredients for porcelain were not available. The advantages of hard paste over the artificial, or soft paste, porcelain were well known by the time kaolin was discovered at Saint Yrieix. Possession of both the formula and the basic ingredient in that area nat-

urally led to experiments in the production of hard paste porcelain. The Royal Court of France recognized the importance of the kaolin discovery, and Turgot, in charge of Finance for King Louis XVI, thought it advantageous to help the industry to get started in France.

The first production of hard paste porcelain at Limoges is attributed to the company of Massie, Grellet, and Fourneira. Massie was the owner of a faience factory which had been established by his father near Limoges in 1737. Following the discovery of kaolin in the area, Massie, circa 1770, became partners with brothers by the name of Grellet, and a chemist by the name of Fourneira. Experiments were begun by the company in making hard paste porcelain. The company was granted the permission to make this form of porcelain products by an order of the Council of the Court. In 1777 the company came under the patronage of the Comte d'Artois, brother of King Louis XVI. Patronage, in effect, meant that the company was financed and supported by the Count. The products were required to be marked with the initials "C.D." These initials were written in various forms, sometimes with the coat of arms of the Count, in different colors, or incised into the porcelain. Pieces carrying these marks are in museums today. (I have not included these marks in this book because they do not represent useful information about porcelain available on the market today. For more information on these marks, see sources in the Bibliography.)

The company encountered problems, both financial and technical, during the first years of operation. The owners as early as 1774 had tried to sell the factory to the King. The sale did not take place though until 10 years later, in 1784. In the meantime progress was made in hard paste production. When the firm was taken over by the king, however, it was neither allowed to carry on the type of production it had started nor to remain a separate company. Louis XVI used the factory as a branch of Sèvres, the Royal Porcelain Company that manufactured soft paste porcelain. White wares were made at Limoges and then sent to Sèvres for decoration. Thus many Sèvres pieces during this time were in fact Limoges porcelain. One of the original founders of the Limoges company, the younger Grellet brother, directed the factory after it was taken over by the king. He served as manager from 1784 until 1788. Markings on the Limoges products during this time included the word *roy-*

alle. J. François Alluaud succeeded Grellet as manager of the royal Limoges company. He served from 1788 until 1794. The French *fleur-de-lis* symbol was used as a mark during this period. The operations of the company were interrupted by the French Revolution. About 1794 the factory was sold to three of the workers: Joubert, Cacate, and Joly.

The end of the revolution, circa 1796, allowed the porcelain industry of the Limousine region to progress. Another hard paste company had been established as early as 1774 near Saint Yrieix by the Comte de la Seynie, evidence that interest in this type of production was not confined to the Massie and Grellet company. Following the revolution there was no monopoly in the business, and other companies were formed at Limoges. Alluaud, former director of the Royal Limoges Company, set up a factory of his own circa 1798. Monnerie and Baignol are other names associated with the Limoges industry at the end of the eighteenth century.

The beginning years of the nineteenth century witnessed greater expansion. It is noted that the industry employed approximately 200 workers circa 1807 but by 1830, the number had increased to over 1,800. The period of the mid to late 1800s was actually the golden age for the Limoges porcelain industry. Production became industrialized. New methods of manufacture and decoration were introduced. The companies were able to benefit from mass production techniques. This was important in order to meet the growing demand of a large export market. During this period approximately 75% of the porcelain manufactured in the area was exported. The largest market was American, but the people of other European countries also wanted examples of this fine quality porcelain. The number of companies increased from around 32 during the mid to late 1800s, to 48 in the 1920s. The porcelain industry was the chief employer of the people of the Limoges area. Men were not the only ones employed; in fact whole families often worked for the companies. The numerous processes necessary to bring off a finished piece of porcelain required many hands from the manufacturing of the products down to the shipping of the goods for export. There were many jobs that could be done by women and children.

In America and also Canada, Limoges table china, especially that made by the Haviland Company, became a status symbol for brides. Art objects and decorative accessories made by the Limoges companies were also in demand by the American consumer. These porcelain items were not cheap for the times, but that did not lessen the demand.

Limoges porcelain was prized due to the exquisite quality and beautiful decoration of the pieces. America was in the full swing of a historical era typified by an extremely elaborate life style. Victoriana dictated the tastes of the period. Many different and unusual items were considered not only proper but necessary for the decoration of home and table, not only for the very wealthy but also for those of more modest means. The living and social customs portrayed by books and pictures of that bygone era seem quite lavish when compared to today's standards.

The Limoges manufacturers were happy to take advantage of the wants and whims of the American market. They soon were catering to that market in the types of objects produced. American table customs and tastes differed somewhat from those of the French, thus many products were made and decorated especially for the American market.

In the early years of the 1900s, however, a crisis developed in the industry. The companies were producing more porcelain than the market could absorb. Many of the older companies were forced out of business, unable to compete with the younger companies. The newer firms were able to adapt to new ideas, and they had more capital resources necessary for the large scale production of porcelain. World War I, followed by the world wide economic crises of the late 1920s and 1930s, brought about the end of the prosperity of the porcelain industry in Limoges. It was some years after World War II before the industry was able to be revitalized. The introduction of gas to the factories in the late 1940s enabled more modern, efficient, and less expensive methods of production. Today Limoges is still the center of hard paste porcelain production in France. The quality of the wares is still superb.

However, the porcelain produced in Limoges from the mid 1800s until approximately 1930 is the porcelain that is of interest to antiques collectors. It is the examples from this period that are currently seen on the American antiques market. The year 1930 is of course an arbitrary cut-off date. One of the reasons for this is the age factor. Porcelain made at Limoges before 1930 is from 50 to over 100 years old. The date also reflects the end of an era. The stock market crash of 1929 and the depression of the 1930s brought an end to the lifestyle prior to that time. Undoubtedly the porcelain produced by Limoges factories after 1930 will also be collected by future generations, for quality is always recognized.

Comparing Haviland and Other Limoges Porcelain

Although hard paste porcelain production actually began as early as 1773 in Limoges, France, with numerous companies operating there since the early 1800s, there is really only one company by name that is immediately recognized today, especially in the United States: Haviland and Company. The Haviland factory actually began producing porcelain in Limoges in 1865 (d'Albis and Romanet, p. 134). At that time, hard paste porcelain production had been in progress at Limoges for roughly 90 years.

The porcelain factories which were established at Limoges before and after the Haviland company were primarily French owned and operated. Prior to the mid 1800s, their products were made for the European market. It was only after 1840 that the companies attempted any large scale exportation of their products to the United States. Many of these companies were small, and some were in business for only a short time. Other firms either changed management, consolidated with, or became absorbed by other companies at various points in time. Records of the companies were often not well kept or became lost through the years. As a result, our knowledge about them is not complete.

Why, then, is the Haviland Company so much better known than the other companies? Prior to locating in France, David Haviland had owned and operated a business in New York for importing china, primarily English earthenwares. In order to improve business during the late 1830s, David Haviland and his brother, Daniel, imported some French porcelain. Americans did not find the dishes appealing. They did not object to the dishes being French porcelain rather than English earthenware, but they did not like the decoration, and sets included pieces they were not accustomed to using.

Obviously realizing that hard paste porcelain was superior to earthenware, Haviland sought to answer the objections of his customers. He first traveled to France in 1840 and later settled in Limoges about 1842. During the first several years there, he selected porcelain made by other Limoges companies and exported the wares to his New York firm. He eventually opened his own decorating studio where his artists decorated china made by other Limoges factories. Finally, some 25 years after he had moved to Limoges, Haviland began producing china. His products, primarily dinner services, were designed almost exclusively for the American market. Americans enthusiastically bought these lovely products. The American demand for the china increased at a high rate. Haviland china was sold in stores and through catalog ordering houses. The Jewel Tea Company, a large grocery firm, offered Haviland china as premiums when people purchased Jewel products. In that way many people who might not have been able to buy a set outright collected an entire dinner service over a period of time. These services were greatly prized and handed down to succeeding generations.

The Haviland company gained fame not only in America, but most importantly also in France. David Haviland is considered partly responsible for the turning point of the Limoges porcelain industry that occurred during the mid 1800s. He was instrumental in creating a large demand for Limoges porcelain on the American market which in turn benefited the other companies. Americans liked Limoges products, and the people did not think that the ware necessarily had to be manufactured by the Haviland firm. Large department stores in the United States requested other companies as well as Haviland to make porcelain items especially for them. Marks for these stores are often seen as additional marks on pieces of Limoges porcelain.

Not only did David Haviland aid in opening up the American market for Limoges porcelain, but he also introduced new methods of technology for production and decoration which were superior to those previously used. He was responsible also for changing the practice of the companies of sending their white wares out of the factory to other studios for decoration. He made the decorating workshops part of his factory thus saving time and money, marks of an efficient American businessman! Eventually other companies followed this procedure. Innovative and time-saving techniques were necessary at this period in the history of the industry in order to meet the growing export demand. Those factories which were able to emulate Haviland's techniques, and in effect, compete with the Haviland company, were able to reap the benefits of the American trade. The other companies were in fact anxious to take advantage of this market. Evidence of this is seen by the quantity and various types of articles carrying the marks of so many different Limoges companies which are seen today on the American antiques market.

The porcelain objects which we see today that were manufactured by the Haviland company or by other china companies in Limoges from the mid 1800s to the early 1900s are examples of hard paste porcelain. (Note that Haviland and some of the other companies did make soft paste and faience, but the hard paste wares are the ones typically identified with the name "Limoges" and those companies.) The basic ingredients used by all of the companies to make the porcelain came from the same area, the Limousine region of France. The methods and specific techniques of manufacture of course varied through time and from company to company. The basic differences between Haviland porcelain and the porcelain made by other Limoges companies are not in the quality of the porcelain, but in the types of articles manufactured and the type of decorating employed. The Haviland company primarily produced dinner services, in thousands of different patterns, for the American market. The patterns of the china were characterized by transfer decoration of delicate floral designs. It is this image that comes to mind when one says "Haviland." The other companies also manufactured dinner services, but in lesser quantity than the Haviland company. Usually their designs and colors were much bolder than Haviland's. But dinner services are not the most representative items that we see for these other companies. Their products include a wide range of objects broadly classified as decorative accessories. These pieces were most often vividly decorated, and frequently hand-painted, with floral, fruit, figural, and scenic themes. Pieces were often elaborately fashioned and embellished with gold. The combination of the ornate golden trim with the deep and vibrant colored designs gives the objects a very rich appearance. It is this image that comes to mind when one says "Limoges."

This, of course, is not to say that the Haviland company did not produce decorative accessories and art objects ornately fashioned and richly decorated, or that the other companies did not manufacture dinner services with delicate designs. The difference is in the emphasis on such items. One sees more "Limoges" decorative accessories and art objects than Haviland art objects; likewise one sees more Haviland dinner ware patterns than "Limoges" dinner ware patterns.

Both Haviland and other Limoges companies exported large amounts of undecorated porcelain to the United States. This unpainted porcelain was referred to as white wares or blanks. These pieces were available in almost any type of object that was thought necessary at the time to enhance home and table decoration. Individuals and decorating firms purchased this white ware. China painting was popular during this period of history. Special schools were established to teach that particular art form, and some people even had their own kilns. China painting during this period is often portrayed as the work of women, but one sees many fine examples signed with men's names. These hand-painted white wares are in demand and collected today as well as pieces decorated in France at Limoges. It is interesting to note that the style of decoration typical of the "Limoges" image is also reflected in the American decoration of these white ware items. This was probably an attempt to emulate the Limoges decorative style as well as the preferred artistic tastes of the mid to late Victorian period. Again one sees more white ware items, decorated in this country, with the mark of some other Limoges company than Haviland, another indication of the trend of the exporting practices of the companies.

A large quantity of porcelain made by the Haviland company and the many other Limoges companies during the peak of the industry, from the middle 1800s to the first quarter of the 1900s, is available in the United States today. These porcelain objects, factory decorated or studio and individually decorated, are considered collector's items.

Because of the good records maintained by the Haviland company, one is able, through various reference sources, to identify the different marks used by the company and the dates when the marks were in use. Books identify many of the patterns of Haviland china made during this time. Haviland matching services exist throughout the United States. In the following pages, the reader should be able to learn more about the many other Limoges companies and see from the color photographs the fine and varied porcelain objects made by these firms. (For a more detailed discussion of David Haviland and illustrations of Haviland basically contrary to the "Haviland image," see my book, *Haviland Collectables and Objects of Art*, 1984.)

Identifying Limoges Porcelain

Objects are prized because of their unique qualities. Some types of objects appeal to some people and different types of objects appeal to others — it is a matter of individual taste. We can like or collect certain items because they appeal to us, but the more we know about the items, the more our appreciation is enhanced. Also from a pragmatic view, many people collect certain objects as a form of investment, so facts become important to ensure that such investments are worthwhile.

Information is always gained through study and experience. For Limoges porcelain collectors, it is important to become familiar with the historical period that represents the time when those items which are considered collector's items today were being manufactured. The social customs and artistic tastes of the period influenced the type of items made and the style of decoration. Visiting antiques shops and antiques shows enables one to see the examples of the various firms. In this way one can examine the objects closely and become familiar with the types of items and styles of decoration firsthand. It is also wise to visit gift shops and department stores to compare modern porcelain pieces with those of the earlier period. Through such experiences one becomes able to differentiate more easily between late and early products.

Types of Wares

In discussing the products of the various Limoges companies, the types of objects have been broadly grouped into three categories for simplification.

(1) The category art objects includes large objects such as vases; decorative plaques; tankards; mugs; trays; decorative bowls and plates; paintings; jardinieres.

(2) The category decorative accessories includes small items such as dresser sets; trinket boxes; candleholders; cachepots; baskets, receiving card trays; small vases; tobacco jars, inkwells, stamp boxes.

(3) The category table china includes berry, pudding, and ice cream sets; cake plates; compotes; coffee and demitasse sets; chocolate sets; teapots; cider pitchers; juice pitch-

ers; decorative creamers and sugars; cracker jars; jam jars; pancake dishes; punch bowls; fish and game services. The majority of these pieces are hand decorated entirely or partially. Also included in the category of table china are place settings and serving pieces for dinner services representing different patterns manufactured by Limoges companies. Many items classified as table china would also be considered as art objects, especially the game and fish services and other hand-painted and elaborately decorated serving pieces.

The Importance of Marks: Factory and Decorator

Marks — a special symbol of a particular factory placed on the back of an object during the manufacturing process — are commonly used to identify porcelain. Collectors and dealers usually look at the mark on a piece of china immediately, even though the eye may have told them what type of porcelain the piece is or who the decorator was. The mark is their reassurance. Most Limoges factories did not routinely mark their products until the latter quarter of the nineteenth century, although several companies did occasionally use marks from the 1850s (d'Albis and Romanet, p. 237).

Marks found on Limoges pieces from the nineteenth and early twentieth centuries consist of initials or names of companies written in a certain way and often contained within a special emblem. Sometimes the mark consists of a symbol with no identifying name or initial. Marks indicating that a certain factory made the object are usually stamped under the glaze on the back of the piece. This mark is often in green, or sometimes the mark is incised into the porcelain. Often there is more than one mark on the back of china. Confusion can exist if one does not know what each mark means. In addition to the factory mark, referred to as the white ware mark, there can be marks to indicate factory or studio decoration, importers, exporters, and artists. These other marks are usually over the glaze. By running one's finger over the marks, one can determine this. Marks indicating factory decoration are usually in a different color (often red) from the factory white ware mark. American decorating firms or art studios such as Pickard placed their mark with their name on the pieces they decorated. The French (Paris or Limoges) decorating studios were more likely to use marks with symbols or initials and not to use complete names. It can thus be difficult without research to know if the mark is that of a factory or a decorator. There is often more than one factory mark. Many factories decorated white wares manufactured by other companies. Some factories were decorating firms before they began producing porcelain, and the same mark may have been continued. However, in most cases, upon examination of and familiarity with the marking system, one is able to tell for example that one mark stands for the company of manufacture (the one under the glaze), and a second mark stands for decoration (factory, studio,

individual). David Haviland, in fact, is credited with implementing the unique "double" marking practice used by most Limoges factories after 1876.

A third mark stands for the exporter (in France) or the importer (in America or other country being either a distributor or commercial business). Pieces which have only a white ware mark tell us one of two things: the piece is early, having been decorated in Paris or Limoges before the decoration process became a part of the factory process, or that the piece was sold as a white ware and decorated in this country by a nonprofessional artist. The style and quality of decoration are points in determining this. Artists' signatures are usually found on the fronts of pieces, sometimes they are hidden, and one must look closely to find the mark. Some artists used a special mark on the bottom of the piece. Many times, of course, one sees a name written on the bottom of a piece, with or without a date. This type of signature is common on white wares decorated by nonprofessional artists.

The marks of exporters cannot always be differentiated easily from those of Limoges decorating marks. If there is an overglaze mark, however, it can usually be assumed that the piece was decorated at a Limoges factory or decorating studio. Lack of an overglaze decorating mark does not always indicate that the piece was not decorated at a Limoges factory or decorating studio. Marks could have been omitted by error, and it is not uncommon for all pieces in a set of dinner ware to lack double marks, especially the cups.

The importer marks usually are easily interpreted. They contain the name of a specific department or jewelry store. Sometimes, though, marks for individuals who ordered a specific set of china will be found in conjunction with the factory underglaze and overglaze marks. In the section on marks, I have tried to indicate by company the type of marks used: white ware mark; decorated ware mark; exporter mark; or importer mark.

It is generally accepted that if a mark contains the name of the country of origin, the piece was made after 1891. The United States government enacted the McKinley Tariff Law stating that articles imported to this country after 1891 must include the name of the country where they were produced. So theoretically, if the mark contains the word "France," the piece was made after 1891. There are exceptions to this rule, however, for some companies did use "France" in their marks prior to 1891. Also note that while the white ware marks may contain the word France, the decorating marks usually only include "Limoges," even those decorating marks which are after 1891.

While it is common to see "Made in" as part of English marks, the wording is not routinely found on Limoges marks. I discussed this in the first edition, indicating that such wording implied that the piece was made after 1914 in accordance again with tariff laws. Further examination of Limoges marks, however, clearly indicates that "Made in France," is rarely found on Limoges items made after 1914 until World War II. It is more commonly found on items made after 1945.

Déposé is often found in conjunction with Limoges marks. The French word means "patented." Some Limoges marks, however, actually have "Patent" written or abbreviated in English as part of the mark and include the date when a certain mold or pattern was registered. Bear in mind when seeing such a mark (Pat'd. Nov. 12, 1892, for example), that the date does not indicate that the piece was actually made in 1892. The date only indicates when the design was first copyrighted, and the piece may, in fact, have been made quite a few years later.

In some instances I have found dates of marks attributed to the very first time that a factory was in production at a certain location, even though that factory had changed owners and marks over a long period of time. For example, several sources show that the GDA (see Gérard, Dufraisseix, and Abbot) mark goes back to 1798; in fact the GDA company was established circa 1900. This confusing error results from the fact that the GDA company can be traced back to the old Alluaud firm which actually began in 1798. But it is certainly not accurate to identify a GDA mark on an object as dating from 1798.

Factories did change hands. In fact, this seems to be more the rule than the exception. Sometimes the same marks were continued by the succeeding firms. In most cases the marks changed either completely, or were either altered in some fashion, or a new white ware mark was introduced while the former firm's decorating mark was continued. Also when a certain year is given as the date of a certain mark, that does not mean that all pieces having that mark were made in that one year. The date indicates when the company started using a particular mark. It is often difficult to pinpoint specific dates when a certain mark was used. The approximate time period when a mark was used or when a company was in production is more helpful. Dates for the majority of marks in this book are for approximate time periods. It is also important to realize that a decorating mark may be some years later than the white ware mark on a piece. Items could be manufactured and marked with the factory mark and then placed in stock to be decorated as the need arose. That also can account for finding the same molds with marks of two different companies, usually one mark belongs to the factory which succeeded the other, such as Bernardaud (B&Co.) taking over Délinières (D&Co.).

There are many beautiful examples of hard paste porcelain which have no marks at all. Many of the older Limoges companies and other European hard paste manufacturers did not mark their wares. To collectors this is often exasperating. If the object is not marked Limoges, however, one cannot definitely tell if it is actually Limoges porcelain or porcelain from some other area, like Bavaria, Austria, or Japan. (Of course, some pieces in a set of china might not have the mark on every piece.) For unmarked items, the type of object and style of decoration should give an indication of when it was made, but that is usually all one can say. Unmarked articles do not sell as quickly as marked ones.

This is often not a deterrent to a buyer if the piece fits in with one's collection, and if one is not too concerned about its value appreciating.

Fake and Misleading Limoges Marks

Often one is cautioned in general not to rely on marks as a method of identification. Many porcelain marks have been copied. The more demand for a particular type of porcelain, the more scarce it becomes on the market. As a result, the possibilities are increased that the marks will be copied on reproductions of those objects. When the first edition was written in 1980, there was no problem with fake Limoges marks. A few years later, however, modern pieces made in Taiwan began to appear at flea markets and antique malls. This china was offered for sale by wholesale houses specializing in reproductions. Such wholesale houses continue to sell these reproduction. Advertisements state, "Handpainted Porcelain Sevres — Royal Vienna — Limoges style."

The fake mark was composed of a *fleur-de-lis*, printed in blue or gold, with a banner printed with "LIMOGES CHINA." That fake mark is found on the same items which could also be found with fake Nippon and R. S. Prussia marks. Hatpin holders, tankards, jewel boxes, and chocolate sets are commonly seen. Later, some more elaborate items were made with that particular fake Limoges mark. Urns, bowls, and vases were made with fancy swan-shaped handles. They are decorated in cobalt blue around colorful transfer pastoral scenes. These pieces may confuse knowledgeable collectors, until they look at the mark. Another fake Limoges mark has come on the market in the last few years. This is a crown mark stamped in gold with crossed swords below the crown and "LIMOGES" printed under the crossed swords. The mark is found on other cobalt blue or dark rose colored pieces such as chocolate sets and trays. Another example is an inkwell decorated with a transfer portrait of "Madam Lebrun" (a popular portrait decoration usually found on R. S. Prussia china).

Fake Limoges Mark 1, fleur-de-lis, with "LIMOGES" printed in blue or gold.

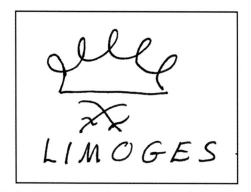

Fake Limoges Mark 2, crown with "LIMOGES" printed in gold.

Undoubtedly, modern fake Limoges marks will continue to be found in the future. Collectors should be aware of certain key indications of reproductions as well as being knowledgeable about the fake marks. If the china is not translucent, it is not Limoges. Some American and English companies marked china with the name "Limoges" during the early 1900s to take advantage of the French Limoges market in America. The china was earthenware, however, and not porcelain. I often receive inquiries about many of the marks used by Limoges China Factory of Sebring, Ohio, on its earthenware production. For information about that company, please see *American Limoges* by Raymonde Limoges, Collector Books, 1996.

The "repro" problem is basically a very small area of concern for today's Limoges collector. The supply of collectible Limoges and Haviland porcelain products has been adequate. The majority of pieces on the American antiques market today date from the latter part of the 1800s and are just now coming into the classification of "true" antiques, over 100 years old. Another deterrent for copying Limoges marks is that some of the companies are still in production. The manufacture of porcelain in Limoges is still a large industry. Modern table china and decorative items from Limoges are seen in department stores and gift shops in the United States today. These modern wares, even if produced by companies whose origins date back to the mid 1800s, are not difficult to differentiate from the old. The type of decoration and marks is a help in distinguishing the old from the new. In new table china, some of the traditional designs are followed, but in new decorative accessories, often seen in gift shops and flea markets, the colors are usually not as rich, but most importantly, the gold in the trim and embellishments is not applied as lavishly. The gold does not have the rich patina of the earlier pieces.

Marks on the modern pieces are also different. There is usually only one mark with no distinction between factory manufactured and factory decorated, even if pieces are factory decorated. The practice of decorating the china at the factory has now been going on so long that there is really no need to double mark. The marks have a "newer" appearance, being more elaborate in form and containing more informa-

tion than the older, simpler, marks. Many of the gift items are marked only "Limoges, France." Several companies operating during the nineteenth century also marked their products in this way. Often this type of marking today is in gold. Gold marks were quite rare during the earlier period. Also the earlier marking "Limoges, France" appears under the glaze, whereas the newer markings are most often over the glaze. For identifying porcelain objects manufactured during the nineteenth and early twentieth centuries at Limoges, marks are helpful.

The Importance of Decoration: Technique and Styles

Decorating techniques changed through the years for the Limoges porcelain industry. Examples of Limoges porcelain found today on the American antiques market, however, appear in one of four categories: (1) unpainted (white ware or blanks), (2) handpainted, (3) transfer decorated, and (4) mixed (a combination of transfer design and handpainted). Decoration may be over or under the glaze. All categories except the first may be further subdivided into factory decorated, studio (professionally) decorated, or individually decorated (amateur or nonprofessional).

Unpainted porcelain does not mean absence of decoration. The article was not "blank" as the term for this type of ware implies. On the contrary, intricate and beautiful designs were molded, incised, or applied to the object in the paste form. Pieces were elaborately fashioned with scalloped borders, scroll work, beading, and fancily shaped handles; knobs and feet were applied or molded into the piece which in turn might have detailed designs. One can inspect a color decorated object to see or feel the design.

Early Limoges porcelain was not decorated until the entire manufacturing process was completed. The white wares or blanks were sent to Paris and handpainted by artists and studios of that city. This type of decoration was over the glaze. It was fine for decorative objects, but it was not very suitable for articles that would come into contact with much use or handling, specifically table china. Decoration over the glaze although done with vitreous paints and refired to "set" the decoration eventually shows signs of wear if used frequently, like with a knife and fork. Pieces subjected to such use can be ruined over a period of time. Objects decorated under the glaze, that is, decoration applied to the bisque form of the piece before the glaze is applied, never show any sign of deterioration — the glaze cannot be penetrated. Objects decorated under the glaze have the vitreous or glassy look all over; they feel smooth to the touch; one cannot feel the painted decoration. Over the glaze, it can be felt; the design has a texture separate from the body of the piece. The appearance is not "slick" as is the case with decoration under glaze. Examine a handpainted vase, for example. If the decoration feels the same as the inside of the vase, the decoration is under the glaze; if it does not, it is over the glaze. Decoration under the glaze was not perfected in the Limoges porcelain industry until the late 1800s.

Décalcomanie is the French term for transfer decoration. A design is made on copper plates or stones in certain colors. The design is pressed onto paper which in turn is pressed onto another object, thus transferring the design to that object. The same design can be used over and over. Transfer designs are a less expensive process of decoration than handpainting. This method of decoration was popular in England from the late 1700s. English potters were able to use this type of decoration under the glaze successfully before the Limoges hard paste factories. English earthenwares were fired at much lower temperatures in the glaze firing than is required for hard paste porcelain. The potters did not have the problem of the designs melting or running together during this second firing. Transfer decoration can also be applied over the glaze; however, the durability of the design is variable. Once the technique of keeping the design intact during the glaze firing had been perfected, this type of decoration was widely used by the Limoges companies, especially for table china.

Mixtion, the French term implying a mixed technique of decoration, was another popular decorating method. Designs were applied in outline or full (colored) form by the transfer method and then filled in or trimmed by handpainting. This style of decoration could be applied either over or under the glaze. Many decorative accessories and serving china pieces show evidence of this particular technique.

Close examination is often necessary in order to differentiate between the categories of methods of decoration: (1) handpainted; (2) transfer; (3) mixed. Items entirely handpainted are the easiest to determine. Most are painted over the glaze. They have a texture which can be felt. Brush strokes and irregularities can be seen when one looks closely. Transfer designs on patterns of table china are usually under the glaze. The pattern is regular and the same on each piece; the design cannot be felt. Pieces decorated by the mixed technique, either over or under the glaze, are the most difficult to determine. When in doubt, a magnifying glass enables better inspection than the eye alone. A pattern of raised dots composing the design or a design pattern outline showing no irregularities indicates that the transfer method has been used.

To summarize, white wares, or unpainted Limoges china, are seen on today's market primarily in the form of table china. Although large amounts of the blanks were exported, one rarely sees an undecorated piece in the form of decorative accessories. The white wares were sold to be decorated, and apparently most were decorated by individuals or art studios. Most examples are handpainted. Early Limoges porcelain was decorated by hand in Paris. From the mid 1800s Limoges porcelain was decorated by special decorating firms or at the factory. Handpainting, transfer, and mixed techniques were all employed. From circa 1870 to the late 1920s, the transfer and mixed methods were used most frequently for table china. Handpainting during this period was primarily reserved for art objects and decorative pieces.

The style of the early decoration of Limoges porcelain consisted largely of gold designs or themes of flowers and people. The "rose de Limoges" is noted as the chief distinction of the early factories. However, decoration tended to reflect the artistic tastes of the historical period. The height of the Art Nouveau period coincided with the height of the golden age of the Limoges porcelain industry, late 1880s – circa 1905. Although the Art Deco period dates from 1925 because of the Paris exhibition titled *"Arts Decoratif"* held that year, examples of that style are seen in pieces of Limoges porcelain dating from the early 1900s.

Floral decor on decorative accessories and art objects, especially roses in all varieties and colors, appears as the most prevalent style of decoration that one sees on Limoges objects. Fruit themes of berries, cherries, and grapes appear as the second most popular form of decoration. Game birds and marine life subjects are evident, especially on elaborate sets of serving china for game, fish, and oysters. Figural, both portrait and allegorical, as well as scenic decor is less common than the other themes.

These various styles of decoration are distinguished by deep and vivid colors and embellishments of gold. There are few objects categorized as decorative accessories or art objects that are decorated in delicate or pale tones. Table china is more likely to be decorated in delicate styles, although table china manufactured by Limoges companies other than Haviland often has a bold and colorful design. Gold trim is, of course, the second chief characteristic of much Limoges porcelain. The gold, referred to as coin gold, was lavishly applied to decorative objects and also to table china during the height of the Limoges porcelain industry. The gold has a rich patina which accents and serves as an outline on the pieces. Objects decorated in such a fashion, especially those professionally handpainted, with vivid floral, fruit, and figural themes enhanced with gold, are unique works of art.

Evaluating Limoges Porcelain For Collectors

For the typical American collector of European hard paste porcelain (Limoges, Austrian, Bavarian), there is usually no attempt to stick zealously to the rule that an item must be over 100 years old before it can be considered worthwhile for collection or investment. The first Limoges hard paste production occurred over 200 years ago, and the Limoges products that have been available through export to the American consumer have been available for only about 150 years. Other European hard paste porcelain also has been produced for less than 300 years, making the porcelain items "young" by European standards of antiquity. Age is important, of course, but porcelain objects which have survived for 50 to 100 years indicate the quality and desirability of the objects. Porcelain is durable, but it is vulnerable to breakage, much more so than some other categories of antiques and collectibles such as furniture. Pieces of porcelain which exist from earlier times show that they have been cared for. The pieces were prized when they were new; they were kept and handed down to future generations. History is preserved: owning a particular piece, whether one inherits or purchases the item, allows one to understand, respect, and share a part of the past. For investment purposes, the objects appreciate in value as years are added to their age.

Marks can be beneficial in determining the approximate age of many pieces of Limoges porcelain. Quality of craftsmanship of the body and quality of decoration on the body are also important factors to consider in addition to age. The thinness (translucency) of a piece of porcelain sometimes is considered an indication of quality. Of course, European hard paste porcelains are all translucent; however, they are not "eggshell" thin as are some Chinese and Japanese pieces. Examples of Limoges hard paste porcelain represent quality craftsmanship, but there are basically small differences in the thickness among the wares of the different Limoges companies, although some companies' products may be more elaborately or exquisitely fashioned than others. The hard paste products should have a deep bell-like ring when gently tapped. If the piece has a break or "hairline" crack, the sound will be dull. Dealers often exhibit this quality of porcelain items to purchasers in order to show that the piece is perfect when sold.

The type and quality of decoration on pieces of Limoges porcelain vary. The marks, or lack of marks, on pieces of Limoges porcelain often give us a clue to how the pieces were decorated (see section on marks). Handpainted objects with only one mark (white ware mark) under the glaze indicates that a certain factory made the piece, but that the decoration was applied by someone else. That decorator could be either a professional French artist or an amateur or professional American artist. If the piece is signed, the name may give a clue as to the origin of the artist. Handpainted pieces having a mark in addition to the white ware mark,

usually over the glaze, indicate that the piece was professionally decorated either by a Limoges (or Paris) studio, a Limoges factory, or by a firm in America (or other country), such as a jewelry company that monogrammed items, or by an art school or studio.

Pieces decorated by the mixed technique primarily have the decorating mark of a factory or decoration studio in addition to the white ware mark. Examples are seen which have been both factory decorated and individually decorated — another form of mixed decor. Plates, bowls, platters, and trays frequently are decorated in this manner. The border glaze or pattern may be the finished product of some factory and show a mark for factory decoration, but the middle or inside of the piece, which was unpainted when it left the factory, may be painted with some scene, theme, or monogram at a later time by someone else, professional or non-professional. If the art work is signed, origin of that particular decoration might be determined.

Pieces decorated by the transfer method are primarily found in examples of table china. Many dinnerware items, however, especially serving pieces, would be considered a type of mixed decoration, having trim, handles, and feet handpainted with gold. Additionally, many transfer designs are often touched up or filled in by hand. Transfer design pieces usually show white ware marks and decorator marks. Sometimes pieces of Limoges porcelain only show a Limoges decorator's mark signifying that the company that manufactured the item did not use a white ware mark. We do not consider the piece unmarked, however, as the decorating mark indicates Limoges. Other pieces having no white ware mark but with a decorating mark that cannot be attributed to Limoges, like Pickard, for example, are not considered Limoges even though the decoration may represent the Limoges image.

Limoges art objects and decorative accessories primarily are handpainted or of mixed decor, as described in the earlier section on decorating techniques. The amount of individual work that goes into the decoration of an object usually serves as the criterion of superiority.

When prices were revised in 1984, I set up a key identifying the type of decoration for each piece. The prices were coded to indicate whether the piece had professional French decoration either by factory or decorating studio (FD); professional American decoration by a specific American decorating studio (PD); quality decoration by a professional or non-professional artist for pieces which had neither a French not an American decorating mark (QD); amateur decoration by an American non-professional china painter (AD); and undecorated white ware, or blanks (UD). Differentiating between the several methods of decoration found on Limoges porcelain is necessary, especially for the serious and advanced collector. There is a very wide variation in quality for items decorated in America.

I elaborated on this system of evaluating Limoges by quality of decoration in an article written for *The Antique Trader Weekly* (July 3, 1985, pp. 56-60). Basically Limoges can be rated on the basis of origin and type of decoration, which can be determined by its marks. First, the most desirable pieces are those which have been handpainted in Limoges factories or decorating studios in Limoges or Paris. Examples will have at least two marks, one underglaze and one overglaze. Some pieces may have an artist's signature or initials on the front of the piece. Sometimes, an artist's mark or initial will be on the base or the back of the item. The *mixtion* type of decoration, such as transfers of portraits or cherubs with partial handpainted work, is also included in this first category. But these examples are valued less than the totally handpainted pieces. Many of the more collectible pieces with figural, scenic, and portrait decoration, however, are of this type.

Second in desirability are pieces handpainted by American decorating studios. Examples will have two marks, the underglaze Limoges factory mark and the overglaze American studio mark such as Pickard or Stouffer. Such pieces usually have a studio artist's signature on the face.

The third category of collectible Limoges is comprised of pieces with Limoges factory transfer designs or patterns. Examples will have at least two marks, the underglaze factory mark and the overglaze decorating mark of the factory or studio.

The fourth category of Limoges consists of items handpainted by American artists or china painters. Examples will have only one mark, underglaze, denoting the Limoges manufacturing company. Pieces may be signed on the front or on the base. This fourth category is the one which poses the most concern for the discriminating collector. Some of the American handpainted work is clearly of a professional quality and should be considered on the same level, or just below that, of American decorating studios. Many other pieces, however, exhibit obviously amateur workmanship,

and these should not be priced in the same range just because they are "handpainted."

A few other points to consider when evaluating Limoges should be noted. Some factories were in production for only a short time, thus examples of their wares, however decorated or even unpainted, may be desirable due to scarcity. Some companies did not export to the United States in quantities as large as others, thus their products are scarce. Certain types of objects appear on the market more than others. Decorative plaques, vases, cachepots, tankards, and fish services are well represented. Whiskey decanters, cuspidors, inkwells, humidors, perfume bottles, baskets, jardinieres, pancake dishes — to name just a few — are not so prevalent. The serving or extra pieces to dinner services such as tea and coffee pots, butter pats, butter dishes, and bone dishes, as well as cups for place settings, make these items desirable if needed to complete a set even though the majority are transfer decorated. Certain themes of decoration such as scenic and animal are more scarce than the other themes. Pieces signed by a specific artist, either professional or in some cases nonprofessional, are often in demand. Determining the specific desirability of Limoges porcelain for individual collection and investment comes through study and experience: reading, looking, touching, examining, and deciding what is personally appealing.

The variety of Limoges porcelain available today provides many ideas for collections. Collections can range from the very general to the very specific. A wide selection of decorative pieces manufactured by different Limoges companies, decorated in different styles by different techniques allows one to enjoy and sample a beautiful array of Limoges porcelain. Personal creativity in putting together a collection for pleasure, investment, or both can be an enjoyable and worthwhile endeavor.

Note: The letters "mc" after a value for an example indicate value for the piece in mint condition. Some flaw on those examples is visible in the photograph.

Charles Ahrenfeldt/Charles J. Ahrenfeldt (CA)

Charles Ahrenfeldt was born in Germany in 1807. He was connected with several different aspects of the porcelain business during his life and was engaged in the china importing business in New York in the 1830s. During the 1840s, he moved to Paris where he had a studio for decorating porcelain. He is noted to have been located in Limoges from about 1860. There he first owned an exporting firm and later a decorating studio, circa 1884. Charles Ahrenfeldt died in 1893 before the Ahrenfeldt factory for making china was in production. A mark attributed to his Limoges decorating studio is shown here along with two examples.

Charles J. Ahrenfeldt was born in 1856 and carried on the porcelain business established by his father. He began producing porcelain about 1894. During the late 1890s, the company carried on an extensive export trade. White wares and decorated table china were the principle articles manufactured. Factory decorated pieces are double marked with the white ware mark in green underglaze and the decorating mark in various colors overglaze. The dates when the various marks were used are not totally clear, and reference sources cite conflicting times for some of the marks. The firm had a long history, active, except during the war years, until about 1969. A number of white ware marks were used as well as several different decorating marks. Mark 1 is probably the earliest mark used by Charles J. It is overglaze in blue and is either a decorating or exporting mark because it is found on porcelain manufactured by other Limoges factories. It is the same type of mark as the one used by his father, except for the color and the addition of the words, "LIMOGES, FRANCE." This is not the elder Ahrenfeldt's mark because some examples have the white ware marks of factories established after the senior Ahrenfeldt's death. Thus, the mark is after 1893 and was probably used before the Ahrenfeldt factory was producing and decorating china to full capacity. Marks 2 – 8 were undoubtedly used during different periods, but no specific times are documented. They were probably used until World War II. Mark 9 appears to be a post World War II mark.

The first two pictures are examples decorated by the Charles Ahrenfeldt Company between 1884 and 1893. The other examples are later, after 1894, and reflect the period when his son, C. J. Ahrenfeldt, became owner. All pieces shown for the Ahrenfeldt factory are factory decorated.

Charles Ahrenfeldt

Mark, overglaze decorating mark in red, ca. 1884 – 1893.

Plate 1. Clam plate, 7½" d, five sections, soft cream finish with brushed gold work on borders and center of plate. Lanternier Mark 2 in green and C. Ahrenfeldt mark in red. **$150.00 – 175.00.**

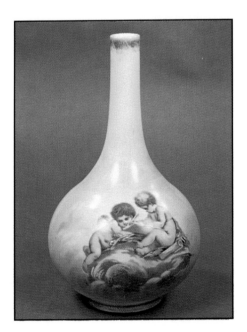

Plate 2. Vase, 8½" h; two cherubs, one writing while the other watches, decorate front of vase. Cherubs and cupids appear to have been a popular decorating theme of the company as is shown by this and several following examples. The designs are *mixtion* in nature combining transfer designs with applied color. Redon Mark 1 in green and C. Ahrenfeldt mark in red. **$300.00 – 325.00.**

Charles J. Ahrenfeldt Marks

Mark 1, overglaze decorating mark in blue, CA monogram with "Limoges, France," after 1893.

Mark 1a, overglaze decorating mark in red-orange, variation of Mark 1 with "Versailles" printed over monogram, after 1893.

Mark 2, underglaze white ware mark in green, CA monogram, after 1894 – 1930s.

Mark 3, underglaze white ware mark in green, CA monogram with a star and "France," after 1894 – 1930s.

Mark 4, underglaze white ware mark in green, CA monogram with "France," after 1894 – 1930s.

Mark 5, underglaze white ware mark in green, CA monogram with star and zig-zag lines, after 1894 – 1930s.

Mark 6, underglaze white ware mark in green, CA monogram with "France, Déposé," after 1894 – 1930s.

Mark 7, overglaze decorating mark in green, CA monogram in a double circle with "Limoges, France," after 1894 – 1930s.

Mark 8a, overglaze decorating mark in green or gold, "C. Ahrenfeldt, Limoges," after 1894 – 1930s.

Mark 8b, variation of mark 8a, overglaze decorating Mark in green, "Made by C. Ahrenfeldt, Limoges," with importer's name, after 1894 – 1930.

Mark 8c, overglaze decorating mark in red, variation of mark 8a, with "FRANCE," after 1894 – 1930.

Mark 9, overglaze decorating mark in blue (incorporating Mark 5), after World War II until 1969.

Charles J. Ahrenfeldt China

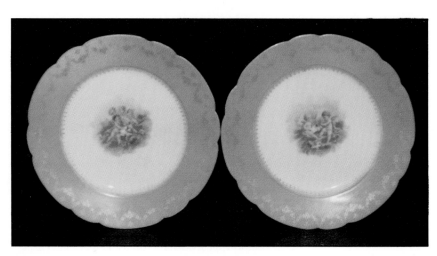

Plate 4. Decorative plates; cherubs compose center decoration on white background highlighted with a deep pink border overlaid with gold stenciled garlands. C. J. Ahrenfeldt Marks 4 and 8a. **$140.00 – 160.00 each.**

Plate 3. Decorative plate; cupids decorate center with heavily gilded fluted border. Laviolette mark in green with C. J. Ahrenfeldt Mark 1 in blue. **$125.00 – 150.00.**

Plate 5. Decorative plate, 9½" d; elaborate scrolled designs in relief accented with gold frame center décor of cherubs frolicking in the clouds. C. J. Ahrenfeldt Mark 1 in blue. **$375.00 – 475.00.**

Plate 6. Game bird plate, scenic décor of birds, water, and marsh decorate center of plate; a wide cobalt blue border trimmed with gold stenciled work accents piece. C. J. Ahrenfeldt Mark 4 in green with an overglaze decorating mark for "Ovington Bros., New York Fabrique à Limoges" in green. **$175.00 – 200.00.**

Plate 7. Turkey service: serving plates, 8¾" d; brightly painted turkeys set against a yard and sky background; the floral transfer border is composed of dark pink and bright yellow roses and is trimmed in gold. The complete service consists of the platter and 12 serving plates. C. J. Ahrenfeldt Marks 4 and 8a in green. **$2,300.00 – 2,500.00 set.**

Plate 8. Platter for turkey service, 19½" l x 13" w.

Plate 9. Commemorative bowls, 7" d; scenes depicting events from the Revolutionary War compose the decorative theme for this and the following two examples. The brightly colored transfer designs include the name of the scene and the artist who painted the original work on which the transfer is based. There were probably other scenes in this series. C. J. Ahrenfeldt Marks 6 and 8a. "Washington Crossing the Delaware — Emanuel Leutre." **$150.00 – 175.00 each.**

Plate 10. "Battle of Bunker Hill — John Trumbull."

Plate 11. "Surrender of Cornwall — John Trumbull."

Plate 12. Basket, 5" l; transfer pattern of orange flowers; sponged gold accents handle. C. J. Ahrenfeldt Marks 3 and 8c. **$75.00 – 95.00.**

Plate 13. Service plate, 11" d; a bouquet of brightly colored flowers, commonly known as "German flowers," forms the center pattern on a white background; a bright yellow-green border between gold bands surrounds the design. C. J. Ahrenfeldt Marks 6 and 8a with a retailer mark "Pour Dulin & Martin Washington, D. C." **$150.00 – 175.00.**

Plate 14. Dinner plate, 9" d, small clusters of pink and red roses with a yellow tulip alternate with a yellow daffodil, a pink tulip, and green feathery leaves for a floral border pattern. The design is enhanced by enameled scrolled work in gold; gold etched bands encircle the outer and inner borders. C. J. Ahrenfeldt Marks 3 and 6. **$100.00 – 125.00.**

Plate 15. Covered serving bowl, 16" d; a bird of paradise is the focal point of this pattern which can be seen on the top of lid; multi-colored flowers decorate six sides of the octagonal-shaped dish; a small floral diaper pattern forms an inner border on lid; the center of the pattern is white while the borders have a cream-colored glaze; handles and trim are painted gold. C. J. Ahrenfeldt Marks 6 and 8a. **$225.00 – 275.00.**

Bawo & Dotter (Elite Works)

Bawo & Dotter was established in the 1860s in New York City for the purpose of importing china, notably Limoges porcelain, for the American consumer. The firm set up its own decorating studio in Limoges during the early 1870s which was named "The Elite Works." The company did not begin manufacturing its own china until about 1896 (d' Albis and Romanet, p. 126). From the 1870s through the 1890s, the company decorated the white ware made by other Limoges factories. Many examples of Bawo & Dotter's decoration and porcelain are found in a variety of items.

The earliest marks used by the company appear to be Marks 1 – 3, a vase shape incorporating the initials "B D" over "L", and the Arms of Limoges. While exact dating is not possible, it is reasonable to assign certain periods to the marks based on examples bearing such marks and by comparing the white ware marks of other companies found in conjunction with the Bawo & Dotter decorating marks. A patent date of "Dec. 12, 82" has been found in conjunction with this type of mark (see Mark 2b).

Later decorating marks are very similar and also include the Arms of Limoges. The white ware marks seem to show the transition from decorating only to manufacturing, with "Limoges" written in script form in both the underglaze mark and overglaze mark (see Marks 4 and 8). Mark 3a has been discovered since the second edition was published. It is an impressed mark of "B D" over "L" and "Déposé." This mark would reflect an early manufacturing mark after 1896. Several other variations of Elite marks have been added.

The company's china production was interrupted in Limoges during World War I. After the war, circa 1920, the company purchased the William Guérin firm. The name of the company became Guérin-Pouyat-Elite, Ltd. (Guérin had previously purchased the Pouyat company.) The individual marks of each of the three companies appear to have been continued from the time of this merger until the business closed in 1932. Apparently, undecorated blanks by either of the three companies were used with a new mark of Guérin-Pouyat-Elite, Ltd. (see Bawo & Dotter Mark 12). This mark is rarely seen, and information on exactly when it was put in use after 1920 has not been found.

The pictures for Bawo & Dotter are arranged first by early table wares decorated before the company began manufacturing china plus two examples with the early impressed manufacturing mark. Most of these pieces have the white ware mark of some other Limoges factory. These are followed by some highly decorated items made and decorated by the company. These include pieces only decorated by Bawo & Dotter as well as china made and decorated by the factory. Many show an Art Nouveau influence. Some table china and dinner ware patterns form a third group of pictures. The last set of photographs illustrates blanks decorated by American china painters.

Some pages from the book, *Limoges, Its People, Its China,* printed in 1900 for the Bawo & Dotter (Elite Works) factory are reprinted here for collector interest. Descriptions of various shapes or molds, decoration, and even prices are shown.

Bawo & Dotter (Elite Works)

There is a distinctiveness about Fish and Game Services coming from the Elite Works that takes them out of the ordinary. The decorative treatment of fish and game subjects by our artists, are not suggested by the time worn studies that have done duty at Limoges for years. There is an originality about Elite conceptions of these subjects just as there is originality in shapes and other decorative treatments that first see the light of day at the Elite Works. You will find very nice ones in the retail shops as low as $12.00 a set and from that up to $100.00. The ware is just as fine quality in the cheaper ones as in the high-cost sets—the elaborateness of the ornamentation only adds to the cost.

FISH
AND
GAME
SETS.

If one thing had to be singled out from our many productions at the Elite Works as the thing of which we are most proud, we would say it is our line of Fancy Plates. The decorations are laid on many shapes but the "Perle" plate with its beaded edges gives the widest scope to the designer and artist. We will state without fear of contradiction that not even the famous English makes of Coalport, Cauldon, Doulton, Wedgwood, Mintons, etc., can boast of more exquisite designs or more effective colorings. You will find "Elite" plates in the finest retail shops in the country. Elaborateness of design; quality of execution and a lower price, make the "Elite" specimens stand out pre-eminently.

FINE
ENTREE
PLATES.

Bawo & Dotter (Elite Works)

The Romeo shape which forms the basis for pattern No. 3004 is one that is exceedingly popular. It is a rococo design with quite a wide bas-relief in the ware on all pieces. The decorative treatment is a border of daisies in the most delicate yellow and green. The effect is a faint greenish one and is very pleasing to the eye. The immense sales testify to its general favor. All handles are stippled with coin gold. Close to the edge a trailing vine takes the place of a gold edge and makes a finish quite as complete. The engraving shows a cake plate and moustache cup—demonstrating the completeness of our open stock patterns. A service of 102 pieces at your dealer's for $37.50. Fancy pieces extra in proportion.

No. 3004. ROMEO SHAPE OPEN STOCK.

The "Marquis" shape is one of the most recent things from the Elite Works. The distinguishing feature is the convex fluting faintly discernable on each piece. With a narrow border in color and supplemented with lace borders in coin gold it is one of the handsomest things ever brought out in china. It is also effective as shown in the engraving. This is a stock pattern with sprays of hawthorn done in pink with leaves in light green. The handles are stippled with coin gold. By the way the handles are very graceful and give an appearance of extra lightness to the covered ware. A set of 102 pieces figures $37.50 and your dealer will supply you at that rate. Separate pieces at the same rate. As in all our open stock patterns the customer has the choice of the old style soup plates with rims or the new coupe shape with no rim. The latter seem to have the call just now.

No. 6076. MARQUIS SHAPE OPEN STOCK.

The variety of Fancy Pieces made at the Elite Works is well-nigh endless. There are shapes aplenty and decorations galore—from the lowest price that good workmanship permits. to the very choicest specimens of the modeler's and decorator's art. These include Manicure Trays, Chocolate Pots, Biscuit Jars, Tankards, Chop Dishes, etc. They cost no more than ordinary French china and each bears that guarantee of excellence – the "Elite" trade-mark – when selecting a bit for a gift or for own use. insist on a piece with the mark. The mark adds naught to the cost. It is a certificate of perfectness.

FANCY PIECES.

There is a greater demand for cups and saucers than for any other single item made in china, with the exception of perhaps those other most necessary articles—plates. So many cups and saucers are bought for presentation purposes; and the fad for "odd" cups and saucers which calls for dozens of cups and saucers no two alike, has greatly argumented the demand. We make a specialty of these goods and in the retail stores you will find hundreds of them in different shapes and decorations selling at from 50c. up. The ones shown in the engraving sell for $1.00 each and the decorations are of a high order of artistic excellence. In no other make of French china will you obtain decorations of such character for the price. On the bottom of the cup or saucer is the tell-tale mark of superiority—the "Elite" stamp. There is no other mark like it on French china—you can't mistake it.

SINGLE CUPS AND SAUCERS.

Bawo & Dotter (Elite Work.

The "Odette" shape is a plain design relieved by a slight rococo edging which admits of exquisite gold tracing and in the absence of tracing , gives the pieces a finish which relieves the otherwise smooth surface. The handles are graceful but very strong. The plates and cups and saucers are of egg-shell thinness. The decoration illustrated is an elaborate one. Each piece bears a continuous stipple about the edges in burnished coin gold, interlined with a running floral vine. The decoration proper is a garland of miniature pinks. Such open piece as cups, gravy boats, etc. have garlands of forget-me-nots on the inside. A set of 102 pieces may be obtained of your dealer for about $60.00. Single pieces may be had at any time at the same proportionate cost. Fancy pieces such as Celery Trays, Chop Dishes. etc. to match.

No. 5001
ODETTE
SHAPE
OPEN
STOCK.

The decoration herewith pictured is one of the best selling ones we ever produced It was designed specially for the Odette shape and is so laid on the ware that the absence of gold on the edges is not noticeable. It is a wreath of conventionalized violets done in a pleasing purplish color with the stems and leaves in a complementary shading The elimination of gold on the edges gives the china an appearance of extra thinness. The handles are all stippled with burnished coin gold and the diverging rococo raised work is traced in gold. Like all our open stock patterns this embraces After-Dinner Coffees. Moustache Coffees. Celery Trays. Chop Dishes. etc. Your dealer will furnish a complete set of 102 pieces for about $37.00 or you can buy a dozen plates at the same rate. If he hasn't this particular pattern he will order it for you.

No. 5000.
ODETTE
SHAPE
OPEN
STOCK.

This illustration shows pieces made in the "Perle" shape besides the ones shown in decoration 5002 on a preceding page. Notice the teapot sugar bowl and cream pitcher: the most beautiful ever made in china. The decoration is a continuous vine of pink and lavender carnations supplemented on the covered ware and in side hollow pieces by an extra vine, similar but of lesser density. The edges of each piece are splashed here and there with burnished coin gold and the handles are carefully traced with gold. This decoration is a very effective one and is nearly one-half less in price than 5002. The ware is exactly the same but there is less detail to the ornamentation A set of 102 pieces at your dealer's for $54.00.

No. 5000
PERLE
SHAPE
OPEN
STOCK.

This shape was designed to go with Colonial silver services and to harmonize with dining room furnishings where the whole decorative scheme is after the colonial renaissance which is the vogue of the present day. The sale of it has not been confined to those who have their dining rooms so furnished by any means. because the graceful lines of each piece instantly create enthusiasm in all lovers of artistically formed china. There are sets on this shape in American homes which cost as high as $500.00. A beaded edge is the distinguishing feature of each piece and besides heightening the effect of coin gold. it greatly strengthens the edges of such pieces as plates without making them weighty. The decoration illustrated —festoons of miniature roses. with solid burnished gold edges—may be had of any dealer in odd pieces or in sets. A set of 102 pieces may be had of your dealer for about $90.00.

No. 5002
PERLE
SHAPE
OPEN
STOCK.

Bawo & Dotter Marks

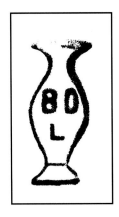

Mark 1, initials "B D" over "L" printed within a vase shape, overglaze decorating mark in a dark neutral color, ca. 1870s – 1880s.

Mark 2, overglaze decorating mark in green with Arms of Limoges (worn in example) and "Limoges" printed underneath, ca. 1870s – 1880.

Mark 2a, overglaze decorating mark in red, like Mark 2, ca. 1870s – 1880s.

Mark 2b, overglaze decorating mark in a dark neutral color, initialed with "PATENTED DEC. 12. 82."

Mark 3, overglaze decorating mark in red or green, like Marks 2 and 2a, plus the initials, "B. D." over "L," ca. 1880s.

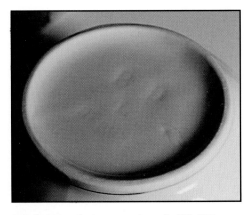

Mark 3a, early impressed mark "B" "D" over "L" with "Déposé," ca. 1896 to 1914.

Mark 4, underglaze white ware mark in green with "Limoges" written in script, ca. 1896 – 1900.

Mark 5, underglaze white ware mark in green, "ELITE/L/FRANCE," ca. after 1900.

Mark 6, overglaze decorating mark in red, without "France," ca. 1880s – 1891.

Mark 7, underglaze white ware mark in green or overglaze decorating mark in red, usually seen in conjuction with an American retailer's mark, ca. 1896 – 1900.

Mark 8, overglaze decorating mark in red with "Limoges" written in script, and "France" printed, ca. 1891 – 1900.

Mark 9, overglaze decorating mark in red with "ELITE WORKS," ca. 1900 – 1914.

Mark 9a, overglaze decorating mark in red, similar to Mark 9a but without "Bawo & Dotter," ca. 1900 – 1914.

Mark 9b, overglaze decorating mark in red like Mark 9, but with "Hand Painted" printed below mark in brown, ca. 1900 – 1914.

Mark 9c, overglaze mark in red like Mark 9a, but with "Hand Painted" printed below mark in brown, ca. 1900 – 1914.

Mark 10, overglaze decorating mark in red, wreath with "ELITE" printed in center and "HAND PAINTED" printed in ribbon on either side of wreath, ca. 1900 – 1914.

Mark 11, overglaze decorating mark in red with "ELITE" printed above Arms and "LIMOGES" printed below, ca. 1920 – 1932.

Mark 11a, underglaze white ware mark in green with "Limoges" and "Elite" printed above Arms, and "France" printed below, ca. 1920 – 1932.

Mark 12, overglaze decorating mark in black and brown, "Guérin, Pouyat, Elite, Ltd.," printed inside ornate emblem, after 1920.

Bawo & Dotter Studio and Factory Decorated China

Early Studio Decorated Table China

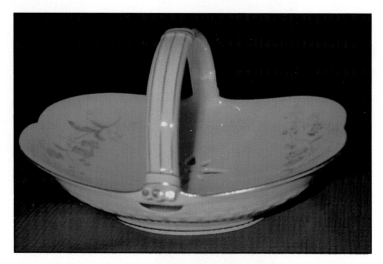

Plate 16. Butter basket; multi-colored floral sprays painted over transfer outlines. Bawo & Dotter Mark 2b. **$250.00 – 300.00.**

Plate 17. Tureen; the same floral pattern as the one on the butter basket decorates this piece, but butterflies have been added. "M R" (Martial Redon) incised and also printed underglaze in a dark neutral color (this odd color probably resulted from the firing process), and Bawo & Dotter Mark 2b. **$400.00 – 500.00.**

Plate 18. Cake plate, 10½" d; transfer outlined floral pattern with hand coloring and gold trim. Bawo & Dotter Mark 2 with "Déposé" printed above vase shape. **$150.00 – 175.00.**

Plate 19. Biscuit jar, 7½" h; hand-painted pink flowers and green leaves on a pastel green background with a gold finial and gold trim on top of jar. Bawo & Dotter Mark 2. **$275.00 – 325.00.**

Plate 20. Square plate, 7"; randomly spaced flowers colored in yellow and pink with green leaves; gold outlining on leaves and stems of bottom left design. Redon Mark 1 and Bawo & Dotter Mark 3. **$65.00 – 85.00.**

Plate 21. Square bowl on a short pedestal base; clusters of flowers with pink centers on long branches with green leaves decorate the interior and exterior of bowl applied with the *mixtion* technique. Bawo & Dotter Mark 3. **$140.00 – 165.00**

Plate 22. Tea set: tray 16" x 13", creamer, covered sugar, teapot; multi-colored flowers decorate body in spray designs, gold trim. Bawo & Dotter Mark 3. Teapot, **$300.00 – 400.00**; creamer, **$150.00 – 175.00**; covered sugar, **$175.00 – 200.00**; tray, **$800.00 – 900.00**.

Plate 23. Tea set: teapot, 8", creamer, and covered sugar; floral sprays painted in autumn colors are scattered over body of pieces and on top of lids. These are part of a 40-piece dessert set. Bawo & Dotter Mark 3. Teapot, **$275.00 – 325.00**; creamer, **125.00 – 150.00**; covered sugar, **$150.00 – 175.00**.

Plate 24. Covered bowl, 10" d plus handles; large blue-gray floral sprays with delicate flowers on thin stems decorate piece; gold trim on finial, handles, and borders. "Limoges, France" Mark 10 and Bawo & Dotter Mark 3. **$250.00 – 300.00**.

Plate 25. Plate, leaves painted in shades of brown and rust with small blue flowers are placed on three parts of the outer border with a butterfly in the center of the plate. Bawo & Dotter Mark 3a. **$70.00 – 85.00**.

Plate 26. Covered sugar bowl, decorated similarly to preceding plate and carrying the same impressed mark, Bawo & Dotter Mark 3a. **$150.00 – 175.00**.

Display China

Plate 27. Decorative plate, 9" d; fancy scrolled designs painted gold with clusters of small blue flowers frame a cupid placed against a stormy blue-gray background. Bawo & Dotter Mark 2a with a gold seal marked "Limoges." **$225.00 – 275.00.**

Plate 28. Chocolate pot, 10" h; enameled gold leaves on the body of the pot and gold sponged work on the handles, spout, and lower part of body distinguish this decoration. Small blue enameled flowers accent some of the gold branches; the body has a matte cream finish. Coiffe Mark 2 and Bawo & Dotter Mark 6. **$550.00 – 650.00.**

Plate 29. Vase, 7" h; floral décor vividly painted in purple, blue, orange, and green decorates lower body of this Moorish style vase; etched designs and small bead work can be seen on the gold handles, neck, and around top of base. Demartial (G. D. & Co.) Mark with Bawo & Dotter Mark 2a. **$650.00 – 750.00.**

Plate 30. Vase, 18" h; handles shaped like griffins make this an unusual piece; hand-painted lilies in shades of purple and dark pink, white daisies, gold floral sprays, and green leaves against a light pink-brown background cover the body of the piece; a deep burgundy finish decorates the arms and base; the griffins' heads are painted gold. Bawo & Dotter Mark 3. **$1,400.00 – 1,600.00.**

Plate 31. Clock case and clock, 17" h; ornately scrolled shape elegantly decorated with gold enameled floral designs and brushed gold high-lighting scrolled work; a reserve below the face of the clock features an eighteenth century style figural scene painted in pastel shades of blue, pink, and mauve and is signed, "Dubois." One woman is in front of a desk and a seated woman and three men are standing; trees and hills are visible in the background; the clock was made by the French firm of Japy Frères. Bawo & Dotter Mark 6 on the case. **$4,500.00 – 5,500.00.**

Plate 33. Vase, 13½" h; large pink roses with green leaves painted against a light green background shading to dark green at the base, accented with gold trim. Bawo & Dotter Mark 8 with "Hand Painted Through Out" printed in brown. **$1,200.00 – 1,400.00.**

Plate 32. Vase, 12½" h; ornately shaped applied handles; large pink and white roses on white body. Latrille Frères mark in green and Bawo & Dotter Mark 8 in red. **$1,000.00 – 1,200.00.**

Plate 34. Vase, 10" h; hand-painted pink and white peonies; applied feet painted gold. Redon Mark 2 and Bawo & Dotter Mark 8. **$600.00 – 700.00.**

Plate 35. Cabinet or display cup and saucer, 2" h; a courtship scene of figures in eighteenth century dress decorate a reserve on the front; gold enameled work frames the scene. Laviolette Mark 1 and Bawo & Dotter Mark 8. **$200.00 – 225.00.**

Plate 36. Vase, 12" h; very elaborate handles shaped as twisted vines with applied leaves; a woman in a lavender gown dances with a cherub, painted against a pastel blue-green background; neck of vase and leaves on handles painted green and accented with gold; gold scrolled work around base of neck and lower part of vase. Bawo & Dotter Mark 8. **$2,000.00 – 2,400.00** (mc.)

Plate 37. Vase, 7" h; cherub décor on a pale pink background; neck, handles, and base trimmed in gold and gold enameled work below cherub. Redon Mark 1 and Bawo & Dotter Mark 8. **$375.00 – 425.00**

Plate 38.

Plate 38. Biscuit jar, 7½" h; two cherubs hold a white dove against a matte pink background; sponged gold trim. Coiffe Mark 2 and Bawo & Dotter Mark 11. **$425.00 – 475.00.**

Plate 39. Jardiniere, 5½" h, 9½" d; deeply scalloped four-footed base, griffin-shaped handles; cupids decorate one side while children fishing decorate the reverse (not shown); pale blue background and heavily gilded handles and trim. Bawo & Dotter Mark 8. **$1,000.00 – 1,200.00.**

Plate 39.

Plate 40. Decorative plate, 8¼" d; heavily scalloped shape; center decoration of pansies painted in pastel colors; scrolled work around outer border highlighted with gold. Laviolette Mark 1 and Bawo & Dotter Mark 8 and the initials, "L. B. G. 2" are also on the back which may refer to the artist or decoration. **$140.00 – 165.00.**

Plate 41. Powder jar, 4" d; hand-painted pink flowers with yellow centers and green leaves decorate top and base; scrolled design on top outlined in gold enamel; dated "Dec. 25, 1894." This date should not refer to the decoration because the piece is marked with Bawo & Dotter Mark 8 which is a decorating mark. It is possible, however, that the piece merely had gold trim and the flowers were applied by an American china painter. Also, the date could refer to a presentation date. **$300.00 – 350.00.**

Plate 42. Punch bowl, 16" d x 9¾" h; large pink flowers and green leaves painted against a light green background with gold trim. Bawo & Dotter Marks 5 and 9. **$1,800.00 – 2,000.00.**

Plate 43. Vase, egg-shaped with applied feet; a reserve on the front is decorated with a bird of paradise perched in a tree covered with multicolored flowers; gold trim. Bawo & Dotter Mark 9. **$400.00 – 450.00.**

Plate 45. Plate, 8¼" d; large white flowers with yellow centers and green leaves cover most of the surface of the piece, artist signed but not decipherable. Bawo & Dotter Marks 5 and 9b. **$140.00 – 160.00.**

Plate 44. Vase, 5¾" h, letter holder style, footed; hand-painted violet flowers with enameled white daisies, gold trim; artist signed, "Ragoll." Redon Mark 2 and Bawo & Dotter Mark 7. **$350.00 – 375.00.**

Plate 46. Plate, 8½" d; a large pink rose and rosebuds are painted in the center of the plate with a dark rust colored background on the left side and a pastel blue with touches of yellow on the right side; artist signed, "Andrée." Bawo & Dotter Marks 5, 9, and 10. **$200.00 – 225.00.**

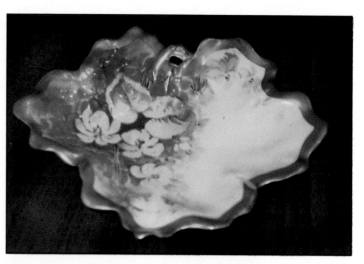

Plate 48. Leaf dish, 6" x 5"; hand-painted pale blue flowers and green leaves against a rust-colored background on the left side with some pink flowers extending to the right side which has a cream-colored background; heavy gold trim; artist signed, "Mullidy." Bawo & Dotter Marks 5 and 9b. **$175.00 – 200.00.**

Plate 47. Plate, 8½" d; large pink flowers painted on a green background cover surface; gold trim; artist signed, "Paula." Bawo & Dotter Mark 10 and Pitkin & Brooks Mark (American retailer, see under Limoges Companies Without Examples.) **$200.00 – 225.00.**

Plate 49. Plate, 8½" d; large orange poppy painted in an Art Nouveau style on a white background decorates center of plate, framed by a wide gold border; artist signed, "Riguel." Bawo & Dotter Marks 5 and 8 with "Hand Painted." **$225.00 – 250.00.**

Plate 50. Bowl, 12" x 10"; a very Art Nouveau shape and décor are evident on this piece; orange poppies are painted on the interior as well as on the exterior; inner border and handles painted gold. Bawo & Dotter Marks 5 and 9b. **$600.00 – 700.00.**

Plate 51. Square dish, 6", with a deeply scalloped border with an applied branch style handle at top; hand painted blue flowers with light green leaves around inner border; heavy gold trim. Bawo & Dotter Marks 5 and 9. **$75.00 – 100.00.**

Plate 52. Charger, 12" d, heavily scalloped and beaded border; Art Nouveau style flowers painted in solid gold and outlined in gold on a white background decorate center of piece, accented by a wide gold border. Bawo & Dotter Marks 5 and 9c. **$275.00 – 325.00.**

Plate 53. Plate, 9" d; large yellow flowers with pink centers and green leaves outlined in gold; light blue inner border and gold outer border; artist signed, "Mary." Bawo & Dotter Marks 5 and 9b. **$225.00 – 250.00.**

Plate 54. Cake plate, 10½" d, decorated with the same floral design as preceding piece and also signed, "Mary." Bawo & Dotter Marks 5 and 9b. **$250.00 – 275.00.**

Plate 55. Scenic plaque, 10½" d; medieval chateau painted in a forest setting on the edge of the sea; artist signed, "R. Parisil." Bawo & Dotter Marks 5, 9a, and 10 with "Chaumont" printed in red, indicating the name of the structure. **$500.00 – 550.00.**

Plate 56. Scenic plate, 9" d; windmill on river bank; artist signed, "E. Vidal." Bawo & Dotter Marks 5 and 9. **$350.00 – 400.00.**

Plate 57. Scenic plate, 10" d; mill on river with trees and mountains in background; yellow flowers and Art Nouveau designs decorate outer border; artist signed, "Lyra." Bawo & Dotter Marks 5 and 9b. **$500.00 – 550.00.**

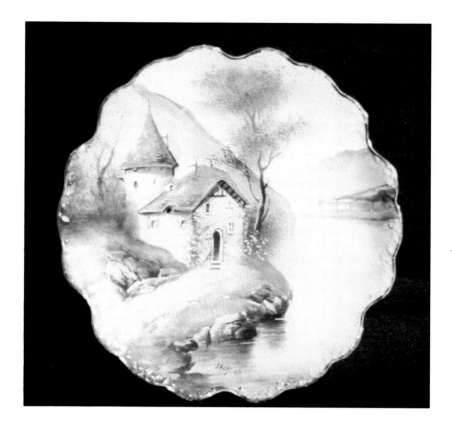

Plate 58. Scenic plaque, 10½" d, mill cottage on river bank with mountains in background; artist signed, "Laurent." Bawo & Dotter Marks 5 and 9. **$500.00 – 550.00.**

Plate 59. Scenic plaque, 10½" d, decorated similarly to the preceding piece, but with a view of a bridge; artist signed, "Laurent." Bawo and Dotter Marks 5 and 9. **$500.00 – 550.00.**

Plate 60. Scenic plaque, 10½" d; seascape portraying boats with rocks and bluffs in the background; artist signed, "E. Vidal." Bawo & Dotter Marks 5 and 9. **$375.00 – 425.00.**

Factory Decorated Table Wares

Plate 61. Mustache cup; a small green floral pattern on exterior with an interior pattern of small blue flowers; brushed gold trim. Coiffe Mark 2 and Bawo & Dotter Mark 8. **$175.00 – 200.00.**

Plate 62. Mustache cup and saucer; white daisies painted against a pale pink background decorate exterior of cup and inner border of saucer; gold accents on scalloped designs, foot, and handle. Redon Mark 2 and Bawo & Dotter Mark 8. **$225.00 – 275.00**

Plate 63. Demitasse set for 12 in a silk-lined presentation case; a delicate floral design forms a border pattern; outer rims and handles painted gold. Redon Mark 1 and Bawo & Dotter Mark 8. **$2,200.00 – 2,400.00 set.**

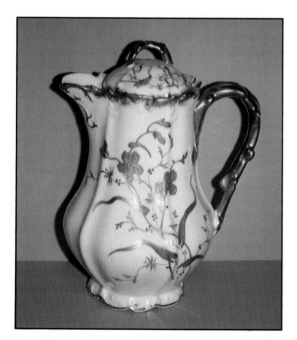

Plate 64. Chocolate pot, 9" h; gold paste floral designs on white body; heavily gilded finial and handle; Coiffe Mark 2 and Bawo & Dotter Mark 6. **$450.00 – 550.00.**

Plate 65. Fish service: platter, 23" l, serving plates (10), 9" d, gravy boat with underplate; scalloped border with shell designs; gold paste flowers, deep pink border, gold trim. C H mark (see Limoges Companies without Examples) and Bawo & Dotter Mark 6. **$2,200.00 – 2,500.00 set.**

Plate 66. Sardine box and seafood dish decorated with hand-painted clam shells and trimmed with brushed gold; artist initialed, "E. J. C." Bawo & Dotter Mark 8. Sardine box, **$275.00 – 325.00;** seafood dish, **$350.00 – 400.00.**

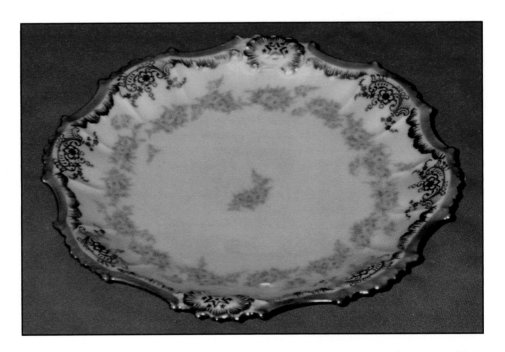

Plate 67. Plate, 9½" d, heavily scalloped border; pattern consists of a spray of light pink roses in the center surrounded by an inner border of rose clusters; fancy gold stenciled designs and brushed gold work accent outer border and accentuate handles of mold; apple green glaze around outer edge with gold trim. Coiffe Mark 2 and Bawo & Dotter Mark 8. **$150.00 – 175.00.**

Plate 68. Ice cream service: platter, 16" x 8½"; serving plates (6), 7" d; lilac and pink-tinted floral sprays decorate inner border of pieces and extend toward center; the scalloped fluted borders are finished in gold. Bawo & Dotter Mark 8. **$800.00 – 1,000.00 set.**

Plate 69. Bowl, 10"d; garlands of pink roses form a pattern in center and around inner border of bowl with outer border trimmed in gold. Bawo & Dotter Marks 5 and 6. **$60.00 – 75.00.**

Plate 70. Strawberry bowl and underplate; bowl is pierced to drain; pink and white floral pattern, gold trim. Bawo & Dotter Marks 5 and 9. **$350.00 – 400.00.**

Plate 71. Creamer and covered sugar bowl; large floral pattern of light blue flowers with yellow centers combined with small white flowers and light green leaves; sponged gold accents handles, feet, and finial; Bawo & Dotter Marks 5 and 9. **$300.00 – 350.00 set.**

Plate 72. Bowl, 10" d; large white roses on a dark green background in three places around bowl with delicate gold leaves framing rose on right. Bawo & Dotter Marks 5 and 8. **$80.00 – 100.00.**

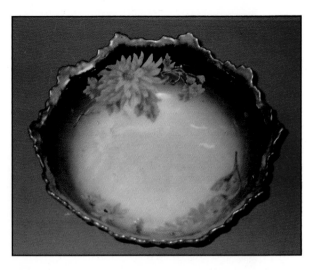

Plate 73. Bowl, 10" d; pink and yellow mums decorate two sides of bowl; dark green inner border with outer border painted gold; center undecorated. Bawo & Dotter Mark 9 with no white ware mark. **$120.00 – 140.00.**

Plate 74. Cup and saucer, pink roses on a cream-colored background and pink flowers on a green background, surrounded by dark blue, form a conventional border pattern. Bawo & Dotter Mark 9a. **$60.00 – 75.00.**

Plate 76. Dinner plate, floral garlands, cameos, and ribbons form outer border pattern; blue inner border overlaid with a gold floral pattern; gold trim. Guérin Mark 3 and Bawo & Dotter Mark 12. **$80.00 – 100.00.**

Plate 75. Dinner plate, birds of paradise compose center pattern with multi-colored floral branches scattered around outer border. Bawo & Dotter Marks 9a and 10. **$65.00 – 80.00.**

Plate 77. Dinner plate, 9½" d; conventional border pattern composed of blue and red flowers overlaid on a gold diaper pattern. Bawo & Dotter Marks 11a and 10. **$55.00 – 65.00.**

Plate 78. Covered vegetable dish, 13" l, oval shape, decorated with the same pattern as dinner plate above. **$150.00 – 175.00.**

Plate 79. Creamer & sugar, match preceding dinner plate and vegetable dish. **$200.00 – 225.00 set.**

American Decorated Blanks

Plate 80. Trinket box, 3½" h x 10" d; large red roses with gold and turquoise enameling are painted on center of lid with the outer border and base painted black; signed, "Adolph Anderson, 1899" on bottom of box. Bawo & Dotter Mark 5. **$400.00 – 450.00.**

Plate 81. Leaf dish, 7" x 5"; hand-painted gold leaves and light green leaves outlined in gold decorate center with a wide gold outer border; Bawo & Dotter Mark 5. Note that while this piece only has a green underglaze factory mark, it may very well be factory decorated. The décor is similar to a preceding plate painted in this Art Nouveau style. **$160.00 – 180.00.**

Plate 82. Dish, 10½" x 7", irregular shape with openwork on two sides; red berries and green leaves are painted on four places around the inner border on a brown background; center is undecorated except for some of the light green leaves extending into it; fluted outer border is heavily gilded. Bawo & Dotter Mark 5. **$175.00 – 225.00.**

Plate 83. Jardiniere, 6" h x 8" w; hand-painted white and yellow daisies with green leaves on a light blue-green background. Bawo & Dotter Mark 5. **$550.00 – 650.00.**

Plate 84. Ferner, 4½" h x 8" w, Art Nouveau shaped handles in branch design are split at top and extend to form feet; hand-painted red cherries on a pastel blue background with pink shading around relief design at top; handles, feet, and parts of upper and lower borders painted gold. Bawo & Dotter Mark 5. **$800.00 – 1,000.00.**

Blakeman & Henderson (B. & H.)

Some new information has surfaced regarding the Blakeman & Henderson marks. In my Revised 2nd Edition in 1992, I separated the Blakeman & Henderson overglaze script mark from the "B. & H." mark printed within a circle, which is found as an overglaze mark as well in green, gray, or red. Examples have now been found which have both the circular and the script marks, so it should be reasonable to say that the two marks were for the same company, that is, Blakeman & Henderson. Other substantiating information has also been conveyed to me in a letter from M. Jacques Plainemaison of the Plainemaison family who informed me that on some examples decorated by the Plainemaison factory, there was a "B. & H." circular mark. That mark, according to French writer Alain Baron, was a mark used by Blakeman & Henderson who were not manufacturers or decorators, but rather were *commissionaires,* or exporters.

There are examples of "B. & H." Mark 1 which have no white ware mark. The Blakeman & Henderson marks, however, are found with other underglaze factory marks. One of the most frequently seen is "Limoges, France" Mark 3, a scrolled banner. Thus, china with the Blakeman & Henderson marks may have actually been decorated by the factories of the white ware mark. But as with other exporting firms, such as Lewis Straus & Sons (L. S. & S.), examples are shown in this edition under the name of the decorating, exporting, or importing company and its overglaze mark rather than under the manufacturing company and its underglaze mark.

Porcelain carrying the Blakeman & Henderson marks is always superbly decorated. Game bird plates, decorative accessories, and vivid and elegant dinner ware patterns are shown in the following examples. The decoration incorporates both transfer and hand-painted work.

Blakeman & Henderson Marks

Mark 1, circle mark with initials, overglaze exporting mark in green, gray, or red, early 1900s.

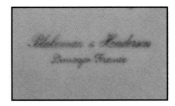

Mark 2, script mark, overglaze exporting mark in green, early 1900s.

Mark 3, circle mark with script mark, overglaze in green, early 1900s.

Decorative China

Plate 85. Tankard, 11¾" h; figural portrait of a girl in a white gown holding a rose; gold stenciled designs and gold trim accent piece; artist signed, "Baumy." Blakeman & Henderson Mark 1. **$1,400.00 – 1,600.00.**

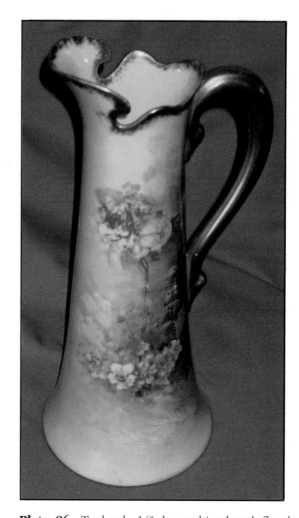

Plate 86. Tankard, 14" h; multi-colored floral décor on a lavender shading to cream background; gold finish on handle and top border; artist signed, "A. Janat." Blakeman & Henderson Mark 3. **$1,200.00 – 1,400.00.**

Plate 87. Plate, 8½" d; clusters of green grapes and leaves hanging from gold enameled branches frame the undecorated center of the plate; a light cream finish has been applied between the inner border of grapes and the outer gold rim; "Limoges, France" Mark 4 and Blakeman & Henderson Mark 2. **$150.00 – 175.00.**

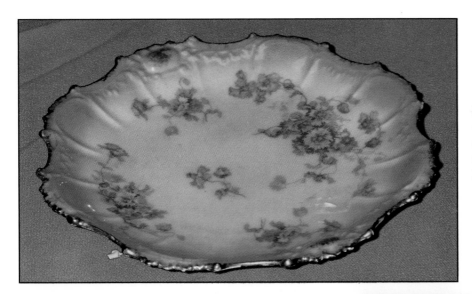

Plate 88. Plate, 8¼" d; transfers of lavender flowers are scattered over interior; a deep pink finish accents the relief work on the outer border; gold trim. Coiffe Mark 2 and Blakeman & Henderson Mark 1. **$100.00 – 125.00.**

Plate 89. Plate, 9½" d; large daisies tinted in pale lavender and blue or in white with green leaves on a cream shading to mauve background cover surface; gold trim. Blakeman & Henderson Mark 1. **$120.00 – 140.00.**

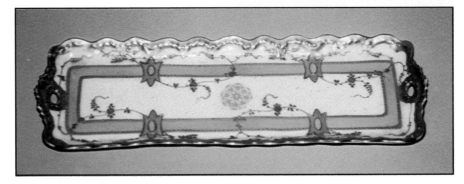

Plate 90. Receiving card tray, 10" x 3", pierced handles and scalloped rim; gold beaded border and enameled gold floral sprays; wide green inner border with gold medallion in center. "Limoges, France" Mark 6 and Blakeman & Henderson Mark 2. **$350.00 – 400.00.**

Plate 91. Plate, 8¼" d; Art Nouveau style décor of light green medallions painted with gold designs are connected and outlined by a fancy gold enameled chain around inner border; gold outer border. "Limoges, France" Mark 3 and Blakeman & Henderson Mark 1. **$100.00 – 125.00.**

Plate 92. Oval bowl, 12" l; large mums painted in vivid colors against a tinted blue and cream background; gold trim; artist signed, "Marsal." Blakeman & Henderson Mark 1 with a retailer mark for "R. L. Litsler, Winchester, Ind. **$275.00 – 325.00.**

Plate 93. One-handled dish or nappy, 7" x 6"; spray of large pink roses on a white background; sponged gold on handle and border. Coiffe Mark 2 and Blakeman & Henderson Mark 2. **$80.00 – 100.00.**

Plate 94. Powder jar, 2" h x 4" x 3"; flowers sculptured in relief at the top of each gilded foot; pattern of large yellow roses on a pastel background; artist signed, "L. Bronssillon." Blakeman & Henderson Mark 2. **$325.00 – 375.00 (mc).**

Plate 95. Oval bowl, 11" x 8"; purple and green grapes on a dark to light green background; gold trim; Coiffe Mark 2 and Blakeman & Henderson Mark 1. **$250.00 – 300.00.**

Plate 96. Ferner (with liner), 4½" h x 7" d; ornately scalloped feet painted gold; top half decorated with small enameled flowers on a light green border divided into sections by darker green triangular shapes. "Limoges, France" Mark 6 and Blakeman & Henderson Mark 1. **$450.00 – 550.00.**

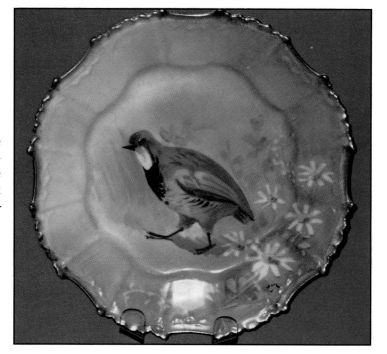

Plate 97. Game bird plate, 8½"; a brown game bird with a white throat is painted against a shaded green background highlighted with white daisies; gold trim; artist signed, "Luc." Coiffe Mark 3 and Blakeman & Henderson Mark 1. **$200.00 – 225.00.**

Plate 98. Game bird plate, 8½", painted with the mate of the game bird in the Plate 97; artist signed, "Luc." Coiffe Mark 3 and Blakeman & Henderson Mark 1. **$200.00 – 225.00.**

Plate 99. Game bird plaque, 11½" d; cockatoo perched on a tree limb with mountains in the background; artist signed, "Baumy." Blakeman & Henderson Mark 1. **$275.00 – 300.00.**

Plate 100. Game bird plaque, 11½" d; bird in flight over mountains; artist signed, "Baumy." Note this and the preceding plaque use the same mold and were painted by the same artist. Blakeman & Henderson Mark 1. **$275.00 – 300.00**.

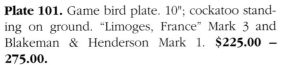

Plate 101. Game bird plate. 10"; cockatoo standing on ground. "Limoges, France" Mark 3 and Blakeman & Henderson Mark 1. **$225.00 – 275.00**.

Plate 102. Game bird plaque, 13½" d; duck flying over lake; artist signed, "Sena." "Limoges, France" Mark 3 and Blakeman & Henderson Mark 1. **$425.00 – 475.00**.

Plate 103. Bird plaque, 10½" d; yellow-breasted bird with vivid dark blue head and wings. "Limoges, France" Mark 3 and Blakeman & Henderson Mark 1. **$225.00 – 250.00.**

Plate 104. Plate, 9½" d; wild duck floating in marsh. Blakeman & Henderson Mark 1. **$175.00 – 200.00.**

Plate 105. Plaque, 11" d; a bird dog is standing at the edge of a lake; gold trim; artist signed, "Y. Golis." Blakeman & Henderson Mark 1. **$350.00 – 400.00.**

Plate 106. Plaque, 10" d; boats with black masts, on blue-gray water, are set against a dark sky with a hint of sun peeking through stormy clouds. Blakeman & Henderson Mark 1. **$325.00 – 375.00.**

Decorative Dinner Ware

Plate 107. Chocolate pot, 8" h; colorful fruit décor painted on a dark green background; top border and handle painted gold, artist signed, "J. Morseys." "Limoges, France" Mark 6 and "Blakeman & Henderson" Mark 1. **$600.00 – 700.00.**

Plate 108. Jam jar with underplate; fruit décor very similar to that on the preceding chocolate pot; both pieces are signed, "J. Morseys." There is some question about the signature; it can look like "Murray." "Limoges, France" Mark 2 and Blakeman & Henderson Mark 1. **$375.00 – 425.00 set.**

Plate 109. Cracker jar, large orange flowers set against a dark burnt-orange background; gold sponged work on finial and handles; artist signed, "J. Morseys." Coiffe Mark 3; Blakeman & Henderson Mark 1; and "J. P. Hale, Akron, Ohio" (retailer). **$400.00 – 450.00.**

Plate 110. Chocolate pot, individual size, 6" h; flowers painted in pink and lavender with green leaves cover body of pot; finial and handle painted gold; artist signed, "Dus." Coiffe Mark 3 and Blakeman & Henderson Mark 1. **$200.00 – 250.00.**

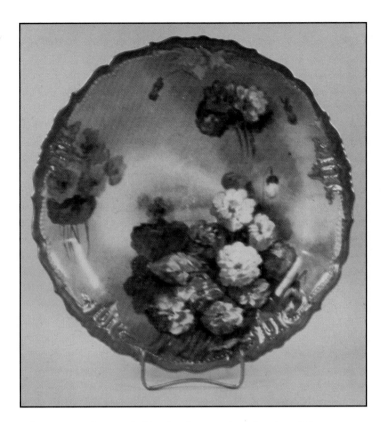

Plate 111. Plaque, 11½" d; white and violet tinted flowers on a shaded purple background; gold trim; "Limoges, France" Mark 2 and Blakeman & Henderson Mark 1. **$425.00 – 475.00.**

Plate 112. Cracker jar, pudding bowl, and jardiniere; white flowers against a pale lavender background; gold trim; each piece artist signed, "J. Morseys." "Limoges, France" Mark 2 and Blakeman & Henderson Mark 1. Cracker jar, **$425.00 – 475.00**; pudding bowl, **$325.00 – 375.00**; jardiniere, **$1,000.00 – 1,200.00.**

Plate 113. Plate, 8½" d; pink and white flowers form an inner border on a dark green background with gold enameled work and gold trim; the decorative border frames a white center decorated with a gold stenciled medallion and gold stenciled border. Coiffe Mark 2 and Blakeman & Henderson Mark 1. **$100.00 – 125.00**.

Plate 114. Plate, 9" d; lavender, pink, and blue floral sprays accented with small yellow flowers are scattered across surface of plate; gold trim. Vultry Frères Mark and Blakeman & Henderson Mark 1. **$65.00 – 85.00**.

Plate 115. Basket, 6" l; violet-colored flowers on a white background. "Limoges, France" Mark 4 and Blakeman & Henderson Mark 2. **$175.00 – 200.00**.

Plate 116. Cake plate, 12" d; small clusters of pink and white flowers around inner border; gold trim. Blakeman & Henderson Mark 1. **$150.00 – 175.00**.

Plate 118. Compote; small red flowers, green *fleur-de-lis,* and gold stenciled scroll designs form interior inner border; two gold bands surround well, and a wide gold band is painted around interior outer border. Blakeman & Henderson Mark 3. **$140.00 – 160.00.**

Plate 117. Plate, 8¾" d; a medallion of small pink roses in center of plate is framed by a rose garland around the well and clusters of small pink roses on a light green background; white outer border highlighted with gold on the molded scroll designs; outer border painted gold. "Limoges, France" Mark 2 and Blakeman & Henderson Mark 1. **$60.00 – 75.00.**

Plate 119. Tea set; green leaves connected by a gold enameled loop chain form an Art Nouveau design; handles, finials, and spout painted gold. "Limoges, France" Mark 3 and Blakeman & Henderson Mark 2. Tea pot, **$300.00 – 350.00;** creamer, **$125.00 – 150.00;** covered sugar bowl, **$150.00 – 175.00.**

Plate 120. Coffee set; wide gold bands overlaid with pink tulips and green leaves outlined in gold compose another Art Nouveau decoration on this set; spout of coffee pot and handles, finials, and rims of all pieces are gilded. "Limoges, France" Mark 4 and Blakeman & Henderson Mark 2. Coffee pot, **$500.00 – 600.00**; creamer, **$125.00 – 150.00**; covered sugar bowl, **$150.00 – 175.00**.

Plate 121. Chocolate set, garlands of pink roses form a border pattern with abstract designs painted in gold scattered randomly over body of piece; outer borders painted gold and outlined in black; Blakeman & Henderson Marks 1 and 2 (pieces marked with either one or the other). Chocolate pot, **$400.00 – 500.00**; creamer, **$110.00 – 125.00**; covered sugar bowl, **$125.00 – 140.00**; dessert plates, **$40.00 – 50.00**; serving plate, 12½" d, **$225.00 – 250.00**; cups and saucers, **$75.00 – 90.00**.

Borgfeldt, George (Coronet)

George Borgfeldt operated a New York based importing company with art studios located in France and Germany. The French studio was located in Paris, but the china was made by various factories in Limoges. The Coiffe and Mavaleix white ware marks are often seen on items with the "Coronet" Mark. Many examples, however, do not have a white ware Mark. Expertly and richly decorated plaques and plates with games bird, floral, and figural themes carry the Coronet Mark. The art studio used the *mixtion* method of decoration, combining transfer designs with hand-painted work. Artist signatures are found on many of the pieces and are in great demand by collectors.

Pieces trimmed with wide gold borders are higher in price than those without gold. Decoration subjects such as the "Cavaliers" are a popular series, and the different figures can make a colorful set. Some table wares were also decorated by the company. Examples of the Borgfeldt company are from about 1906 to the 1920s.

Borgfeldt Marks

Mark 1, overglaze decorating mark in green or blue, crown with "CORONET," ca. 1906-1920.

Mark 2, overglaze decorating mark in green like Mark 1 but with "TRADE MARK," after 1920.

Portrait Plaques and Figural Decorations

Plate 122. Plaque, 10½" d; cavalier holding a meerschaum pipe with a white plume of smoke escaping from his mouth; gold trim. Artist signed, "L. Coudert." Mavaleix Mark and Borgfeldt Mark 1. **$425.00 – 475.00.**

Plate 123. Plaque, 10½" d; portrait of a smiling cavalier, tweaking his mustache; gold trim; artist signed, "L. Coudert." Mavaleix Mark and Borgfeldt Mark 1. **$425.00 – 475.00.**

Plate 124. Plaque, 10" d; seated cavalier dressed in a colorful costume; gold border; artist signed, "Le Pic." Borgfeldt Mark 1. **$425.00 – 475.00.**

Plate 125. Plaque, 10" d; standing figure dressed in a pink tunic, white shirt, and green cape; artist signed, "Luc." Borgfeldt Mark 1. **$300.00 – 350.00.**

Plate 126. Plaque, 10" d; cavalier standing, dressed in a yellow tunic with a purple cape; artist signed, "Luc." Borgfeldt Mark 2. **$300.00 – 350.00.**

Plate 132. Plaque, 10" d; portrait of a monk holding a wine glass; artist signed, "Le Pic." Borgfeldt Mark 1. **$225.00 – 275.00.**

Plate 133. Plaque, 10" d; portrait of a monk smoking a pipe; artist signed, "Le Pic." Borgfeldt Mark 2. **$225.00 – 275.00.**

Plate 134. Plaque, 10" d; portrait of an Indian in full regalia with one feather in his hair; artist signed, "Luc." Borgfeldt Mark 1. **$550.00 – 650.00.**

Plate 136. Plaque, 18" d; figural scene of a seated woman hugging a child, painted in an outdoor setting; gold trim; artist signed, "E. Furlaud." Borgfeldt Mark 1. **$2,200.00 – 2,500.00.**

Plate 135. Plaque, 10" d; portrait of an Indian with long black hair, dressed with a hat, beads, and medals; artist signed, "Luc." Borgfeldt Mark 1. **$550.00 – 650.00.**

Plate 138. Vase, 25" h; portrait of a barefooted woman, dressed in white and holding a broken vase, placed in an outdoor setting; green floral designs painted in an Art Nouveau style decorate borders; gold enameled leaves accent the piece; handles, neck, and base trimmed in gold. Borgfeldt Mark 1 overlaid with gold. **$2,200.00 – 2,400.00 (mc).**

Plate 137. Square dish, 6½", reticulated border; figural portrait of a woman strumming a lute; gold trim; artist signed, "J. Yarin." "L. B. LIMOGES, FRANCE" printed as an underglaze Mark in green (unidentified company) and Borgfeldt Mark 2. **$325.00 – 375.00.**

Bird, Fish, Animal, and Scenic Decorations

Plate 139. Plaque, 10" d; rooster and hen; artist signed, "L. Coudert." Borgfeldt Mark 1. **$200.00 – 225.00.**

Plate 140. Plaque, 9½" d; turkey gobbler and hen; artist signed, "L. Coudert." Mavaleix Mark and Borgfeldt Mark 1. **$175.00 – 200.00.**

Plate 141. Game bird set: platter, 18" x 13"; plates, 8¾" d; a brightly painted cockatoo decorates the platter and two of the plates; wild ducks and game birds are painted on the other four plates; the background is a light green, shading to yellow and accented with yellow flowers; gold trim; artist signed, "Noryl." Borgfeldt Mark 1. Platter, **$1,000.00 – 1,200.00.**

Plate 142. Plates to game set: wild ducks, 8¾"d. **$200.00 – 225.00 each.**

Plate 143. Plates to game set: cockatoos, 8¾"d. **$200.00 – 225.00 each.**

Plate 144. Plates to game set: game birds, 8¾"d. **$200.00 – 225.00 each.**

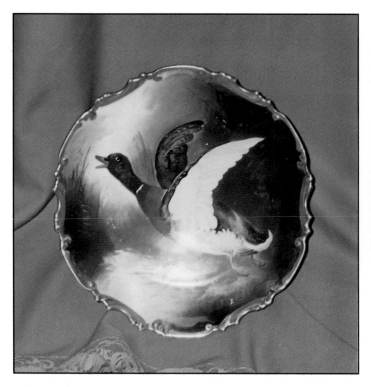

Plate 145. Plaque, 11½" d; wild duck flying over marsh against a dark cobalt blue background highlighted with yellow; gold trim; artist signed, "Duval." Borgfeldt Mark 1. **$400.00 – 500.00.**

Plate 146. Plaque, 11½" d; large white-breasted bird is set against green grasses with a village in the background; gold trim; artist signed, "Duval." Borgfeldt Mark 1. **$350.00 – 400.00.**

Plate 147. Plaque, 10" d; ring neck pheasant; artist signed, "L. Coudert." Borgfeldt Mark 1. **$200.00 – 225.00.**

Plate 148. Plaque, 12½" d; game bird and two chicks; gold trim; artist signed, "C. Rosier." Borgfeldt Mark 1. **$375.00 – 425.00.**

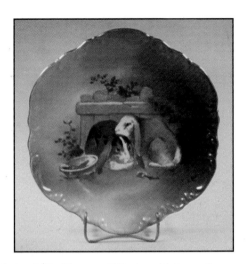

Plate 149. Plaque, 10" d; rabbits eating carrots; artist signed, "L. Coudert." Borgfeldt Mark 1. **$325.00 – 375.00.**

Plate 150. Plaque, 10" d; wild boars cavorting in a winter setting; artist signed, "Pradet." Coiffe Mark 2 and Borgfeldt Mark 1. **$300.00 – 350.00.**

Plate 151. Plaque, 9½" d; a pair of red foxes are painted against a green and lavender background; artist signed, "Pradet." Latrille Frères Mark 1 and Borgfeldt Mark 1. **$350.00 – 375.00.**

Plate 152. Plaque, 9½" d; a buck and a doe are set against a background similar to that of the foxes; artist signed, "Pradet." Latrille Frères Mark 1 and Borgfeldt Mark 1. **$350.00 – 375.00.**

Plate 153. Plaque, 10" d; portrait of a dog; artist signed, "L. Coudert." Borgfeldt Mark 1. **$300.00 – 350.00.**

Plate 154. Plaque, 9¾" d; portrait of a cat with a dragonfly in the background; artist signed, "L. Coudert." Borgfeldt Mark 1. **$300.00 – 350.00.**

Plate 155. Plaque, 11½" d; monochrome portrait of a kitten; gold trim; artist signed, "Dubois." Borgheldt Mark 1. **$325.00 – 375.00.**

Plate 156. 9½" d; underwater view of a fish; artist signed, "Naillat." Mavaleix Mark and Borgfeldt Mark 1. **$150.00 – 175.00.**

Plate 157. Plate, 10" d; outdoor winter scene; artist signed, "Rory." "Limoges, France" Mark 6 and Borgfeldt Mark 2. **$250.00 – 275.00.**

Plate 158. Plaque, 10" d; scenic décor of two people in a large boat with sail; artist signed, "Duval." Borgfeldt Mark 1. **$325.00 – 375.00.**

Plate 159. Plaque, 10" d; another boat scene painted by "Duval" on the same blank as in Plate 158. Borgfeldt Mark 1. **$325.00 – 375.00.**

Floral and Fruit Decorations

Plate 160. Bowl, 8" d; deep mauve and light pink roses with green leaves decorate interior. Mavaleix Mark and Borgfeldt Mark 1. **$120.00 – 135.00.**

Plate 161. Plate, 8½"; small white bell-shaped flowers with yellow enameled centers and large green leaves are painted over surface of plate; gold trim. Mavaleix Mark and Borgfeldt Mark 1. **$130.00 – 145.00.**

Plate 162. Charger, 12" d; autumn-colored leaves and red berries; gold trim; artist signed, "Duval." Latrille Frères Mark 1 and Borgfeldt Mark 1. **$450.00 – 500.00.**

Plate 163. Plate, 8½" d; white roses are tinted with pink on a white background; gold trim. Coiffe Mark 3 and Borgfeldt Mark 1. **$130.00 – 145.00.**

Plate 165. Charger, 13" d; large pink roses on a dark green background; gold trim. Borgfeldt Mark 1. **$550.00 – 650.00.**

Plate 164. Charger, 13½" d; two large pink leaves and white flowers with enameled gold centers and dark green leaves on wine stems form an Art Nouveau design over a scenic lake background; gold trim; artist signed, "J. Barin." **$600.00 – 700.00.**

Plate 166. Plate, 9½" d; pink roses on a white background accented by a dark green finish on scroll work around border; gold trim. Coiffe Mark 3 and Borgfeldt Mark 1. **$150.00 – 175.00.**

Plate 167. Plate, 8¾" d; large pink dahlias are painted against a light green shading to cream background; gold trim; artist signed, "Barin." Latrille Frères Mark 1 and Borgfeldt Mark 1. **$200.00 – 225.00.**

Plate 168. Charger, 15" d; a basket holds a bouquet of brightly colored roses; gold trim; artist signed, "Duval." Borgfeldt Mark 1 in green and in gray. **$1,200.00 – 1,400.00.**

Plate 169. Charger, 11½" d; basket of multi-colored dahlias; artist signed, "Duval." Borgfeldt Mark 1. **$700.00 – 800.00.**

Plate 171. Ferner, 5½" h x 7" d; pink roses accented with white enamel against a pale yellow to deep burnt-orange background; heavily gilded feet; artist signed, "Gex." Borgfeldt Mark 1. **$600.00 – 700.00.**

Plate 170. Plate, 10¼" d; vividly painted fruit decor featuring a sliced orange and purple grapes; gold trim; artist signed, "Barbet," Borgfeldt Mark 1. **$500.00 – 600.00.**

Plate 172. Vase, 15" h; pink and yellow roses with green leaves cover body; artist signed, "A. Bronssillon." Mavaleix Mark and Borgfeldt Mark 1. **$1,600.00 – 1,800.00.**

Plate 174. Triangular dish, 9¾" x 10½"; pattern of pink floral sprays; gold trim. Coiffe Mark 3 and Borgfeldt Mark 2. **$175.00 – 225.00.**

Plate 173. Chocolate pot, 10" h; dark and light pink roses cover body; gold trim. Latrille Frères Mark 1 and Borgfeldt Mark 1. **$500.00 – 600.00.**

Plate 175. Tea set; pink roses on curling stems with green leaves form an Art Nouveau pattern accented with heavily molded scrolled designs around borders. Latrille Frères Mark 1 and Borgfeldt Mark 1. Tea pot, **$325.00 – 375.00;** creamer, **$150.00 – 175.00;** covered sugar bowl, **$175.00 – 200.00.**

Plate 176. Chocolate cup and saucer, pink flowers with white daisies are scattered over body; gold trim. "Limoges, France" Mark 4 and Borgfeldt Mark 1. **$80.00 – 100.00.**

Plate 177. Chocolate pot, 13" h, matches cup and saucer above. **$450.00 – 550.00.**

Coiffe

The distinctive star mark used by the Coiffe factory is one of the most frequently seen on various pieces of Limoges porcelain. The factory produced large quantities of china which were decorated by other Limoges factories and studios. The Coiffe mark is usually accompanied by one of these other Limoges marks. Coiffe blanks decorated by American china painters are also found, but not as frequently as Coiffe blanks decorated by other French companies or carrying the marks of French or American exporting firms. It is possible that the Coiffe china with exporter marks such as Lewis Straus & Sons (L. S. & S) and others was actually decorated by the Coiffe factory. Examples with the exporter marks all exhibit French factory or studio decoration. That is, pieces with an exporter mark do not appear to be blanks which were exported for the American china painting market.

When the Coiffe mark is the only mark on an object, the decoration also often appears to be professional and, more-over, of Limoges origin. Several pieces of this nature are shown here as well as a few Coiffe blanks decorated by American china painters. I have included Coiffe in this chapter even though few examples are shown here under their name. Numerous other items made by Coiffe, however, are found throughout the book under the name of other Limoges companies. It is evident that the Coiffe factory was prolific and manufactured quality porcelain, often ornately fashioned, ranging from table china to decorative accessories.

The company had several associates during its history which dates from the 1870s to the mid 1920s. The same mark is shown for L. Coiffe and E. Coiffe, jeune (younger or Junior) by Lesur and Tardy (pp. 55, 108). L. Coiffe is noted as being in business during the mid 1870s, and E. Coiffe, jeune, operating in Limoges from 1887.

Coiffe Marks

Mark 1, underglaze white ware mark in green without "FRANCE," before 1890.

Mark 2, underglaze white ware mark in green with "FRANCE," after 1891 – 1914.

Mark 3, underglaze white ware mark in green with "LIMOGES, FRANCE," after 1891 – 1914.

Mark 4, underglaze white ware mark in green with "MADE in FRANCE," after 1914 – 1920s.

Coiffe Professionally Decorated China

Plate 178. Plaque, 10" d; fruit décor painted and signed by "Luc" on a pair of plates shown in this and the following example: hand-painted peaches, one whole and one split. Coiffe Mark 3. **$200.00 – 225.00.**

Plate 189. Oval plaque, 9½" x 13", made with a fluted frame; hand-painted cottage and mill scene; frame painted gold. This piece is unusual because most plaques were made with smooth edges and not any framework. Coiffe Mark 1. **$400.00 – 500.00.**

Plate 190. Vase, 7" h, fashioned with a wrap-around or napkin fold design on top third of piece and scalloped shell designs above pedestal base; hand-painted berries with light to dark green leaves; gold trim. Coiffe Mark 2. **$250.00 – 275.00.**

Plate 191. Clock case, 8" h x 5" d; ornately scrolled body design accented with gold; a large reserve on the front is decorated with a hand-painted boat scene which is complemented by a similar scene in a small reserve at the top of the case; artist initialed "A. F.," and dated "189-" (the last digit of the year is not clear) in gold, on the lower left side of reserve. Coiffe Mark 2. **$2,000.00 – 2,200.00.**

Délinières (D. & Co.)/Bernardaud (B. & Co.)

Remy Délinières was associated with P. Guéry during the 1860s. No marks have been attributed to the association of Guéry and Délinières. Some collectors, however, have written to me about examples which have impressed initials "G. D." It is possible that such a mark could have been used by Guéry and Délinières, but without more information, I will not attribute that mark to them. According to d'Albis and Romanet (pp. 161, 162), Délinières became head of the company after 1879. Wood (p. 31) notes that the Délinières Company did not decorate its production until after 1881 when a decorating workshop became part of the factory. In 1900, the company became L. Bernardaud and Co. Leon Bernardaud and his father had worked for Délinières. Although they were the successors of Délinières circa 1900, the year 1863 is often cited as the founding date of Bernardaud & Co. That time, though, actually marks the beginning of the Guéry firm which preceded Guéry and Délinières. Leon Bernardaud's company was continued by his family and is currently in operation.

Examples of Délinières and Bernardaud china are found mostly in the form of white wares painted by American china painters. Factory decorated art objects, accessory items, and fish and game services seem to more frequently carry Délinières marks. Factory decoration on Bernardaud marked china is generally confined to table wares. The blanks or white wares, however, illustrate that the companies produced a large amount of porcelain in a variety of objects and shapes. The large jardinieres are especially popular among collectors. Examples made by both Délinières and Bernardaud are illustrated together in this section with the particular mark for each noted in the caption. Factory decorated china precedes the non-factory decorated china.

D. & Co. Marks 1 and 2, underglaze green marks, represent early white ware marks, and Mark 4, an overglaze red mark, represents an early decorating mark. These were in use before 1891. According to Wood (p. 31), Mark 4 was the company's first decorating mark and was continued until 1893. Mark 3 is the most commonly seen D. & Co. mark, dating after 1891 until 1900. It is found on many decorative white wares which have American hand-painted decoration. Factory-decorated items with Mark 5, an overglaze mark in red of "R. Délinières & Cie., Limoges" written in script form, is usually found on table wares or decorative fish and game services. Pieces which appear to be factory decorated are sometimes found without an overglaze decorating mark, notably some early hand-colored patterns on dinner ware which are included here. The early white ware mark (Mark 1) of Bernardaud closely resembles the style of Délinières' marks. Examples are also found with the D. & Co. white ware mark and the decorating mark of Bernardaud, indicating the transition in ownership. Bernardaud Mark 2 is sometimes cited as dating from after 1930. That mark, however, was probably in use after World War I. An example has been found with that Bernardaud Mark 2 and a Pickard decorating mark which was in use between 1912 – 1919 (Platt, p. 74). The decorating mark, of course, had to have been applied after the white mark.

Délinières & Co. Marks

Mark 1, underglaze white ware mark in green, ca. 1870s.

Mark 2, underglaze white ware mark in green with one line under initials, ca. 1879 – 1893.

Mark 3, underglaze white ware mark in green with "FRANCE," ca. 1894 –1900.

Mark 4, overglaze decorating mark in red, pot or vase design, ca. 1881 – 1893.

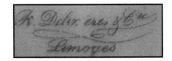

Mark 5, overglaze decorating mark in red, name written in script form, ca. 1894 – 1900.

Mark 6, overglaze decorating mark in red, printed name in oval shape with name of Scottish importer.

Bernardaud & Co. Marks

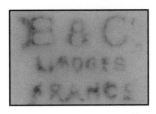

Mark 3, overglaze decorating mark in red "L. Bernardaud & Cie.," ca. 1900 – 1930s and after.

Mark 1, underglaze white ware mark in green, "B&CO." over "FRANCE," ca. 1900 – 1914.

Mark 2, underglaze white ware Mark in green, "B&CO." over "LIMOGES, FRANCE," 1914 – 1930s and after.

Mark 4, underglaze white ware mark in green of "D. & Co." over "FRANCE" (D. & Co. mark 3) with an overglaze mark in red of "L. Bernardaud & Cie.," after 1900, a transition mark showing the succession of Bernardaud & Co. to Délinières & Co.

Délinières/Bernardaud Factory Decorated China

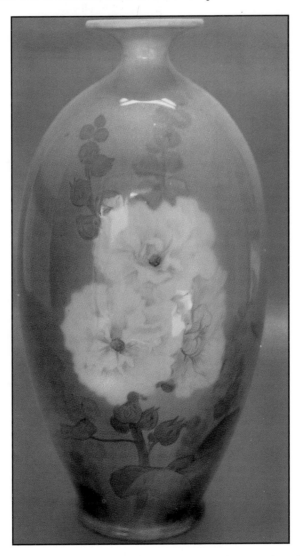

Plate 192. Vase, 12" h; large white flowers on a blue background painted underglaze; artist signed, "Berg." D. & Co. Mark 4 on a circular pad on base with an artist mark in underglaze blue; there is no overglaze decorating mark except the artist mark. Underglaze painted decoration is rarely found. **$1,200.00 – 1,400.00.**

Plate 194. Plate, 9" d; cherub holding a flower; gold stenciled designs around border. D. & Co. Mark 4, no white ware mark. **$200.00 – 225.00.**

Plate 193. Vase, 12" h; underglaze decoration like the preceding vase but painted with a large white bird in flight; artist signed, "Berg," and marked as above. **$1,200.00 – 1,400.00.**

Plate 195. Portrait plate, 9" d; "Louis XV" printed on back with D. & Co. Marks 3 and 5. There are other plates in this series including one of "Louis XVI." **$225.00 – 275.00.**

Plate 196. Tray, 11" x 8½"; figural and scenic décor of a cavalier galloping on horseback with a river and castle in the background; the scene is framed by gold enameled flowers and scroll designs; pompadour rose glaze on wide border with gold trim. D. & Co. Marks 3 and 4. **$400.00 – 500.00.**

Plate 197. Cachepot, 8" h x 8" w; blue and pink enameled flowers with green leaves on a light pink ground with borders trimmed in deep wine with gold trim. D. & Co. Marks 2 and 4. **$500.00 – 600.00.**

Plate 199. Gravy boat and underplate matching fish plate. D. & Co. Mark 1. **$325.00 – 375.00 set.**

Plate 198. Fish serving plate, 9" d; a fish on the bank composes center decoration; the border has a vivid teal blue glaze overlaid with enameled gold floral designs. D. & Co. Mark 1 with no overglaze decorating mark, but set is factory decorated. **$220.00 – 240.00.**

Plate 200. Platter for fish service, 22" l x 9" w. D. & Co. Mark 1. **$1,200.00 – 1,400.00.**

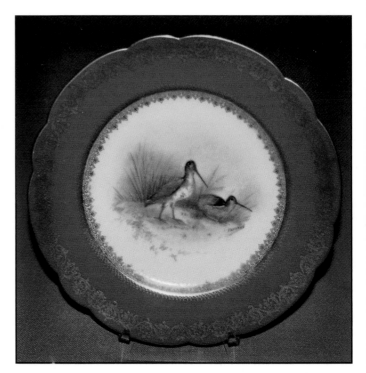

Plate 201. Game bird plate, 8¾" d; a wide wine-colored border overlaid with gold stenciled designs frames birds; artist signed, "Faynaud." D. & Co. Marks 3 and 5. **$200.00 – 225.00.**

Plate 202. Fish platter, 24" l x 9" w; a large fish decorates center of platter; blue and green floral border, gold trim; the set includes serving plates decorated with a different fish on each and a sauce boat (not shown). D. & Co. Marks 2 and 4. **$2,800.00 – 3,000.00 set.**

Plate 204. Open bowl, 4" h x 10½" d; a similar floral design as on plate, composed of a spray of multi-colored enameled flowers and leaves; thin gold outlining on handle and spout. D. & Co. Mark 1. **$100.00 – 120.00.**

Plate 203. Plate, 7¼" d; pink roses with purple and blue flowers arranged in a large spray on right side with a small cluster of purple flowers on the left. This floral design is hand-colored over a transfer outline. This and the following four examples appear to be early factory decorations, although there is no overglaze decorating mark on them. There is an exporting mark on some examples. D. & Co. Mark 1 with T. & V. Mark 1a, an exporting mark in blue. **$45.00 – 55.00.**

Plate 206. Covered vegetable bowl, 101/4" l, painted with a variation of preceding pattern. D. & Co. Mark 1. **$225.00 – 275.00.**

Plate 205. Pitcher, 8" h, bamboo-shaped handle, decorated with the same floral pattern as bowl. D. & Co. Mark 1. **$300.00 – 325.00.**

Plate 208. Dessert or sandwich set; blue floral pattern with sponged gold around borders. D. & Co. Marks 3 and 5. **$175.00 – 225.00**

Plate 207. Tea set decorated like covered bowl. D. & Co. Mark 1 with T. & V. Mark 1a, an exporting mark in blue. Covered sugar bowl, **$150.00 – 200.00**; creamer, **$125.00 – 150.00**; cup & saucer, **$75.00 – 90.00 set.**

Plate 209. Plates, 8¼" d; floral designs are hand enameled in pink, blue, and yellow and vary on each plate; brushed gold on fluted border. D. & Co. Marks 2 and 4. **$75.00 – 90.00 each.**

Plate 210. Platter, 14" l; white floral transfer pattern on a light turquoise ground; brushed gold and gold stenciled designs on a cream border highlight pattern. D. & Co. Marks 3 and 5. **$325.00 – 375.00.**

Plate 211. Compote, 9¼" d x 2½" h; pink, lavender, and orange flowers scattered over surface; sponged gold on scallops around border. D. & Co. Marks 3 and 6. **$300.00 – 350.00.**

Plate 212. Decorative dish, 10" l, with handle; irregular shape with open work around border on top side; spray of yellow-gold flowers on interior and part of exterior; salmon tinted glaze on border; gold trim; D. & Co. Mark 3 and "for Hodson and Sons, Leeds," overglaze decorating mark. **$300.00 – 350.00.**

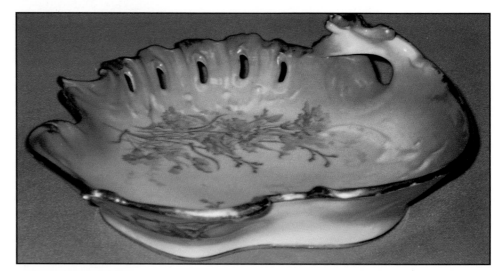

Plate 213. Cake plate, 10½" d; blue, gold, and burnt-orange flowers form an inner border pattern; handles heavily gilded. B. & Co. Mark 4. **$150.00 – 175.00.**

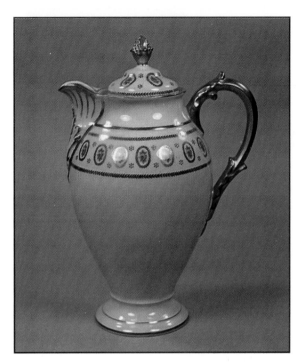

Plate 214. Chocolate pot, 9½" h; clusters of pink roses between fancy gold stenciled designs decorate upper part of pot and lid; gold trim. B. & Co. Mark 4. **$275.00 – 325.00.**

Plate 215. Chocolate pot, 10½" h; pink rose cameos are on lid and upper border; gold trim. B. & Co. Mark 4. **$325.00 – 375.00.**

Plate 216. Demitasse set; floral garlands compose pattern around borders; gold trim. B. & Co. Mark 4. Demitasse pot, **$300.00 – 350.00;** cup and saucer, **$75.00 – 100.00 each;** tray, **$275.00 – 325.00.**

Plate 217. Chamber stick and ring tree, 5" d; pattern of large dark green leaves with gold sponged work accenting borders and handles. D. & Co. Marks 3 and 5. **$225.00 – 275.00.**

Plate 218. Ferner, 5" h x 8½" w, footed; green leaf pattern accented with sponged gold. D. & Co. Marks 3 and 5. **$450.00 – 550.00.**

Plate 219. Lamp, 9½" (originally fueled by oil); pattern of violets on a white ground; brushed gold on base. D. & Co. Mark 3 without a decorating mark, but piece is factory decorated. **$1,000.00 – 1,200.00.**

Luncheon service: This is a unique set made especially by Bernardaud for a reception honoring Queen Elizabeth II when she visited France in 1957. The set was commissioned by French president, Jules Gustave Coty. The reception was held in the Hall of Mirrors at Versailles in April, 1957. The occasion was an attempt by both nations to heal the breach that had developed between the two countries during the Suez Canal War in 1956. The Phoenix bird in this pattern symbolized the new relationship between those two world powers. The value of these pieces would ultimately be determined by the desire of a collector. Because of the special history of the china and its nature as a royal commemorative, a minimum value of **$1,200.00 – 1,500.00** per place setting is listed here.

Plate 220. Bernardaud marks on luncheon service.

Plate 221. Dinner plate; pattern of Phoenix birds and flowers enameled in gold.

Plate 222. Cup and saucer shows the decoration on the interior of the cup as well as on the exterior.

American Decorated White Wares
Display Pieces with Figural and Scenic Themes

Plate 223. Vase, 7½" h; portrait of a woman dressed in a pink gown with a cherub perched on her shoulder; grape vines are in the background; dark green finish around reserve with portrait; artist signed, "L. E. Hummel 1900." D. & Co. Mark 3. **$800.00 – 1,000.00.**

Plate 224. Portrait charger, 14½" d; portrait of a girl wearing a colorful beret on her dark hair; green leaves are in the background. D. & Co. Mark 3. **$1,200.00 – 1,400.00.**

Plate 225. Painting on porcelain, 14" x 11"; figure of a girl dressed in a white gown with exposed shoulders; a river and river bluffs are in the background. D. & Co. Mark 3. **$1,200.00 – 1,400.00.**

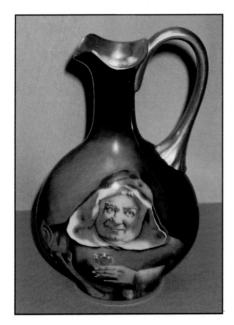

Plate 226. Ewer, 8" h; portrait of a hooded monk holding a glass of wine painted on a dark brown background; gold finish on interior and handle. D. & Co. Mark 3. **$375.00 – 425.00.**

Plate 227. Whiskey or wine jug, 6½" h; portrait of a monk drinking from a wine bottle; dark brown glaze around reserve; stopper monogrammed in gold; artist signed on the bottom with the year, 1905. D. & Co. Mark 3. **$350.00 – 400.00.**

Plate 228. Cider pitcher, 5" h; 7" d at base; hand-painted windmill scene around top half of pitcher; gold trim. D. & Co. Mark 3. **$275.00 – 325.00.**

Plate 229. Painting on porcelain, 13" x 8¾"; hand-painted scenic décor of a river and bridge. D. & Co. Mark 3. **$400.00 – 500.00.**

Table Wares and Accessory Items with Floral and Fruit Themes

Plate 230. Leaf dish, 6½" x 7"; small white flowers on a light green background enhanced with gold enameled scroll designs and gold trim. D. & Co. Mark 3. **$175.00 – 200.00.**

Plate 231. Basket, 6½" x 7"; ornate handle with relief work; blue flowers on a cream background; sponged gold and gold outlining accent flowers; gilded handle; interior has a pink glaze. D. & Co. Mark 1. **$175.00 – 200.00.**

Plate 232. Round tray painted with red and purple grapes; D. & Co. Mark 3. **$350.00 – 400.00.**

Plate 233. Powder bowl or jar; pink roses painted on a light pink background and accented with gold. B. & Co. Mark 1. **$400.00 – 450.00.**

Plate 234. Covered sugar bowl and creamer; *fleur-de-lis* painted gold on a dark blue background; gold trim. B. & Co. Mark 1. **$75.00 – 100.00 set.**

Plate 235. Cider pitcher, 5½" h; hand-painted pots of flowers decorate each panel of pitcher; gold trim. B. & Co. Mark 2. **$200.00 – 250.00.**

Plate 236. Two-handled cup, 2½" h x 3" d; abstract geometric designs around top border with a pearl luster finish on the body; artist signed on the base "McCully." D. & Co. Mark 3. **$45.00 – 55.00.**

Plate 237. Cruet, 6" h; small pink and red flowers and green leaves form a pattern below the handle; gold trim. B. & Co. Mark 2. **$75.00 – 90.00.**

Plate 238. Perfume bottle, 5½" h; a border around bottle is painted with blue and pink flowers against a dark blue or black band; stopper painted gold. B. & Co. Mark 1. **$100.00 – 125.00.**

Plate 239. Tankard, 9½" h; red and purple grapes. D. & Co. Mark 3. **$400.00 – 450.00.**

Plate 240. Tankard, 13½" h; purple grapes; handle and base painted gold. D. & Co. Mark 3. **$700.00 – 800.00.**

Plate 241. Mug, 6" h; unusual handle fashioned with the applied head and bust of woman; hand-painted purple and green grapes; borders and handle painted gold. D. & Co. Mark 3. **$225.00 – 275.00.**

Plate 242. Pitcher, 6½" h; hand-painted blackberries with green leaves. D. & Co. Mark 3. **$250.00 – 300.00.**

Plate 243. Condensed milk container and underplate; hand-painted red currants and green leaves on a tinted light green background; gold trim. D. & Co. Mark 3. **$400.00 – 450.00 set.**

Plate 244. Cider pitcher, 6½" h; hand-painted cherries; artist signed and dated "Z. Goodrick, '15." B. & Co. Mark 1. **$425.00 – 475.00.**

Jardinieres and Vases with Floral Themes

Plate 245. Covered potpourri jar, 13½" h; heavily gilded applied work on sides of jar, around feet, and on lid; there are pierced openings on the lid which causes this to be a potpourri jar rather than an urn; light pink flowers with green leaves. D. & Co. Mark 1. **$1,000.00 – 1,200.00.**

Plate 246. Jardiniere, 9¼" x 13", on separate claw-footed stand, with handles shaped in the form of lions' heads; lavender flowers with yellow centers and green leaves; base, handles, and neck heavily gilded. D. & Co. Mark 3. **$3,000.00 – 3,500.00.**

Plate 247. Jardiniere, 8" x 12"; separate base with embossed designs painted in green and brown tones, and mauve; large dark pink roses; border painted gold in an irregular design; artist signed and dated "L. M. N. April 1898." D. & Co. Mark 1. **$2,000.00 – 2,500.00.**

Plate 248. Jardiniere, 8" x 12" h; lion head handles and separate base with paw feet; multi-colored roses on a pastel background; lions' heads and base painted gold. D. & Co. Mark 1. **$3,500.00 – 4,000.00.**

Plate 249. Jardiniere, large size; ornately scalloped feet and handles painted gold; large white mums with green leaves painted on a pastel ground. D. & Co. Mark 3. **$2,200.00 – 2,600.00.**

Plate 250. Jardiniere, 11¾" x 14"; lion head handles and separate base with paw feet; yellow, light pink, and dark pink roses decorate one side; lions' heads and paw feet on base painted gold. D. & Co. Mark 3. **$3,500.00 – 4,000.00.**

Plate 251. Reverse of jardiniere above right painted with light and dark pink roses.

Plate 252. Jardiniere, 6" x 6½" (note small size); yellow mums cover body; gold trim. B. & Co. Mark 1. **$450.00 – 550.00.**

Plate 253. Jardiniere, 9" x 11"; large pink roses painted on a light green background; artist signed, "Mel." B. & Co. Mark 1. **$500.00 – 600.00.**

Plate 254. Vase, 5" h; dark pink and light pink roses are painted in a garland and chain design around center with a green finish above and below flowers; gold trim. D. & Co. Mark 3. **$275.00 – 325.00.**

Plate 255. Letter holder or vase, 6" h, footed; lavender flowers with green leaves and butterflies are outlined in gold on a matte cream background. D. & Co. Mark 3. **$325.00 – 375.00.**

Plate 256. Vase, 16" h, straight sides with a slight flare at base; large pink roses are accented with gold scrolled designs and a wide gold border; artist signed, "Anna Peters Denver." D. & Co. Mark 1. **$800.00 – 1,000.00.**

Plate 257. Vase, 12" h, same shape as preceding vase; light pink flowers and buds with green leaves are painted on a light yellow background; a gold border encircles the interior. B. & Co. Mark 1. **$500.00 – 600.00.**

Plate 258. Vase, 10" h; lavender and light orange poppies on a light to dark green background. B. & Co. Mark 1. **$550.00 – 650.00.**

Plate 259. Vase, 11½" h, reticulated border; applied ring-shaped handles painted gold; pink roses form a large garland on front of vase; gold trim. B. & Co. Mark 1. **$700.00 – 800.00.**

Plate 260. Vase, 12" h, same reticulated style as preceding vase; a scenic ruin is painted on a light matte cream background on one side; handles painted gold with sponged gold around border and at top of handles. D. & Co. Mark 3. **$800.00 – 900.00.**

Plate 261. Reverse of vase above decorated with gold paste flowers.

Plate 262. Vase, 8" h; openwork handles fashioned in an Egyptian style are painted gold; small purple flowers and multi-colored leaves decorate body of vase on a cream background; the neck of the vase is decorated with gold webbed designs in imitation of a crackle finish. D. & Co. Mark 2. **$700.00 – 800.00.**

Plate 263. Vase, 9" h, made in the same shape as the preceding vase; large white daisies and pink flowers with green leaves outlined with gold enameled work are painted on lower part of vase; sponged gold on border of neck; gilded handles. D. & Co. Mark 2. **$800.00 – 900.00.**

Plate 264. Vase, 10" h; rose décor with pink and yellow roses on body and white roses on interior; handles painted gold; artist signed, "Meg." D. & Co. Mark 3. **$900.00 – 1,000.00.**

Flambeau China (L. D. B. & Co.)

According to two marks, this company is identified by the name, "Flambeau China." (See Marks 3 and 5.) The company who used the initials "L. D. B. & Co." and "Flambeau China," accompanied by a distinctive torch mark, remains unidentified. The torch and flame composing the mark are obviously the insignia for the company's name. Sometimes the marks are difficult to read, and the "B." in the group of initials may look like an ampersand. A mark similar to Mark 5 is also noted to have been used on Bavarian china. Some of the Flambeau China examples have a white ware mark (see Mark 1). But many pieces only have one of the deco-rating marks with or without the white ware mark of another Limoges factory. From the dates of the other factories' white ware marks, it is apparent that Flambeau China was in business from the late 1890s until World War I. Its first operations were also probably confined to decorating, rather than manufacturing, porcelain. The company may well have been American based as was common at this time. China with the Flambeau marks is highly decorated and often hand-painted. No examples have been found of blanks decorated by American artists.

Flambeau China Marks

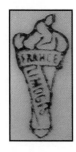

Mark 1, underglaze white ware mark in green, torch with "Limoges, France," ca. 1890s – 1914.

Mark 2, overglaze decorating mark in red, torch with initials and "Limoges, France," ca. 1890s, probably used before the company manufactured porcelain.

Mark 3, overglaze deco-rating mark in green, red, or blue with "Flambeau," ca. 1890s – 1900s.

Mark 4, overglaze decorating Mark in green with "Flambeau, Limoges, France" printed in ban-ner around torch with "Hand Painted," ca. 1890s – 1900s.

Mark 4a, overglaze decorat-ing mark like Mark 4 but with "Hand Painted" printed rather than in script.

Mark 5, overglaze decorating mark in green, torch in oval shape with initials and "Flam-beau China," before 1914 and after Marks 2, 3, and 4.

Mark 6, overglaze decorating mark in green, initials and "Flam-beau China" printed in circular design around torch with "Hand Painted," before 1914, and after Marks 2, 3, and 4.

Flambeau Game Bird and Animal Decorations

Plate 265. Plate, 9½" d; game bird poised to fly; artist signed, "René." Flambeau Mark 2. **$175.00 – 200.00.**

Plate 266. Plaque, 10" d; cockatoo standing in the marsh with a lake in the background. Flambeau Marks 1 and 3. **$200.00 – 225.00**

Plate 267. Plaque, 9¾" d; bird in flight above a cluster of flowers; gold trim; artist signed, "Dubois." Flambeau Marks 1 and 2. **$250.00 – 275.00.**

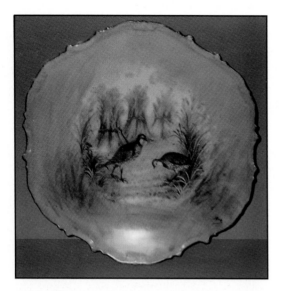

Plate 268. Plaque, 9" d; game birds in a wheat field; narrow gold trim; artist signed, "René." Flambeau Mark 6. **$200.00 – 225.00.**

Plate 269. Plate, 10" d; game bird in flight over a large white water lily; artist signed, "René." Flambeau Mark 4 without "Hand Painted." **$175.00 – 200.00.**

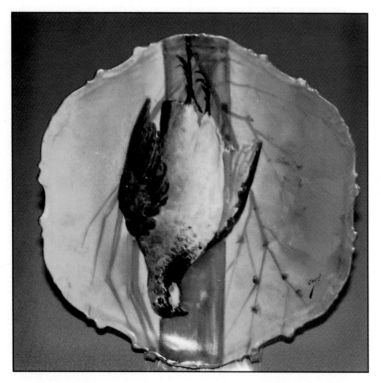

Plate 270. Plaque, 10" d; dead game bird; artist signed, "Canvi." Flambeau Mark 4. **$150.00 – 175.00.**

Plate 272. Plaque, 10" d; pair of game birds standing in a field; a large white daisy is in the foreground; gold trim; artist signed, "René." Flambeau Mark 4. **$250.00 – 275.00.**

Plate 271. Plaque, 9½" d; game bird in flight over water with pastel flowers in the background; gold trim; artist signed, "Dubois." Flambeau Marks 1 and 4. **$250.00 – 275.00.**

Plate 273. Plate, 9½" d; black-feathered and white-breasted game bird in flight; orange flowers at top of plate; artist signed, "Max." "Limoges, France" Mark 6 and Flambeau Mark 2. **$200.00 – 225.00.**

Plate 274. Plate, 8½" d; a rabbit decorates center; artist signed, "Dubois." Laviolette Mark and Flambeau Mark 2. **$120.00 – 140.00.**

Plate 275. Plate, 8½" d; a matching decoration to Plate 274; the rabbit is hopping across the grass. **$120.00 – 140.00.**

Plate 276. Plate; red foxes painted in a winter scene; brushed gold trim; artist signed, "TOG." The following two plates are part of a winter series by this artist. Coiffe Mark 3 and Flambeau Mark 4 without "Hand Painted." **$350.00 – 375.00.**

Plate 277. Plate decorated with wolves. **$350.00 – 375.00.**

Plate 278. Plate decorated with wild boar. **$350.00 – 375.00.**

Flambeau Fish Decorations

Plate 279. Plaque, 10½" d; large fish with purple iris in the foreground; artist signed, "Levy." Flambeau Marks 1 and 3. **$200.00 – 225.00.**

Plate 280. Plaque, 10" d; a pair of fish on a pale blue background surrounded by large pink flowers; gold trim; artist signed, "Dubois." Flambeau Mark 3. **$225.00 – 250.00.**

Plate 281. Charger, 12" d; two large fish on bank with a basket in the background; gold trim; artist signed, "Brisson." Flambeau Mark 2. **$400.00 – 450.00.**

Plate 282. Plate, 8¾" d; fish painted with a lake setting in the background; pink flowers on the right side appear only partially finished; artist signed, "Levy." Flambeau Marks 1 and 4a. **$60.00 – 75.00.**

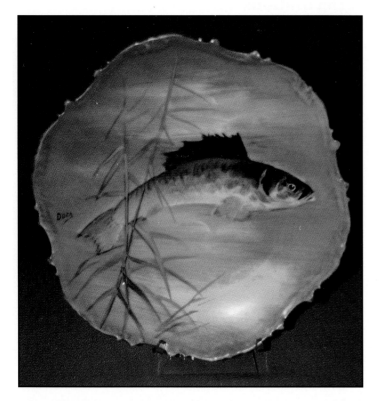

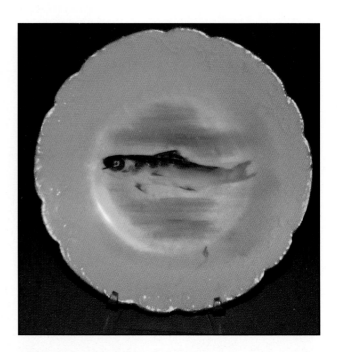

Plate 284. Plate, 8½" d; fish decorates center with a sky and water background; artist signed, "René." Flambeau Marks 1 and 4 (without "Hand Painted"). **$100.00 – 125.00.**

Plate 283. Plate, 9½"; large fish on a green tinted ground; artist signed, "Duca." Flambeau Mark is like Mark 6, but in solid green. **$200.00 – 225.00.**

Plate 285. Platter, 19" x 8", matches plate above right; a very large fish covers center of platter with the same sky and water background; artist signed, "René," and marked like plate. **$375.00 – 425.00.**

Plate 286. Platter to fish set, 10½" x 24"; a single large fish decorates each piece on a green shading to rust-orange background with large white lily pads in the foreground; gold trim; artist signed, "René." Flambeau Mark 2. Set with platter, gravy dish and underplate, and 12 serving plates, **$3,500.00 – 3,700.00.**

Plate 287. Gravy dish and underplate to fish set.

Plate 288. Individual serving plates to fish set, 9½" d.

Fruit and Floral Decorations

Plate 289. Plaque, 10" d; a peach and a pear are painted against a dark green background; artist signed, but name is illegible. Flambeau Marks 1 and 4. **$200.00 – 225.00.**

Plate 290. Plaque, 9½" d; two pears on a bed of green leaves; artist signed, but name is illegible. Flambeau Mark 1. **$200.00 – 225.00.**

Plate 291. Cake plate, 10" d; peaches and pink blossoms with green leaves form inner border; gold trim. Coiffe Mark 3 and Flambeau Mark 4. **$175.00 – 200.00.**

Plate 292. Plaque, 10¾" d; large yellow apples with pink flowers and green leaves cover surface; gold trim. Flambeau marks 1 and 4. **$375.00 – 425.00.**

Plate 293. Plate, 8½" d; enameled gold flowers; gold trim; artist signed, "Gilbert." "Limoges, France" Mark 4 and Flambeau Mark 3. **$150.00 – 175.00.**

Plate 294. Cake plate, yellow daffodils with green leaves; gold trim; artist signed, "Bay." "Limoges, France" Mark 4 and Flambeau Mark 3. **$325.00 – 375.00.**

Plate 295. Plate, 8½" d; one red-gold rose stands out among large pink roses; gold trim. "Limoges, France" Mark 6 and Flambeau Mark 3. **$150.00 – 175.00.**

Plate 296. Plaque, 10¼" d; one large pink rose, on a bent stem with large green leaves, appears to be painted to show a water reflection; artist signed, but signature is not legible. Flambeau Marks 1 and 3. **$225.00 – 250.00.**

Plate 297. Berry set: serving bowl, 10" d and 6 individual bowls, 5½" d; pink and white roses decorate lower part of bowls; gold trim; artist signed, "André." Coiffe Mark 3 and Flambeau Mark 4. **$800.00 – 1,000.00 set.**

Plate 298. Celery dish, 12½" x 5½"; pink and green floral designs in an Art Nouveau style around border; gold trim; artist signed, "Luc." Coiffe Mark 3 and Flambeau Mark 3. **$350.00 – 400.00.**

Plate 299. Mug, 5½" h; hand-painted medallions with black centers alternate with smaller gold medallions connected with a gold chain; black outer border; gold handle; artist signed, "Max." Paroutaud Mark 1 and Flambeau Mark 4. **$175.00 – 200.00.**

Plate 300. Plaque, 11½" d; flowers painted a vivid red, purple, and yellow, with long green leaves, decorate right half of plate with a faint image of a castle in the background on the left side; artist signed, "René." Flambeau Marks 1 and 4a. **$375.00 – 425.00.**

Plate 301. Plaque, 10½" d; one pink rose and two red roses are set against a dark mauve ground; artist signed, but name is illegible. "Limoges, France" Mark 2 and Flambeau Mark 4. **$325.00 – 375.00.**

Flambeau Portrait and Scenic Decorations

Plate 302. Plaque, 18" d; figural portrait of two Dutch girls with scenic seaside background; heavily gilded border; artist signed, "Dubois." Flambeau Mark 2. **$2,500.00 – 3,000.00.**

Plate 303. Plaque, 17½ d; figural scene of a woman giving money to a child with a beggar; heavily gilded border; artist signed, "Dubois." Flambeau Mark 2. **$2,500.00 – 3,000.00.**

Plate 304. Plaque, 11" d; portrait of an 18th century woman; gold trim; artist signed, "Dubois." Flambeau Mark 4. **$1,200.00 – 1,400.00.**

Plate 306. Plaque, 9½" d; country barn scene; artist signed, "Max." Flambeau Marks 1 and 3. **$250.00 – 275.00.**

Plate 305. Plate, 10½" d; scenic décor of a man with a cane, walking on a farm road; a house and barn are in the background; artist signed, but signature is not legible; "Limoges, France" Mark 6 and Flambeau Mark 3. **$275.00 – 325.00.**

William Guérin (W. G. & Co.)

During the early 1870s, William Guérin became the owner of the Utzschneider porcelain factory in Limoges, where he had been the director. The firm carried on a large export business. Most Guérin-marked china which is found on the American market is in the form of white wares decorated by American china painters or factory decorated table china. In the white ware line, Guérin seems to have had an exclusive on "cachepots." That word literally means a pot made to hide something such as plants, letters, or even rubbish, depending on the size which ranges from 6" to 12". Relatively few factory-decorated art objects are found with the exception of some vases.

Shortly before World War I, the Pouyat firm merged with Guérin. It appears that both the Pouyat marks and the Guérin marks were used after that time. Two years after the war, however, the Guérin Company was purchased by Bawo & Dotter (Elite Works). Due to the war years, from the time Pouyat and Guérin were joined and the short period after the war before the company was sold, it is difficult to know how much of the new production would have actually carried a Pouyat mark. It is probable that the remaining Pouyat stock, which was already marked, was sold through the Guérin company, or that the former Pouyat factory merely continued to produce china and marked it with the same Pouyat marks which had been in use prior to the merger.

It is also noted by French references that all three companies' marks were continued after 1920 by Bawo & Dotter when they purchased Guérin-Pouyat. Bawo & Dotter Mark 12, an overglaze mark, incorporates the words "Guérin-Pouyat-Elite, Ltd." That overglaze mark was found in conjunction with a Guérin marked blank. Thus the new mark seems to have been added to blanks already marked with either the Guérin, Pouyat, or Elite marks. The Bawo & Dotter Mark 12 is rarely seen. Bawo & Dotter closed in 1932, and thus Guérin marks are no later than that year. (See Bawo & Dotter and Pouyat in this section.)

Mark 1, "WG & Ce," (for *compagnie*) is a mark attributed to Guérin when he was associated with Utzschneider. It would date in the 1870s, and it is rarely found. Mark 2, although printed with "FRANCE," should date prior to 1891. Mark 3, printed with both "LIMOGES," and "FRANCE," is after 1900; this is the mark most frequently found on Guérin examples. Mark 4 is a decorating mark, certainly in use after 1891, and perhaps some years earlier. The mark seems to have remained essentially the same with some variations which are infrequently seen and were probably not intended for use on exported wares. Examples of such marks are "Wm. Guérin & Co. de Limoges, France," and "W. Guérin and Cie., Paris & Limoges" printed in an oval shape. A torch printed with "Guérin Feu de Four" may be found as a mark on some pieces, indicating a special firing process.

The Guérin examples, while showing a limited amount of factory decorated china, do illustrate a wide variety of items, including not only table china, but accessory items for the dresser and desk, and jardinieres and vases as well. It is easy to see why so much of American-painted china carries a Guérin white ware mark. A number of Guérin blanks with hand-painted decoration have been selected to show the range of the company's production.

Guérin Marks

Mark 1, underglaze white ware mark in green, "W G & Ce," ca. 1870s.

Mark 2, underglaze white ware mark in green, "WG & Co. FRANCE," before 1891 – 1900.

Mark 3, underglaze white ware mark in green, with "LIMOGES" and "FRANCE," 1900 – 1932.

Mark 4, overglaze decorating mark in red, blue, green, brown, or gold, late 1800s to 1932.

Factory Decorated China

Plate 307. Game service: a wild duck in flight over a marsh setting decorates each piece; a dark cobalt blue outer border overlaid with gold stenciled designs accentuates decoration; the use of different game birds on the pieces combined with the cobalt trim makes this a striking set. Plate, 8¾" d. Guérin Marks 3 and 4. Set with 12 plates, **$3,800.00 – 4,000.00**

Plate 308. Plate from game service showing a different game bird.

Plate 309. Platter to game service, 18½" x 10½", heavily gilded handles.

Plate 310. Vase, 15" h; white irises accented with purple on a green background; gold trim. Guérin Marks 3 and 4. **$1,400.00 – 1,600.00.**

Plate 311. Vase, 13" h; gold paste roses and leaves applied over a dark cobalt blue background with a high glaze. Guérin Marks 3 and 4. **$1,600.00 – 1,800.00.**

Plate 312. Tea caddy, 3" h; salmon and white lilies decorate each side and top of lid; relief scroll work brushed with gold. Guérin Marks 2 and 4. **$275.00 – 300.00.**

Plate 313. Coffee pot, 8½" h; pink and blue-gray floral transfer pattern on body and lid; gold sponged work on handle, finial, and spout; the piece appears to be factory decorated although there is no overglaze decorating mark. Guérin impressed initials "W. G. & C." over "L," and Guérin Mark 2. **$350.00 – 400.00.**

Plate 314. Tureen, 7" h x 13" l; deeply scalloped handles and finial lightly brushed with gold; pink, blue, and gray floral transfer pattern. Guérin Marks 2 and 4. **$400.00 – 450.00.**

Plate 315. Serving bowl; a bold blue, yellow, and red border pattern with floral garlands around inner border; "The Mandarin" is printed in red within a wreath on each piece and indicates that the china was made for a Chinese restaurant. Guérin Marks 3 and 4. **$125.00 – 150.00.**

Plate 316. Chop plate, 13½" d; a gold stenciled medallion decorates center and is enhanced by a wide cobalt blue border with gold stenciled designs around edge. Guérin Marks 2 and 4. **$225.00 – 275.00** (mc).

Plate 317. Platter, 17½" l; small pink roses around inner border and in center; gold trim on handles; Guérin Marks 3 and 4. **$300.00 – 350.00.**

American Decorated White Wares

Display Pieces with Figural Decoration

Plate 318. One-handled plate, 10" d; center decoration of a cherub holding a bow in one hand and a fish in the other, framed with enameled gold scroll work, on a pink background; gold trim. Guérin Mark 2. **$275.00 – 325.00.**

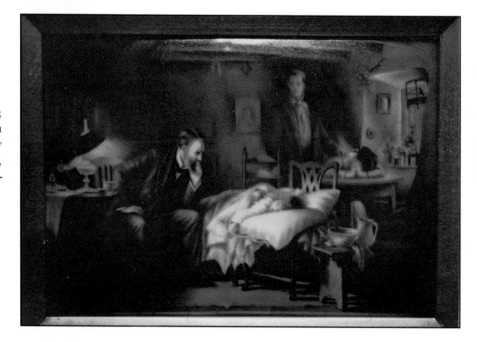

Plate 319. Painting on porcelain, 4" x 6"; a portrait of a doctor and child based on the original painting of "The Doctor," by Sir Luke Fidles; artist signed, "Aug. 1899, J. Gorin." Guérin Mark 2. **$3,000.00 – 3,500.00.**

Plate 320. Miniature vase, 3½" h, possibly a salesman's sample; a portrait of a woman dressed in white with a pink headdress is painted in a reserve on the front; artist signed, "Lorme." Guérin Mark 3. **$250.00 – 300.00.**

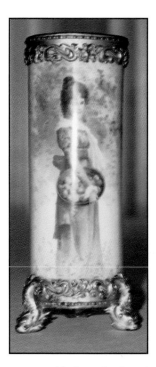

Plate 321. Vase, 7½" h; cylinder shape mounted with gilded metal at top and base; feet shaped in dolphin form; the decoration is a transfer of a Victorian girl holding a basket of apples; this transfer is also seen in china decorated by other European factories. It is possible that the vase was decorated at the Guérin factory, or some professional studio, but it does not have an overglaze decorating Mark. Guérin Mark 3. **$1,200.00 – 1,400.00.**

Plate 323. Tankard, 14¾" h; figural portrait of a monk drinking from a wine jug is painted in sepia tones. "Here's Looking 15th Century" is printed below figure. This decoration was to commemorate the beginning of the 20th century, with this side hailing the discovery of America in 1492. The reverse side is printed with, "20th Century," and portrays a woman preparing a punch to toast the new century. Art Nouveau style white flowers, dark green trim and gold accents enhance the decoration; artist signed, "E. L. Ferguson, 1901." Guérin Mark 3. **$2,000.00 – 2,200.00.**

Plate 322. Potpourri jar, 15" h; figural portrait of a woman in a white gown sitting on a river framed by gold enameled designs on a cream background; a dark green finish on the lid and base complement the background of the portrait reserve; artist signed, "C. J. Doyle." Guérin Mark 2. **$1,800.00 – 2,000.00.**

Plate 324. Reverse side of tankard in Plate 323.

Plate 325. Tankard, 14½" h; portrait of a cavalier sitting on a white and gold draped bench holding an ale tankard in one hand; artist signed, "Graue." Guérin Mark 3. **$1,400.00 – 1,600.00.**

Plate 326. Tankard, 14½" h; portrait painted in brown tones of a monk in a wine cellar. Guérin Mark 3. **$600.00 – 700.00.**

Vanity, Desk Items, and Trays

Plate 327. Hand mirror, 5" d; white and lavender daisies painted on porcelain back of mirror. Guérin Mark 3. **$275.00 – 300.00.**

Plate 328. Powder jar, 4½" d; sprays of multi-colored flowers decorate china; the bowl has burnished gold metal fittings on top of bowl base and on lid. Guérin Mark 2. **$225.00 – 275.00.**

Plate 329. Desk set: tray, ink pot holder; blotter and stamp box; note the relief scrolled work at the back of the tray which serves as pen rests; hand-painted pansies decorate center of pieces accented by gold scrolled designs and pink-beige borders; artist signed, "MC, X-Mas 1897." Guérin Mark 2 on all pieces except the stamp box which has T. & V. Mark 5a. **$700.00 – 800.00 set.**

Plate 330. Miniature vase, 4" h; white daisies on a tinted green background with neck painted gold. Guérin Mark 2. **$100.00 – 125.00.**

Plate 331. Leaf dish, 6" x 5"; large white daisies on a tinted blue background; gold trim. Guérin Mark 3. **$60.00 – 75.00.**

Plate 332. Dresser tray, 16½" x 12"; swan and lily pads scenic theme. Guérin Mark 3. **$200.00 – 225.00.**

Plate 333. Tray, 11" l x 6" w; split center handle painted gold; pink roses; artist signed, "L. C. D., 1905." Guérin Mark 3. **$300.00 – 350.00.**

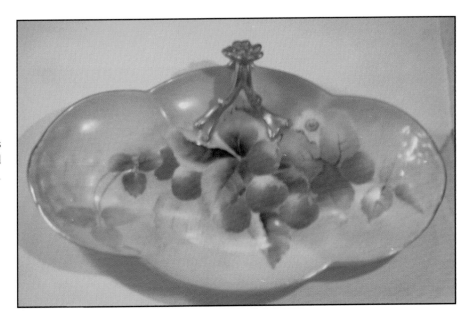

Plate 334. Tray, 11" l, 6" w; red cherries and green leaves; artist signed and marked the same as the preceding example. **$300.00 – 350.00**.

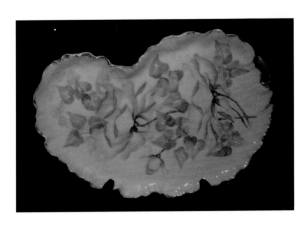

Plate 335. Tray, 7" x 11", kidney-shaped with fluted border; large pink roses and green leaves on a white background; gold trim; Guérin Mark 3. **$200.00 – 250.00.**

Plate 336. Dresser tray, 12" x 9"; irregular scalloped shape; a large spray of yellow flowers is in the center; gold enameling accents flowers and scroll work around parts of border which have been painted in green and extend toward center of tray; artist signed, "E. M. A., 1895." Guérin Mark 2. **$225.00 – 275.00.**

Plate 337. Dresser tray, like the preceding one, but decorated with a transfer of cherubs framed by a garland of roses with a blue bow; gold trim. Guérin Mark 3. **$250.00 – 300.00** (mc).

Table Wares

Plate 338. Plate, 9" d; hand-painted violets with light green leaves. Guérin Mark 2. **$75.00 – 100.00.**

Plate 339. Chocolate pot, 9" h; Art Deco design of stylized flowers painted in yellow, green, and brown on a light tan background. Guérin Mark 3. **$225.00 – 275.00.**

Plate 340. Punch bowl, 7" h x 14" d; red, green, and purple grapes decorate interior and exterior; gold trim; artist signed, "E. Hancock, Nov. 1911." Guérin Mark 3. **$1,000.00 – 1,200.00.**

Plate 341. Mug, 6" h; hand-painted blackberries with multi-colored leaves. Guérin Mark 3. **$150.00 – 175.00.**

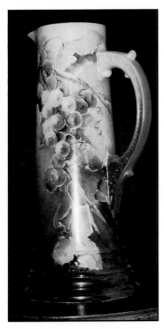

Plate 342. Tankard, 14" h; purple grapes with dark green leaves accented with brown; artist signed, "A. Fuller." Guérin Mark 3. **$600.00 – 700.00.**

Plate 343. Cider pitcher, 6½" h; large purple plums and small white flowers; gold trim. Guérin Mark 3. **$400.00 – 450.00.**

Plate 344. Cider pitcher, 6¾" h; red raspberries painted on a pastel background. Guérin Mark 3. **$400.00 – 450.00.**

Plate 345. Cider pitcher, 6½" h; small red berries with green leaves set against a shaded rust-colored background; gold trim. Guérin Mark 3. **$425.00 – 475.00.**

Plate 346. Ewer, 17" h; Art Nouveau shape; applied scrolled work around base and neck; handle is heavily gilded; light and dark pink roses are painted on lower part of ewer. Guérin Mark 3. **$1,600.00 – 1,800.00.**

Plate 347. Tankard, 14" h; magenta and light yellow mums; dark green finish on top and base; handle painted gold. Guérin Mark 3. **$700.00 – 800.00.**

Cachepots, Jardinieres, and Vases

Plate 348. Cachepot, 9" h; lighthouse scene with large sea gulls in the foreground; gold trim. Guérin Mark 3. **$500.00 – 600.00.**

Plate 349. Cachepot, 6" h, small size designed to hold letters or other desk accessories; large roses painted in pink and dark pink with green leaves; gold trim. Guérin Mark 3. **$600.00 – 700.00.**

Plate 350. Cachepot, 9" h; mixed bouquet of pink and white flowers; gold trim. Guérin Mark 3. **$1,000.00 – 1,200.00.**

Plate 351. Cachepot, 12" h; large light pink, dark pink, and purple flowers painted on a light green shading to white ground; gold trim; artist signed, "Brown." Guérin Mark 2. **$1,200.00 – 1,400.00.**

Plate 352. Cachepot, 12" h, vivid light and dark pink roses on a shaded green background decorate one side; gold trim. Guérin Mark 3. **$1,200.00 – 1,400.00.**

Plate 353. Reverse of Plate 352, painted with purple, lavender, and yellow pansies.

Plate 354. Jardiniere style planter but only 4½" h x 5" w; salmon-pink flowers with green leaves; gold trim; artist signed, "Smith." Guérin Mark 3. **$250.00 – 300.00.**

Plate 355. Jardiniere, 8" h x 11" d; purple grapes outlined in gold with blue leaves painted in an Art Nouveau style on a matte blue-green background. Guérin Mark 3. **$500.00 – 600.00.**

Plate 356. Urn, 14" h; split branch style handles and unique stopper painted gold; light and dark pink roses painted on a pastel ground with a darker finish on foot of urn. Guérin Mark 2. **$1,400.00 – 1,600.00.**

Plate 357. Vase, 14½" h; ornately shaped feet painted gold; light pink and white roses with green leaves. Guérin Mark 3. **$1,200.00 – 1,400.00.**

Plate 358. Vase, 14" h, made in the same shape as the preceding vase; pink, white, and red roses on a green background; gold trim on neck. Guérin Mark 3. **$1,000.00 – 1,200.00.**

Plate 359. Vase, 13" h; purple irises on a matte cream background; scalloped foot and neck brushed with gold. Guérin Mark 2. **$800.00 – 1,000.00.**

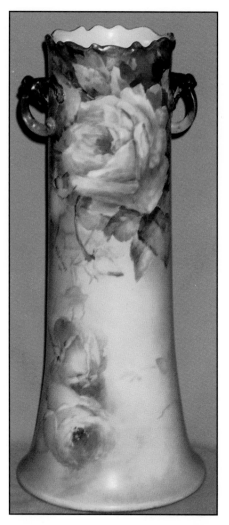

Plate 360. Vase, 13" h; large white roses with pastel tints on a cream background; artist signed, "F. R. Callaway, 1902." Guérin Mark 3. **$700.00 – 900.00.**

Charles Field Haviland (CFH)/Gérard, Duffraisseix & Morel (GDM)/Gérard, Dufraisseix & Abbot (GDA)

Charles Field Haviland left America for Limoges in the early 1850s to work for his uncle, David Haviland, founder of Haviland & Company. After a few years, however, Charles Field established his own porcelain decorating studio. He acquired his first porcelain manufacturing company about 1868. Later, he married the granddaughter of François Alluaud, Sr., and in 1876, he took charge of the Alluaud porcelain factory, one of the oldest Limoges factories. It is possible that early Charles Field decorated items were not marked. Only one form of decorating mark for him has been documented (see Mark 3). This particular mark is most often found on objects made by the successors to his company rather than on pieces carrying only his white ware marks (see Marks 1, 2, and 4).

In 1881, Charles Field retired from the business, and Gérard, Dufraisseix, and Morel took over the operations. That company continued to use Charles Field Haviland's Mark 3 as the overglaze decorating mark, but they changed the white ware mark by adding their own initials, "GDM" under "CFH."

Morel ceased to be a partner around 1890, thus leaving the business in the name of Gérard and Dufraisseix until 1900. Before the departure of Morel, Edgar Abbot, about 1886, became associated with the American importing firm which represented Charles Field Haviland, Haviland and Gagner (d'Albis and Romanet, p. 148). An overglaze importing mark in red of "Haviland and Abbot" is found on some china reflecting this partnership. Subsequently, circa 1900, Abbot became a partner in the Gérard, Dufraisseix firm. The white ware mark was changed to "GDA" over "France." The company was known as "Porcelaines GDA." The Gérard, Dufraisseix, and Abbot company continued to use the old "Charles Field Haviland" circular decorating mark until 1941. The mark appears to have been only in red, whereas, the same mark is found in other colors for the GDM company and the original CFH company. The GDA company was also using another overglaze decorating mark in 1910 as well as the circular Charles Field Haviland mark, according to an advertisement for the company. This other mark was a wreath with the initials "G. D. A." printed over "Limoges" (see GDA Mark 4). After 1941, the old "CFH" decorating mark was sold to the Haviland and Parlon Company, which was a separate company and not part of, nor a successor to, the Charles Field Haviland company, although Robert Haviland was the grandson of Charles Field Haviland (see Robert Haviland under Other Limoges Factories). The last successor to the Charles Field Haviland Company, Gérard, Dufraisseix, and Abbot, is still in operation.

The production of Charles Field Haviland and his successors was heavily concentrated on table wares. Artistic porcelain and display pieces were made, but few of those are available on the American market. The GDA factory is noted to have made porcelain art objects for the L'Art Nouveau firm of Samuel Bing's company in Paris during the early 1900s. The large vase with figures in relief which is shown first in this chapter was made by GDM. One like it has been on display in Limoges at the Musée National Adrien Dubouché.

The "Charles Field Haviland" decorating mark can be confusing. The white ware mark determines the specific company and time period for all pieces with a "CFH" decorating mark. If the mark is accompanied by a white ware mark of just "CFH," then it was made by Charles Field Haviland between 1859 – 1881. If the mark is accompanied by "CFH" over "GDM," it was made by Gérard, Dufraisseix, and Morel between 1882 – 1890. If it is accompanied by "GDA" over "France," it was made by Gérard, Dufraisseix, and Abbot circa 1900 – 1941. If a piece of china has only the "CFH" decorating mark, it was made by the Robert Haviland company after 1941 and not by the Charles Field Haviland company or either of its successors.

The marks for Charles Field Haviland; Gérard, Dufraisseix, and Morel; and Gérard, Dufraisseix, and Abbot are shown separately for each company. Descriptions of the china illustrated note the specific marks on the pieces which are arranged according to decoration and not by mark. It is not always possible to determine by mark if the china was decorated by the Charles Field Haviland Company or either of his successors. There is not always an overglaze decorating mark on the china. Some pieces are obviously factory decorated, such as transfer patterned pieces, but have only a white ware mark. This will be seen in the first examples of table wares which include the Moss Rose pattern and other early floral designs. Other examples with only a white ware mark are certainly professionally decorated. The last several pictures in this chapter include some of these examples. Some pictures from advertisements for the companies precede the photographs.

Charles Field Haviland Marks

Mark 1, impressed initials "CFH" on white ware, 1868 – 1881.

Mark 2, underglaze white ware mark in green, "CFH," 1868 – 1881.

Mark 3, overglaze decorating mark in black, brown, or blue, 1859 – 1881.

Mark 4, "PORCELAINES A FEU," stamped on white ware in black, 1868 – 1881.

Gérard, Dufraisseix, and Morel Marks

Mark 1, underglaze white ware mark in green, ca. 1882 – 1890.

Mark 2, underglaze white ware mark in green with "FRANCE," 1891 – 1900.

Mark 3, overglaze decorating mark in red, blue, gray, brown, or black "CH. FIELD HAVILAND" printed inside double circle, ca. 1882 – 1900.

Haviland & Abbot Mark

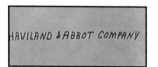

Overglaze importing mark in red, after 1886.

Gérard, Dufraisseix, and Abbot Marks

Mark 1, underglaze white ware mark in green, ca. 1900 – 1941.

Mark 2, underglaze white ware mark in green, "Porcelaine de Feu," ca. early 1900s.

Mark 3, overglaze decorating mark in red, "CH. FIELD HAVILAND" printed inside double circle, ca. 1900 – 1941.

Mark 4, overglaze decorating mark in red or green, ca. 1941 to present.

Charles Field Haviland Advertisement

Several pictures from an undated brochure feature the mold "Brittany," along with a few others. Notice that only a number indicates the type of decoration. The description of the pieces and their uses shows how the china was advertised in the late 1890s. While there is no date indicated, other information in the booklet places its publication circa 1897 or 1898.

Advertisement for Gérard, Dufraisseix, and Abbot China

These ads, distributed by Haviland & Abbot in New York, were printed in 1904 (butter dish and sandwich set) and 1914 (cup and saucer).

Advertisement for Porcelaines G. D. A.

This ad illustrates the marks used on the china in 1910. The notation that the factory was founded in 1797 refers to the historic Alluaud factory. Charles Field Haviland became successor to that factory in 1876.

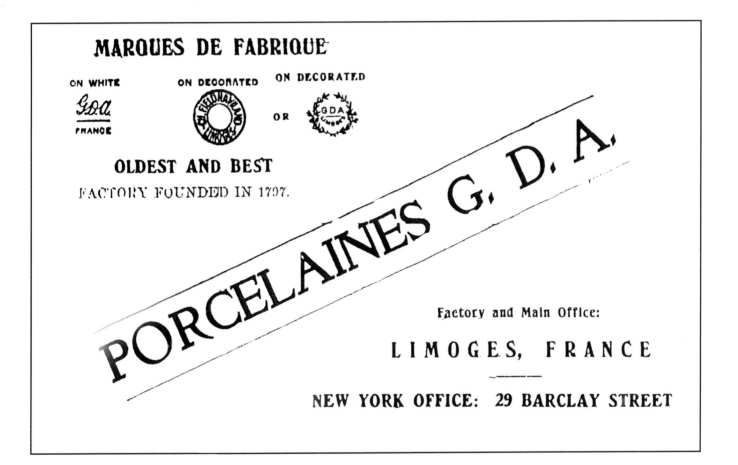

Charles Field Haviland and Successors' China Production

Display Piece

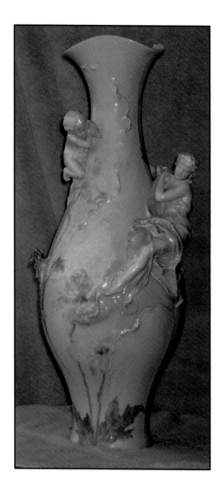

Plate 361. Vase, 21" h; applied figures of a woman and cherub are sculptured in fine detail; scalloped designs in relief and hand-painted flowers together with the pastel glazes show the Art Nouveau influence. GDM Mark 2 without a decorating Mark. **$6,500.00 – 7,500.00.**

Table Wares

Plate 362. Coffee set, Wedding Ring pattern; simple gold band with gold outlining on finials, handles, and spouts. CFH Mark 2. Plate, **$35.00 – 45.00**; coffee cup and saucer, **$45.00 – 55.00.**

Plate 363. Covered sugar and creamer in Wedding Ring pattern. **$250.00 – 275.00 set.**

Plate 364. Coffee pot in Wedding Ring pattern. **$300.00 – 325.00.**

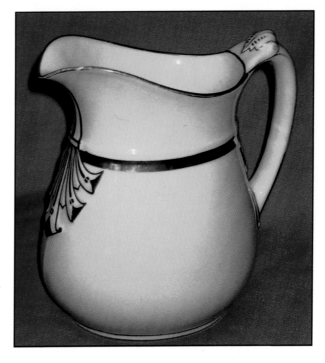

Plate 365. Water pitcher; GDM Marks 1 and 3. **$225.00 – 275.00.**

Plate 366. Mustache cup, Moss Rose pattern accented with gold. CFH Mark 1. **$250.00 – 300.00.**

Plate 367. Soap dish, 5" x 4" with drainer, Moss Rose pattern; gold trim. CFH Mark 1. **$175.00 – 200.00.**

Plate 368. Pitcher, 8" h; Moss Rose pattern; gold trim. CFH Mark 1. **$250.00 – 300.00.**

Plate 369. Tea tile, 6½" d; Moss Rose pattern. CFH Mark 3. **$125.00 – 150.00.**

Plate 370. Platter, 12½" l; Moss Rose pattern with a blue-gray inner border; gold outlining on embossed designs. CFH Mark 1. **$300.00 – 350.00.**

Plate 371. Pitcher, 8" h; a pattern composed of sprays of small blue flowers with yellow centers, gray-brown stems, and leaves decorates the surface of this pitcher and the following two pieces. GDM Mark 1. **$150.00 – 175.00.**

Plate 372. Pancake dish, 10" d; GDM Marks 2 and 3. **$325.00 – 375.00.**

Plate 373. Tureen, 12" x 17"; handles decorated with raised gold flowers and gold stenciled designs. GDM Mark 1. **$500.00 – 600.00.**

Plate 374. Cup and saucer; large flowers tinted pink on a white background. GDM Marks 1 and 3 with the importer Mark of "J. McD & S," (unidentified company, see Mark under Limoges Companies Without Examples). **$50.00 – 60.00.**

Plate 375. Butter dish with drainer, 4½" square; this piece has the same floral pattern as Plate 374; gold trim. GDM Marks 2 and 3. **$250.00 – 275.00.**

Plate 376. Creamer and covered sugar bowl, double ring handles; large blue flowers with yellow centers; brushed gold on borders, finial, and handles. This particular mold or shape is a good example to show how the same molds were used by the successive owners of the company. This piece is marked with CFH Marks 2 and 3, while the others have a GDA or a GDM Mark. **$250.00 – 325.00 set.**

Plate 377. Coffee pot, 11" h; this blue floral pattern is different from the one on the creamer and sugar in Plate 376; gold stenciled leaves decorate spout. GDA Marks 1 and 3. **$325.00 – 375.00.**

Plate 378. Chocolate pot, 11" h; another example of the double ring handle design with yet another blue floral pattern; finial and handle heavily gilded. GDM Mark 2. **$375.00 – 400.00.**

Plate 379. Covered sauce tureen with attached underplate; blue flowers with yellow centers and rust and gray-brown leaves form a border pattern; gold trim. GDM Marks 2 and 3. **$225.00 – 275.00.**

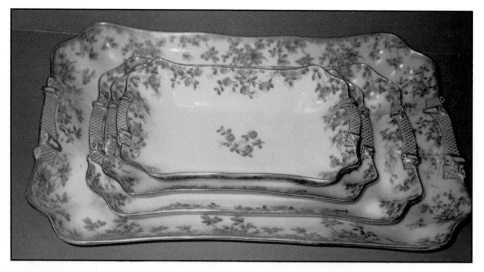

Plate 380. Set of platters: these are decorated with the same blue floral pattern as the sauce tureen in Plate 379; brushed gold trim on edges with a gold diamond pattern painted on the handles. GDM Marks 1 and 3. 18" x 12", **$400.00 – 450.00;** 14" x 8", **$350.00 – 400.00;** 11½" x 6½", **$250.00 – 300.00;** 10" x 5½", **$175.00 – 225.00.**

Plate 381. Covered bowl, 4" d, with attached underplate, 5" d, for sauce or jam; pattern of pink, blue, and yellow flowers scattered over surface; brushed gold trim; GDM Marks 1 and 3. **$150.00 – 175.00.**

Plate 383. Cheese dish, 7" h, with underplate, 8¼" square; finial shaped in Egyptian "Isis" style; yellow flowers with brown leaves scattered randomly over surface. GDM Marks 1 and 3. **$350.00 – 400.00**

Plate 382. Demitasse cup and saucer; shell-shaped handle; pattern composed of autumn colored leaves; gold trim. GDM Marks 1 and 3. **$120.00 – 140.00.**

Plate 385. Demitasse cup and saucer; large pink roses with green leaves form pattern on exterior and interior of cup and around border of saucer; a double ring of brushed gold accents outer borders and handle. GDA Marks 1 and 3. **$80.00 – 95.00.**

Plate 384. Pitcher, 9" h, with ice lip; sprays of yellow flowers with green and blue-gray leaves decorate body; gold trim. GDM Mark 1. **$275.00 – 325.00**

Plate 386. Demitasse cup and saucer, clusters of small pink roses with dark green leaves form a pattern around inner border of pieces with an outer border composed of light green leaves; gold trim. GDM Marks 2 and 3. **$70.00 – 85.00.**

Plate 387. Tea set: tray, 21" x 14", covered sugar bowl, creamer, and cups and saucers; small pink flowers with green leaves are scattered over surface of pieces; brushed gold trim. GDA Mark 1. **$1,600.00 – 1,800.00 set.**

Plate 388. Chocolate pot, 6½" h; small pink and white flowers form borders on lid and around top and base of pot with a few scattered around middle of body; gold trim. GDA Mark 1 and Haviland & Abbot Mark. **$300.00 – 350.00.**

Plate 389. Chocolate pot, 10" h; embossed floral design near base and top of pot; sprays of pink and blue flowers in varying sizes scattered over body; brushed gold trim. GDA Marks 1 and 4. **$325.00 – 375.00.**

Plate 390. Bowl, 9½" d; clusters of pink flowers with a white one in the center are placed around inner border; a smaller cluster is in the center; light green finish on outer border; gold trim. GDA Marks 1 and 3. **$60.00 – 75.00.**

Plate 391. Chocolate cup and saucer; pink and white floral pattern enhanced by gold stenciled designs and gold trim; a dark shading to light green finish decorates borders. GDA Marks 1 and 3. **$80.00 – 95.00.**

Plate 393. Covered bouillon cup and mug, 3" h; both fashioned with the "Isis" design handles and finial; pastel floral patterns and gold trim. GDM Marks 1 and 3 on bouillon cup, **$175.00 – 200.00;** GDM Marks 2 and 3 on mug, **$100.00 – 120.00.**

Plate 392. Chocolate pot (lid missing), 11" h; pattern matches the preceding cup and saucer; it is marked the same; the embossed work on the lower body is highlighted in gold, and gold leaves are painted around the handle. Notice that this gold work is not on the cup and saucer. GDA Marks 1 and 3. **$350.00 – 400.00** with lid.

Plate 394. Covered bouillon cup and saucer; small pink roses framed by light green leaves in a scrolled design form pattern around inner borders; gold trim. GDA Marks 1 and 4. **$150.00 – 175.00.**

Plate 395. Cake plate, 10½" d; green and red geometric pattern on outer border with like-colored medallions scattered around inner border; gold trim. GDA Marks 1 and 3. **$75.00 – 85.00.**

Plate 396. Baking dish, 12" d; scallop shell-shaped handles painted gold; branches with small pink flowers over body; brushed gold on outer border. CFH Mark 4. **$175.00 – 200.00.**

Plate 397. Plate, 7" d; this piece is decorated with a very similar, if not the same, floral design as the baking dish; brushed gold trim. GDA Marks 1 and 3. **$35.00 – 45.00.**

Plate 398. Plate, 9½" d; wine-glazed border overlaid with gold leaves. GDM Mark 1. **$140.00 – 160.00.**

Plate 399. Tray, 9" x 16"; large pink roses with green leaves form a random pattern over surface; gold trim. GDM Marks 2 and 3. **$350.00 – 400.00.**

Plate 400. Demitasse cups and saucers; bamboo-shaped handles; cobalt blue finish overlaid with gold paste leaves and beaded work; small yellow flowers on interior; gold trim. GDM Mark 1. **$150.00 – 175.00 set.**

Plate 401. Bowl, 13" x 8", decorated with the same pattern as the demitasse cups in Plate 400 and marked the same. **$425.00 – 475.00.**

Plate 402. Tray, 13" x 8", matching the preceding pieces. **$550.00 – 650.00.**

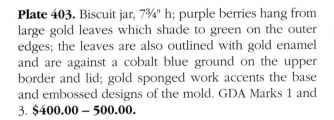

Plate 403. Biscuit jar, 7¾" h; purple berries hang from large gold leaves which shade to green on the outer edges; the leaves are also outlined with gold enamel and are against a cobalt blue ground on the upper border and lid; gold sponged work accents the base and embossed designs of the mold. GDA Marks 1 and 3. **$400.00 – 500.00.**

Plate 404. Salt dip, 2¼" d; small white and violet blossoms; brushed gold trim. GDM Marks 2 and 3. **$35.00 – 40.00.**

Plate 405. One-handle bowl, 6" l; pattern of small blue flowers over surface; gold trim. GDM Marks 1 and 3. **$60.00 – 75.00.**

Plate 407. Oyster plate, three sections; blue floral pattern; brushed gold trim. GDM Marks 1 and 3. **$150.00 – 175.00.**

Plate 406. Egg dish, 9¼" d; gold trim on fluted borders. GDM Marks 1 and 3. **$300.00 – 325.00.**

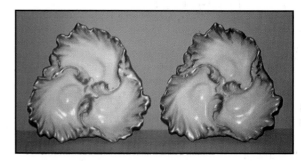

Plate 408. Oyster plates, 6" d; three sections; fluted borders tinted with a pale pink finish; gold trim. GDM Mark 1. **$150.00 – 175.00 each.**

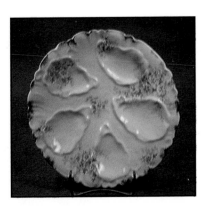

Plate 409. Oyster plate, 8¾" d; five shell-shaped sections; large lavender flowers form an irregular pattern; brushed gold trim. GDA Marks 1 and 3. **$200.00 – 225.00.**

Plate 410. Shell fish plate, 9" d; five shell-shaped sections; pink and white floral pattern; brushed gold accents sections and border. GDM Marks 1 and 3. **$220.00 – 240.00.**

Plate 411. Oyster plate, square shape; this very decorative plate exhibits a pink pearl luster finish on three sections; a cameo boat scene painted on one section, and a small sea shell on another; floral designs in yellow-orange and magenta as well as gold trim enhance the piece. GDM Mark 1. **$375.00 – 425.00.**

Plate 412. Game bird plate, 8¼" d; wild ducks in a marsh and one in flight are surrounded by a large pink flowering vine and a stand of yellow flowers; gold trim. CHF Marks 2 and 3. **$175.00 – 200.00.**

Plate 413. Game plate, 9¾" d; forest scene featuring a deer at sunrise, colored in brown tones with yellow-gold highlights. CFH Mark 3. **$200.00 – 225.00.**

Plate 414. Game bird plate, 7" square; the very fancy mold with embossed floral designs is decorated with a dark yellow-gold glaze; game birds in the center are framed by gold stenciled designs. GDM Mark 1. **$250.00 – 275.00.**

Plate 415. Ice cream set: tray, 13¾" l, with 4 serving dishes, 5" square; a cameo winter scene is featured on each piece; large blue floral sprays enhanced by gold and enameling cover surface of pieces around cameos. GDM Marks 1 and 3. **$1,400.00 – 1,600.00 set.**

Decorative China

The following examples do not have an overglaze decorating mark; but unlike the transfer-patterned dinner wares, it is not as easy to attribute the decoration to the factory, although all of these pieces are finely decorated.

Plate 416. Plate, 7¼" d; hand-painted scenic décor of a shepherd and sheep with trees and a house in the background; gold stenciled pattern around outer border. CFH Mark 2. **$300.00 – 350.00.**

Plate 417. Plate, 7¼" d, like the preceding piece, but decorated with an outdoor scene of a little girl holding an umbrella, standing by a pond with ducks at her feet. CFH Mark 2. **$300.00 – 350.00.**

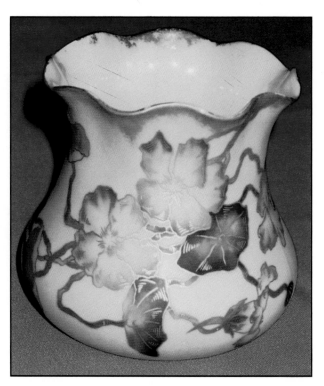

Plate 418. Plate, 9" d; a brightly colored transfer courting scene decorates center of plate; cobalt blue finish on border highlighted with gold. GDM Mark 1. **$175.00 – 225.00.**

Plate 419. Vase, 5" h; large flowers tinted in shades of pink and wine with gold accents, on a matte cream background, cover body; brushed gold around neck. GDM Mark 1. **$175.00 – 225.00.**

Plate 420. Creamer and open sugar basket; purple flowers scattered over surface; brushed gold trim. GDM Mark 1. **$300.00 – 350.00 set.**

Plate 421. Powder jar, 5" d; enameled gold flowers and leaves decorate lid with sponged gold around borders. GDM Mark 1. **$350.00 – 400.00.**

Plate 422. Dresser set: pair of candle holders, 6" h, **$150.00 – 175.00 each;** powder jar, **$250.00 – 275.00;** pin box, **$200.00 – 225.00;** ring tray, **$225.00 – 250.00;** and two cologne bottles, 4" h, **$250.00 – 300.00 each;** bright red-orange and purple flowers, highlighted by a deep pink finish shading to white, decorate pieces; gold trim. GDM Mark 2.

David Haviland/
Theodore Haviland/Frank Haviland

David Haviland played a very important role in bringing Limoges porcelain to the attention of the American public. He began his career as an importer of French porcelain in New York during the late 1830s and early 1840s. He moved to France in 1841 and settled in Limoges about 1842. Haviland operated an exporting business for several years, choosing porcelain made by Limoges factories to be shipped to his New York company. In 1847, he opened a decorating studio in Limoges. He had other Limoges factories make porcelain items according to his specifications which, in turn, were decorated at his studio and shipped to New York.

David Haviland did not produce any porcelain until 1865 (d'Albis and Romanet, p. 134). His sons, Charles Edward and Theodore, were involved in the business which was quite prosperous for many years. David Haviland died in 1879, and Charles and Theodore became partners. In 1891, however, Theodore left the company and formed his own business in 1892 under the name of "Theodore Haviland." Haviland and Company was continued by Charles. He died in 1921, and his son, George, carried on the business until 1930 when it closed due to bankruptcy. The company was reorganized after 1941 when Theodore's son, William, was able to obtain the rights to the old Haviland and Co. marks and models which had been sold in 1931. The Theodore Haviland Company in Limoges reverted to the name of Haviland and Company. William retired in 1957, and the company was carried on by his sons. They retired in 1972, and the management of the company was turned over to the Cerabati group under the name of "Haviland SA." The company remains in business today.

Marks used by Haviland & Co. and Theodore Haviland are shown together in this chapter. They are numbered sequentially, and specific numbers are listed in the captions of the photographs. Examples for each company are shown together as well. Marks 19 – 22 are found on Haviland art pottery. Examples of the art pottery are not included in this edition because they are not porcelain. The marks may be of interest to collectors, however. A few changes have been made in the dates of the marks, based on information in *Haviland,* a book published in 1988 by Jean d'Albis, where the dating of Haviland marks has been refined from his earlier work with Céleste Romanet in 1980, *La Porcelaine de Limoges.*

Marks used by Frank Haviland, the youngest son of Charles Edward Haviland, are also illustrated here. Frank Haviland was an artist and operated his own decorating studio from about 1910 – 1925. Various marks incorporated his full name. These marks are sometimes found on Haviland marked blanks. Additionally, Haviland & Co. marked some china with an underglaze white ware mark specifically for Frank Haviland (d'Albis, p. 123), see Frank Haviland Mark 4. Some pieces of Frank Haviland's china have been included in the photographs.

A pamphlet titled *Porcelaine Theodore Haviland,* published in August, 1912, shows several views of the factory, its workers, and various stages of china production. A few of those pages have been reprinted before the marks. These illustrate the modeling of pieces, the blanks, and the decorated ware before it was exported.

The Haviland company made its name by exporting, manufacturing, and decorating table china as discussed on pages 13 and 14, "Comparing Haviland and Other Limoges Porcelain." Pieces of Haviland table ware patterns are found more frequently than art objects and decorative accessories. A selection of dinner ware patterns, beginning with some early pieces decorated by the company before it began manufacturing china, are shown first. Popular patterns such as Moss Rose, Old Blackberry, Wedding Ring, and Silver Anniversary are represented as well as a number of others. Some of the early pieces exhibit *mixtion* decoration with hand coloring added to the transfer outline. The majority of these patterns do not have factory assigned names, and no attempt has been made to devise names for them. A pattern name is used only if it is a common one coined by popular usage or a documented factory name. Documented shapes or forms are noted for some pieces.

Examples of decorative china or display wares, as opposed to dinner wares, follow the Haviland patterns. A few pieces from services designed for American presidents are shown in this section because of their unique and decorative nature. It is hard to imagine even a President dining off some of this china. The last section features Haviland white wares decorated by American china painters. In the chapter on Undecorated Limoges Porcelain, several pieces of Haviland's very popular Ranson shape are shown. (For a more thorough study of the Haviland companies, see the entries in the Bibliography. Please note that my book published in 1984, *Haviland Collectables and Objects of Art,* is out of print; however, it is available at many public libraries.)

Theodore Haviland

Theodore Haviland

Theodore Haviland

Haviland & Co. Marks

Mark 1, applied mark of impressed name, indicates pieces made for Haviland Bros. by other Limoges companies, but presumably decorated by the Haviland studio, early 1850s to about 1865.

Mark 2, applied mark of impressed name, similar to Mark 1, early 1850s to about 1865.

Mark 3, applied mark of impressed name with "Déposé," similar to Marks 1 and 2, mid 1850s to about 1865.

Mark 4, impressed name, not attached, but impressed directly into base, mid 1850s to about 1865.

Mark 5, impressed initials, used during first period of porcelain manufacture by Haviland & Cie., 1865 – 1875.

Mark 6, underglaze initials in green, 1876 – 1880.

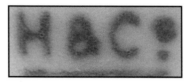

Mark 7, underglaze initials in green, underscored, 1877.

Mark 8, underglaze initials in green, underscored with two lines, 1876 – 1886.

Mark 9, underglaze intials in green, underscored with "L" added to indicate "Limoges," 1888 – 1896. Note: this same mark was used overglaze as a decorating mark in various colors for a short time from about 1878.

Mark 10, underglaze initials in green, underscored with "Déposé," adopted about 1887.

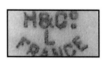

Mark 11, underglaze, initials in green with "L" for "Limoges" and "FRANCE," 1888 – 1896.

Mark 12, underglaze, full name with "France," in green, 1894 – 1931.

Mark 13, overglaze full name with "Limoges" in red, 1876 – 1878 1889 – 1931.

Mark 14, same as Mark 13, in blue. "Feu de Four" added to indicate special firing technique. Red overglaze mark indicates pieces were made for the "R. B. Gray Co., St. Louis," Missouri.

Mark 15, overglaze in red, importer mark of "Davis, Collamore, & Co., Importers, 24.7 Broadway, New York." Also impressed English Registry Mark, indicating particular design had been registered with the English Registry Office.

Mark 16, overglaze in blue, full name, 1897 – 1883.

Mark 17, overglaze, in blue (or other colors) double circle mark with full name. 1879 – 1889.

Mark 18, overglaze, in green, same as Mark 17, 1879 – 1889.

Mark 19, round paper label with initials over "Elite" in green, 1878 – 1883. This mark was used to grade the whiteware, but it is overglaze. Another similar mark of "Special" under "H & Co" in reddish-brown was used at the same time. It is extremely rare to find examples with these paper marks.

Mark 20, impressed full name underscored with "Limoges," art pottery mark, 1873 – 1882.

Mark 21, impressed initials, art pottery mark, 1873 – 1882. Also paper label for L'Escalier de Cristal, exclusive outlet for the Haviland art pottery.

Mark 22, impressed initials on stoneware with Chaplet's artist mark symbolizing a rosary, 1882 – 1886.

Theodore Haviland Marks

Mark 23, overglaze decorating mark, initials, in red, before 1892.

Mark 23a, underglaze, in green, initials with "FRANCE" printed above and an "L" on either side of the "H," ca. 1892.

Mark 24, underglaze, in green, "Mont-Mery" over three castle towers, initials, "FRANCE," ca. 1892.

Mark 25, underglaze, in green, "TH. HAVILAND" over three castle towers. "Limoges" in script. "FRANCE" printed, ca. early 1890s (probably after 1892).

Mark 26, underglaze, in green, "Theo. Haviland," with "Limoges" in script, "FRANCE" printed, ca. 1893.

Mark 27, impressed intials with the Legion of Honor symbol, primary white ware mark used to identify factory from 1894 to 1957.

Mark 28, impressed full name with "Theodore" underscored, the same design as overglaze Mark 34, ca. 1904 to mid 1920s.

Mark 29, underglaze, full name written in horseshoe shape, with "FRANCE" in center of mark, in green, ca. 1920 – 1936.

Mark 30. Underglaze, full name with "FRANCE" in shield shape with "Limoges" in rectangular shape above, ca. 1936 – 1945.

Mark 31, overglaze, in green, initials with "Porcelaine Mousseline" separated by Legion of Honor symbol and "FRANCE," in circular shape, 1894 – 1903. Mark also was written horizontally with "Limoges" in script form under the initial "T." and "FRANCE" printed under the initial "H." 1894 – 1903.

Mark 32, overglaze, in red, full name with the Legion of Honor symbol (may appear with "Theodore" abbreviated to "Théo."). 1895 to probably 1903.

Mark 33, overglaze, in red, full name in printed script, slanted, with "Limoges" in written script, and "FRANCE" printed, 1903 – 1925.

Mark 34, overglaze, in red, same as in Mark 33, except "Theodore" is underscored, c. 1904 to mid 1920s.

Mark 35, overglaze, in red, similar to Marks 33 and 34, except the name is written with the letters straight aligned rather than slanted, 1925 to probably mid 1940s.

Haviland, S. A. (Post World War II Marks)

Mark 36, underglaze, in green, ca. 1946 – 1962 (same as Mark 12 used from 1894 – 1932).

Mark 37, overglaze mark of a tower with "HAVILAND, LIMOGES, FRANCE," ca. 1958 and similar to present.

Frank Haviland Marks

Mark 1, overglaze decorating mark in red, or underglaze white ware mark in green, ca. 1910 – 1914.

Mark 2, overglaze decorating mark in red, variation of mark 1, ca. 1914 – 1926.

Early Haviland Decorated China

Plate 423. Compote, 4½" h, 9" d; simple rose-colored bands decorate piece. Marked "Fabrique Par Haviland & Co. Pour W. Boteler & Bro., Washington," in red, circa 1850s; no white ware mark. **$600.00 – 700.00.**

Plate 424. Covered bowl, 12" l, with nut finial; dark blue band borders with gold trim. H. & Co. Mark 1. **$425.00 – 475.00.**

Plate 425. Morning glory vase, 6" h; an example of early Haviland decoration, circa mid 1850s. H. & Co. Mark 4. **$1,200.00 – 1,400.00.**

Factory-Decorated Table Ware Patterns

Plate 426. The following six pieces are examples of the Moss Rose pattern. Soup bowl, 9½" d, gold trim; H. & Co. Mark 9. **$45.00 – 55.00.**

Plate 427. Cake plate, 9½" d; handles, leaf designs, and inner and outer borders outlined in pink. H. & Co. Marks 9 and 17. **$125.00 – 150.00.**

Plate 428. Chamber stick, applied ring-shaped handle; blue trim highlights Moss Rose pattern. H. & Co. Mark 16 with "Pour Glover Harrison Toronto." **$200.00 – 225.00.**

Plate 429. Sugar bowl, 7½" h; blue trim outlines borders, handles, finial and molded rope designs. H. & Co. Marks 5 and 9. **$175.00 – 200.00.**

Plate 430. Covered bowl, 4" h x 10" d, gold trim. H. & Co. Mark 5. **$250.00 – 300.00** (mc).

Plate 431. Pitcher, 11" h, gold trim around spout. H. & Co. Mark 5. **$300.00 – 350.00.**

Plate 432. Tea set: tea pot, sugar bowl, creamer; Wedding Ring pattern. H. & Co. Mark 5. **$375.00 – 425.00 set**.

Plate 433. Tea set: sugar bowl, tea pot, creamer; Ivy mold; transfer floral pattern colored with turquoise blue, highlighted by a dark pink; gold outlining on finial, handles, and molded ivy designs around handles. H. & Co. Mark 5. **$500.00 – 600.00 set.**

Plate 434. Plates, 9½" d; sprays of brightly colored flowers decorate centers of plates with a light pink border around well and on edges; each of four plates is decorated with a different floral design. H. & Co. Marks 9 and 17. **$75.00 – 100.00 each.**

Plate 435. Other plates from preceding set.

Plate 436. Coffee pot, 9½" h; triangular shape and Anchor design with braided handle and finial; a spray of multi-colored flowers on body and lid; blue trim. H. & Co. Marks 6 and 17. **$325.00 – 375.00.**

Plate 437. Sugar bowl, 7" h, same handle design as preceding coffee pot; large floral pattern composed of dark pink flowers; blue borders outlined with gold. H. & Co. Marks 6 and 17. **$175.00 – 200.00.**

Plate 438. Coffee set: coffee pot, 9" h; creamer, 6" h, sugar bowl, 7" h; large pink flowers with green leaves scattered over body, highlighted by blue outlining. H. & Co. Mark 6. **$550.00 – 650.00 set.**

Plate 439. Cup and saucer, Napkin Fold shape; large blue roses form a random design; folded edges highlighted with touches of gold. H. & Co. Mark 8 on saucer and Marks 9 and 17 on cup. **$100.00 – 120.00.**

Plate 440. Dessert dishes, 4" square, Napkin Fold shape, Old Blackberry pattern. H. & Co. Marks 9 and 18. **$40.00 – 50.00 each.**

Plate 441. Covered vegetable dish, rectangular shape; Old Blackberry pattern with gold outlining on handles and finial. H. & Co. Marks 9 and an overglaze decorating mark of "Haviland & Co. Pour F. J. Blair & Andree Co., Milwaukee, Wis." **$350.00 – 400.00.**

Plate 442. Place setting decorated with a pattern of blue bachelor buttons and wheat stalks. H. & Co. Marks 9, 11, or 12 with Mark 13 are found on the various pieces. Dinner plate, **$50.00 – 65.00;** bread and butter plate, **$25.00 – 35.00;** butter pat, **$30.00 – 40.00;** dessert bowl, **$25.00 – 35.00;** cup and saucer, **$60.00 – 75.00.**

Plate 443. Gravy or sauce tureen with attached underplate; yellow, burnt-orange and blue flowers; gold trim. H. & Co. Marks 10 and 18. **$150.00 – 175.00.**

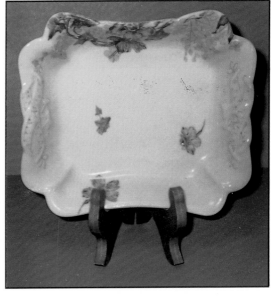

Plate 444. Bowl, 10" square; large blue flowers and brown leaves form a random pattern on borders and center. H. & Co. Marks 8 and 10. **$60.00 – 75.00.**

Plate 445. Covered bowl, 10" d; sprays of small blue flowers with brown and green leaves form a large border pattern extending toward center of pieces; gold trim. H. & Co. Marks 9 and 13. **$175.00 – 225.00.**

Plate 446. Bowl, 12" x 8"; brown flowers highlighted with yellow; gold outlining on embossed work under the deep scallops of the border. H. & Co. Marks 9 and 13. **$70.00 – 95.00**

Plate 447. Tea pot and sugar bowl, matching preceding pattern; sponged gold on handles, spout, and finials. H. & Co. Marks 6 and 13. Tea pot, **$225.00 – 250.00;** sugar bowl, **$100.00 – 125.00.**

Plate 448. Plate, 9" d, Marseille shape; clusters of pale orange flowers with gray stems and leaves are placed around border; gold enameled designs and gold trim enhance pattern. H. & Co. Marks 13 and 14. **$120.00 – 140.00.**

Plate 449. Compote, 3" h x 9" d, decorated with the same floral pattern and carrying the same marks as the preceding plate. **$300.00 – 350.00.**

Plate 450. Plate, 10" d; bouquets of pink, white, yellow, and purple flowers form a random pattern; brushed gold on four places around outer border. Theodore Haviland Mark 33. **$60.00 – 75.00.**

Plate 451. Platter, 12" x 7", same floral pattern as preceding plate. **$150.00 – 175.00.**

Plate 452. Creamer, 3¼" h, Ranson shape; large yellow flowers and small blue blossoms decorate interior and exterior; brushed gold on handle and borders. H. & Co. Marks 11 and 13. **$60.00 – 75.00.**

Plate 453. Coffee pot, 9¾" h and cups and saucers; sprays of white roses with pink flowers form pattern; brushed gold trim. H. & Co. Mark 11 with "Haviland & Co. for Meyberg Bros." Coffee pot, **$300.00 – 350.00;** cup and saucer, **$75.00 – 100.00 set.**

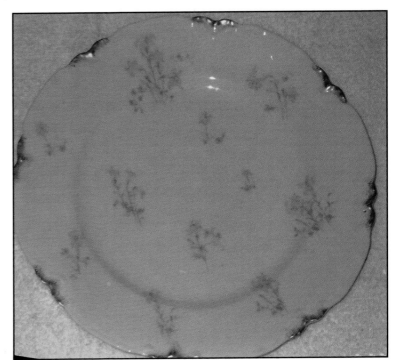

Plate 454. Plate, 10" d; floral pattern of small blue and pink flowers; brushed gold on embossed scallops around border. H. & Co. Marks 11 and 13. **$50.00 – 60.00.**

Plate 455. Plate, 10" d; inner beaded border; sprays of small pink roses scattered over surface; gold trim. H. & Co. Marks 12 and 13. **$50.00 – 60.00.**

Plate 456. Platter, 13½" l; Ranson shape, decorated with the same pink floral pattern as preceding plate. H. & Co. Marks 12 and 13. **$175.00 – 225.00.**

Plate 457. Bowl, 9¼" d, one handle; large pink roses and green leaves form a border pattern; gold trim. H. & Co. Marks 12 and 13. **$50.00 – 60.00.**

Plate 458. Cake plate, 10¾" d; Dubarry pattern, a Dresden type floral pattern decorates center and border; gold trim. Theodore Haviland Mark 29 with "Ivory China" and "Dubarry," plus Mark 35. **$150.00 – 175.00.**

Plate 459. Plate, 10" d; Autumn Leaf pattern. H. & Co. Marks 12 and 13. **$45.00 – 55.00.**

Plate 460. Plate, 10" d; Ranson blank with Silver Anniversary pattern. H. & Co. Marks 12 and 13. **$45.00 – 55.00.**

Plate 461. Soup tureen; large blue floral sprays with light green leaves form a body pattern; brushed gold trim. Theodore Haviland Mark 24 with "MANUFACTURED BY" over "LIMOGES" over "THEODORE HAVI-LAND." **$400.00 – 500.00.**

Plate 462. Place setting, simple gold trim around inner and outer borders. Theodore Haviland Mark 32. Dinner plate, **$45.00 – 55.00;** salad plate, **$25.00 – 35.00;** bread & butter plate, **$15.00 – 20.00;** cup and saucer, **$45.00 – 55.00.**

Plate 463. Open vegetable bowl, 10" x 7½", matching place setting; the decoration is enhanced by gold scroll work on and around handles. **$70.00 – 85.00.**

Plate 464. Platter, 12" x 14½", with well, from Theodore Haviland set. **$300.00 – 350.00.**

Plate 465. Cup and saucer; Vermicelle blank; blue flowers, accented with yellow and brown, form a wide border pattern. H. & Co. Marks 8 and 17 on cup, and Marks 9 and 17 on saucer. **$60.00 – 75.00.**

Plate 466. Demitasse cups and saucers in a presentation case; yellow, blue, and wine glazes, embellished with gold, decorate pieces. Notice the variation in the arrangement of the color on the cups and saucers. H. & Co. Marks 8 and 17. **$1,000.00 – 1,200.00 (mc).**

Haviland China
Factory Decorated with Birds, Insects, Fish, and Game

Plate 467. Game bird plate, 9" d; transfers of small birds in light brown tones decorate center and are overlaid on the wine glazed outer border. Other examples from this set have either a deep yellow or a teal blue border. H. & Co. Marks 10 and 17. **$140.00 – 165.00.**

Plate 468. Cup and saucer decorated with butterflies and small floral design highlighted by bright blue bands. H. & Co. Marks 6 and 17. **$75.00 – 100.00.**

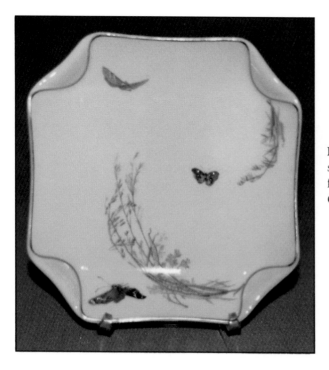

Plate 469. Dessert plate, 7" square, Napkin Fold shape; three butterflies and flowering branches form the pattern called Meadow Visitors. H. & Co. Marks 9 and 17. **$70.00 – 85.00.**

Plate 470. Tea pot, 6" l, Basket-Weave mold; bird and leaf decoration, another version of the Meadow Visitors pattern. H. & Co. Marks 8 and 18. **$250.00 – 275.00.**

Plate 471. Plate, 9" d; game birds and a butterfly; gold stenciled border pattern. H. & Co. Marks 8 and 16 with "Davis Collamore & Co., New York." **$120.00 – 135.00.**

Plate 472. Cake plate, 11" d; a colorful bird surrounded with small multi-colored flowers forms center pattern with another bird, fruit, and flowers at points around outer border; handles heavily gilded. H. & Co. Mark 12 and Frank Haviland Mark 2. **$300.00 – 350.00.**

Plate 473. Reticulated basket on a pedestal base; magenta transfer pattern of a bird and flowers decorates base of pedestal; gold stenciled border around base; gold accents the middle part of the lattice work and trims the border. Theodore Haviland Mark 23. **$400.00 – 500.00.**

Plate 474. Plate, 9½" square, Napkin Fold shape; brown monochrome scenic decoration of a hunter in woods with a raccoon perched in a tree. H. & Co. Marks 9 and 17. **$250.00 – 275.00.**

Plate 475. Plate, 9¼" d; scenic decoration of a rabbit and dog in the woods; light pink glaze on a wide outer border; gold trim. Theodore Haviland Mark 23. **$200.00 – 225.00.**

Plate 476. Plate, 9½" d; pair of game birds in the brush. H. & Co. Mark 9 and "For the Tynedale Company, Philadelphia." **$120.00 – 140.00.**

Haviland Presidential China

Plate 483. Soup plate, 9½" d; an example from President Rutherford B. Hays' service. The decoration was made from designs based on nature themes by Theo. R. Davis which were patented in 1880. The Mountain Laurel decorates this piece. See the Marks in the following picture. **$2,000.00 – 2,200.00.**

Plate 484. Mark on soup plate: H & Co. Mark 8 in green and "Fabrique Par Haviland & Co. d' apres les dessins des" in red, signature, "Theo. R. Davis," in black, and "Patented August 10th 1880, No. 11833," in blue.

Plate 485. Fruit plate, 8" l, shaped like the leaf of a wild apple, from a design for the Hays service. The decoration is of "Locust Blossoms" with an apple orchard in the background. The piece is marked like the preceding soup plate. The artist's initials, "H. J.," are on the front bottom edge of the piece. **$1,200.00 – 1,400.00.**

Plate 486. Plate from a design for the Hays service but made later. Klapthor (pp. 122 – 125) notes that the same designs were ordered during the Arthur and Cleveland administrations. The decoration is called "The Cranes Walk 'Round," representing cranes dancing at sunset. It is marked like preceding examples, but with patent number "11936." **$1,000.00 – 1,200.00.**

Plate 487. Leaf bowl, 12" d; another example made by Haviland from a design by Theo. R. Davis. This piece exhibits a garden theme with red fruit, a beetle, and a rabbit; brushed gold on fluted border. **$6,500.00 – 7,000.00.**

Plate 488. Base of leaf bowl above, showing the various marks on the piece which include the signature of Davis and the U. S. Eagle and Laurel Branch insignia.

Haviland Artist Signed and Display China

Plate 490. Vase, 11" h, Marseille form; white flowers scattered over a rust-colored ground shading to white at base; gold trim. H. & Co. Marks 9 and 13. **$800.00 – 900.00.**

Plate 489. Pitcher, 7" h; Penguin design by "Sandoz," reflecting the Art Deco influence; artist signed. Theodore Haviland Mark 34. **$500.00 – 600.00.**

Plate 491. Ewer, 11" h; reserves are decorated with figural scenes; a light green finish on the body is overlaid with gold embellishments. H. & Co. Mark 11 and "H. & Co." written in gold script. One of the reserves has a signature and date, "A. Nice 1893," in brown. The gold mark should be indicative of factory decoration, although the signature and date are unusual. **$2,200.00 – 2,400.00.**

Plate 492. Plate, 10½" d; gold flowers and leaves form a six-point star outlining center of plate which is decorated with scattered multi-colored flowers; wide cobalt blue border; beaded gold rim; artist signed, "Ernest Barbeau." H. & Co. Mark 12 in green and in gold. **$350.00 – 400.00.**

Plate 493. Plate, 9½" d; large pink roses accented with white enamel; gold trim; artist signed, "M. Naudin." H. & Co. Marks 12 and 13. **$300.00 – 350.00.**

Plate 494. Plate, 8¾" d; lake and mountain scenic décor overlaid with a large spray of pink roses; gold border; artist signed, "Berton." H. & Co. Marks 12 and 13 and "Hand Painted" printed over Mark 12. **$375.00 – 425.00.**

Plate 495. Plate, 9½" d; Marseille form; seascape in cobalt blue shading to white; gold trim; artist signed, "P. Wallestirz." H. & Co. Marks 9 and 14. **$450.00 – 500.00.**

Plate 496. Charger, 13¾" d; an Oriental scene in the center is framed by a large white flower and leaf design outlined in gold on a highly glazed turquoise ground; gold stenciled designs around border; gold trim. H. & Co. Marks 9 and 18. **$600.00 – 700.00.**

Plate 497. Plate, 10" d; colorful figural mythological scene is framed by a deep lavender border overlaid with gold floral designs accented with white enamel beads; "Kauffman" appears as a signature, but the name actually refers to original art by Angelica Kauffman on which the transfer is based. Theodore Haviland Mark 34. **$350.00 – 400.00.**

Plate 498. Plate decorated with another Kauffman scene by Theodore Haviland. **$350.00 – 400.00.**

Plate 499. Portrait plate, 10" d; terrace and garden scene featuring a woman dressed in a long white gown with an apricot-colored sash; wide cobalt blue border overlaid with elaborate gold work; artist signed, "J. Soustre." H. & Co. Mark 11 with "Floreal gold" and "Haviland and Co. pour E. Offner, New Orleans." **$1,400.00 – 1,600.00.**

Haviland American Decorated White Ware

Plate 500. Shaving mug, 3½" h; "P. H. Reegan," inscribed in gold; gold trim. H. & Co. Mark 8. **$175.00 – 200.00.**

Plate 501. Cuspidor, 7" x 9"; hand-painted pink roses on a tinted blue ground; gold trim. H. & Co. Mark 7. **$500.00 – 600.00.**

Plate 502. Humidor, 7" h; dark brown finish on bottom half; yellow roses form borders around middle of jar and on lid; monogrammed. H. & Co. Mark 12. **$250.00 – 300.00.**

Plate 503. Cup and saucer, *Papillon* (butterfly) handle; hand-painted holly with red berries; monogrammed. H. & Co. Mark 12. **$75.00 – 100.00.**

Plate 504. Individual size coffee pot, 6" h; butterfly handle; hand-painted flowers on front with a butterfly on the back. H. & Co. Mark 9. **$225.00 – 275.00.**

Plate 505. Chocolate pot, 9½" h; border and reserve of yellow roses outlined in gold. H. & Co. Mark 12. **$250.00 – 300.00.**

Plate 506. Chocolate pot, 12" h; large yellow and white flowers with a dark brown finish at base of pot; handle and finial painted gold. H. & Co. Mark 12. **$200.00 – 250.00.**

Plate 507. Bowl, 9" x 11"; Marseille shape; large blue flowers outlined in gold on a cream-colored background decorate exterior; interior has a deep pink finish; brushed gold on border and scalloped work on mold accents decoration. H. & Co. Mark 11. **$220.00 – 240.00.**

Plate 508. Tray, 10½" x 17½"; hand-painted scene of a church on a river bank; a person can be seen in a boat in the background; molded floral designs, handles, and rim painted gold; artist signed, "E. Garber, 1892." H. & Co. Mark 9. **$600.00 – 800.00.**

Plate 509. Covered jar or sugar bowl, tri-angular shape, three handles; dark and light pink roses on a pastel background; handles and finial painted gold. H. & Co. Mark 7. **$175.00 – 200.00.**

Plate 510. Punch cup, dark purple grapes and gold leaves painted in an Art Nouveau style; artist signed, "Giles." H. & Co. Mark 12. **$80.00 – 100.00.**

Plate 511. Charger, 12½" d; hand-painted blackberries and green leaves; gold trim. H. & Co. Mark 12. **$350.00 – 400.00.**

Plate 512. Charger, 13½" d; hand-painted cherries. H. & Co. Mark 12. **$375.00 – 425.00.**

Plate 513. Plate, 11½" d; clusters of yellow roses connected by trailing vines painted around outer border. H. & Co. Mark 12. **$75.00 – 100.00.**

Plate 514. Plate, 8½" d; large yellow flowers and gold enameled scroll designs decorate half of plate. H. & Co. Mark 11. **$100.00 – 125.00.**

Plate 515. Bowl, 9" x 7½"; large yellow flowers and green leaves cover interior; brushed gold on points around border; dated 1890. H. & Co. Mark 10. **$175.00 – 200.00.**

Plate 516. Plate, 8" d; peacocks painted dark blue-black are perched on flowering tree limbs; gold trim; dated 1887. H. & Co. Mark 9. **$100.00 – 125.00.**

Plate 517. Pitcher, 6½" h. and bowl, 3½" h x 7" d; evergreens are painted on the pitcher with similar trees on the bowl with a cow in the foreground; a deep pink finish applied to handle and top of pitcher and base of bowl. H. & Co. Mark 7. **$225.00 – 275.00 set**.

Plate 518. Compote, 9" x 10"; vividly hand-painted pink flowers and red and black berries cover interior and exterior; gold trim; artist signed, "Andrew." H. & Co. Mark 11. **$700.00 – 800.00.**

Plate 519. Covered soup tureen, 13" d; decoration matches compote and is signed by the same artist. H. & Co. Mark 11. **$1,000.00 – 1,200.00.**

Klingenberg, A. (AK)/Charles Dwenger (AKCD)

A Limoges porcelain factory and decorating studio were owned by A. Klingenberg from the 1880s until about 1910 (Wood, p. 32). In the first edition, this company was identified as Kittel and Klingenberg. Subsequent research shows that "Kitel" Klingenberg was an exporter of Limoges china. Very little documentation has been found for Klingenberg. Wood (p. 32) notes when writing about Limoges factories other than Haviland that "first mention should be to the A. Klingenberg pottery whose product and Mark were very prevalent in the American market from 1880 to 1910." The only mark shown in Wood's book, however, is "AKCD," which is the same mark attributed to Charles Dwenger by Röntgen (p. 262), but with the words "Carlsbad, Austria," instead of "Limoges, France." Röntgen also lists Charles Dwenger as a New York based importing company for Bohemian china from before 1895 to after 1917 (p. 455). Lesur and Tardy (p. 129) list Kitel Klingenberg Cie. as an exporter in Limoges from 1867 – 1872, followed by Klingenberg associated with Leonard (P. Leonard?) in 1873, and then Klingenberg alone from 1883 – 1887. No marks are illustrated, however.

White ware marks of "AK" over "D" are found in conjunction with decorating marks of "AK Limoges" as well as with "AKCD Limoges." D'Albis and Romanet (p. 157) mention a "Dwenger" as operating a decorating studio in Limoges dur-ing the early 1900s. Because the "AK Limoges" decorating mark is exactly the same style as the "AKCD" mark, the probability is almost certain that Klingenberg and Dwenger merged, or that Dwenger took over Klingenberg. The "AK" decorating marks should precede those of "AKCD," reflecting Klingenberg decorating activities prior to his china production. One example has been seen, however, which has the "AK" decorating mark on an "AK/D" blank, perhaps only indicating that the "AK" decorating mark was used for some time after the white ware mark changed to include "D" and before the "AKCD" mark was instituted.

The general time period for the Klingenberg marks alone ("AK") is probably early 1880s until 1890s. The Dwenger mark (AKCD) should be 1895 or a few years earlier until 1910 or prior to World War I, perhaps as late as 1920. The AKCD mark showing the Klingenberg and Dwenger association is listed here as Mark 9.

A variety of finely decorated pieces carry the "AK" or "AKCD" marks. Transfers enhanced with some hand coloring and the use of a lot of gold are found on many factory decorated pieces. The decorating marks are also found on white wares made by other Limoges factories. White ware Marks 3 through 8 are found on china decorated by American china painters.

Klingenberg and Dwenger Marks

Mark 1, overglaze decorating mark in red, wine glass with initials, early 1880s.

Mark 2, overglaze decorating mark in red or blue, initials in circle, ca. 1880s – 1890s.

Mark 3, impressed or underglaze white ware mark in green, "AK," ca. 1880s – 1890.

Mark 4, underglaze white ware mark in green, initials with "FRANCE," after 1891.

Mark 5, underglaze white ware mark in green, initials underscored with "FRANCE," ca. 1890s.

Mark 6, underglaze white ware mark in green, "AK" over "D," (showing Dwenger association), ca. 1890s – 1910 but after Mark 5.

Mark 7, underglaze white ware mark in green, "AK" over "D," with "FRANCE," ca. 1890s – 1910.

Mark 8, underglaze white ware mark in green "AK" over "D," underscored with "FRANCE," ca. 1890s – 1910.

Mark 9, overglaze decorating mark in red "AKCD," ca. 1900 – 1910.

Factory Decorative China

Plate 520. Plate, 10" d; heavily gilded scalloped border; cherubs decorate center and two reserves on sides. Klingenberg Mark similar to Mark 4, but with "FRANCE" printed above the initials. **$325.00 – 375.00.**

Plate 521. Plate, 9½" d; cherubs, framed by gold enameled scrolled designs; pink flowers around outer border; heavy gold trim. Coiffe Mark 3 and Klingenberg & Dwenger Mark 9. **$250.00 – 300.00.**

Plate 523. Plate, 9" d; scenic decoration of a large bird with rocks, water, and flowers in the foreground; brushed gold around border. "FRANCE" underglaze Mark and Klingenberg & Dwenger Mark 9. **$175.00 – 225.00.**

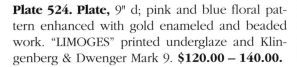

Plate 522. Vase, 9" h; gilded handles shaped in the form of an open-mouthed fish or creature; two cherubs holding a white dove are framed by gold enameled shell and scroll designs on a matte pink background. Klingenberg Marks 4 and 5. **$700.00 – 800.00.**

Plate 524. Plate, 9" d; pink and blue floral pattern enhanced with gold enameled and beaded work. "LIMOGES" printed underglaze and Klingenberg & Dwenger Mark 9. **$120.00 – 140.00.**

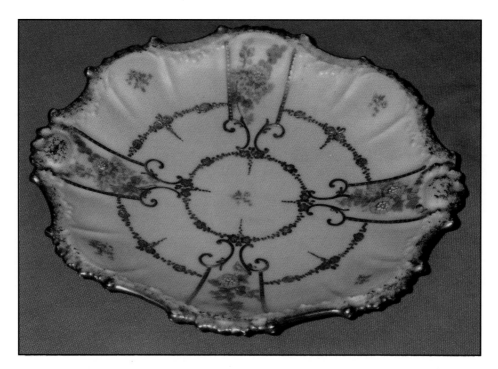

Plate 525. Plate, 8½"; reserves of pink and blue floral clusters on four sides of piece are outlined with gold enameled designs; gold trim. Coiffe Mark 2 and Klingenberg & Dwenger Mark 9. **$100.00 – 120.00.**

Plate 526. Cuspidor; hand-painted water and mountains decorate reserves on exterior and interior; deep wine finish overlaid with large white flowers. "DÉPOSÉ" impressed Mark and Klingenberg Mark 1. **$1,000.00 – 1,200.00.**

Plate 527. Chocolate pot, 10" h; brilliant purple iris are accented with gold enameled designs and brushed gold trim; spout, handle, and finial painted gold. Klingenberg Mark 4 and Klingenberg & Dwenger Mark 9. **$600.00 – 700.00.**

Plate 528. Toast tray, 7½" l; gold enameled leaves surround two small pearl type flowers; gold trim. Klingenberg Mark 7 and Klingenberg & Dwenger Mark 9. **$70.00 – 95.00.**

Plate 529. Plate, 10" d; sections of cobalt blue and light blue around border are overlaid with gold enameled flowers; gold scrolled designs around inner border frame a gold stenciled center medallion. "Limoges, France" Mark 7 and Klingenberg & Dwenger Mark 9. **$150.00 – 175.00.**

Plate 530. Syrup jug, 5" h; gold enameled vines with small green leaves on a white ground; spout and handle painted gold. Klingenberg Marks 2 and 3. **$175.00 – 200.00.**

Plate 531. Covered bouillon cup and saucer; autumn-colored flowers and leaves; brushed gold trim. Klingenberg Marks 2 and 3. **$200.00 – 225.00.**

Plate 532. Demitasse mustache cup and saucer; gold enameled floral décor. Klingenberg Mark 1. **$250.00 – 275.00.**

Plate 533. Oyster plate, 9" d; six sections with center sauce dip; large violet flowers decorate each section; gold trim. Illegible white ware Mark with Klingenberg Mark 2. **$220.00 – 240.00.**

Plate 534. Fish plate, 9½" d; a pair of fish are surrounded by yellow-gold flowers; gold trim. Klingenberg Mark 2. **$150.00 – 175.00.**

Klingenberg and Dwenger American Decorated White Wares

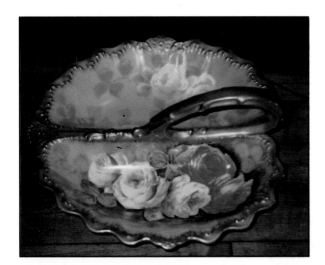

Plate 535. Divided dish, 7" l; dark multi-colored roses on a dark to light green background; heavy gold trim. Klingenberg Mark 3. **$250.00 – 275.00.**

Plate 536. Hair receiver, 2¾" h x 4¼" d; large pink roses are highlighted with gold enameled work and brushed gold around borders. Klingenberg & Dwenger Mark 7. **$200.00 – 250.00.**

Plate 537. Caberet: decanter, cups, and tray; red cherries and green leaves on a light green background; gold trim. Klingenberg & Dwenger Mark 7. **$700.00 – 800.00 set.**

Plate 538. Creamer, sugar bowl and tray, small blue flowers are scattered over surface; gold trim. Klingenberg & Dwenger Mark 7 on sugar bowl; other pieces unmarked. **$300.00 – 400.00 set**.

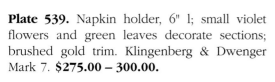

Plate 539. Napkin holder, 6" l; small violet flowers and green leaves decorate sections; brushed gold trim. Klingenberg & Dwenger Mark 7. **$275.00 – 300.00.**

Plate 540. Bowl, 7¾" d, three feet; hand-painted blackberries decorate both interior and exterior; gold trim. Klingenberg & Dwenger Mark 7. **$350.00 – 400.00.**

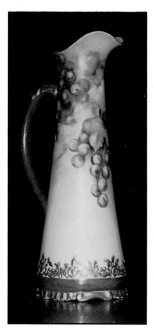

Plate 541. Pitcher, 12½" h; hand-painted purple grapes; enameled gold designs around base above a green border; handle is similarly decorated. Klingenberg & Dwenger Mark 7. **$600.00 – 700.00.**

Plate 542. Ferner, 3½" h x 7¾" d; pink and white flowers accented with green scrolls; pink finish around top and base. Klingenberg & Dwenger Mark 7. **$325.00 – 375.00.**

Plate 543. Ferner, 8½" d, with liner, footed; pink and white mums; heavy gold trim; artist signed, "M. E. K. 1898." Klingenberg & Dwenger Mark 7. **$450.00 – 550.00.**

Plate 544. Ewer, 6" h; large white flowers with yellow centers painted around base of piece; iridescent gold finish on neck. Klingenberg Mark 3 impressed and Mark 4. **$250.00 – 300.00.**

Plate 545. Vase, 9" h, sawtooth cut neck; lightly tinted pink flowers painted on bulbous base; gold trim. Klingenberg & Dwenger Mark 7. **$150.00 – 175.00.**

Plate 546. Vase, 7½": h; yellow and orange flowers with green and gray leaves decorate body; handles painted gold. Klingenberg & Dwenger Mark 7. **$120.00 – 140.00.**

A. Lanternier

The Lanternier family exported porcelain from Limoges during the 1850s. Some sources note the year 1855 as the beginning date of the Lanternier porcelain factory, but the company did not actually become engaged in manufacturing porcelain until the mid 1880s when Frederic Lanternier, Alfred's father, decided to make porcelain as well as decorate and export Limoges china. Production dates from circa 1890s. The company carried on an extensive export trade with table china being its chief product. The Lanternier white wares are often seen with the decorating mark of other Limoges companies or decorating studios. The Lanternier marks reflect the son's name, "Alfred." Mark 5, a blue mark with "Lanternier" printed inside a double circle, appears to be an exporting mark, and examples with just that mark were probably decorated by another Limoges company and date prior to 1890.

In addition to table wares, Lanternier china is found in decorative pieces. Some hand-painted examples bear the signature of familiar Limoges artists, such as "Duval." Note that most of the examples here have some other factories' white ware marks and only the Lanternier decorating mark. The Lanternier mark is also well-known in the area of doll collecting. *La tête de poupée* (doll head) was a porcelain product made by Lanternier during the latter part of World War I, circa 1917 (d' Albis and Romanet, p. 167). Two fashion dolls are shown at the end of this chapter. The non-factory decorated china illustrated here exhibits professional and quality art work. It is possible that a few pieces were decorated by either Lanternier or another Limoges studio. The four compotes (pgs. 232-233) are examples of Lanternier white wares which seem to have been decorated by an English china painter, as the origin of the pieces is England. The signature and date indicate that they are non-factory decorated, but the painting is very professional in appearance.

Lanternier Marks

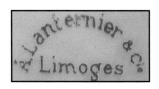

Mark 1, overglaze decorating mark in red, full name with "Limoges," ca. 1890s.

Mark 2, underglaze white ware mark in green, "A. L. DÉPOSÉ," ca. 1890s.

Mark 3, underglaze white ware mark in green with anchor and "DÉPOSÉ," ca. 1890s.

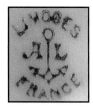

Mark 4, underglaze white ware mark in green with anchor and "LIMOGES, FRANCE," ca. 1891 – 1914.

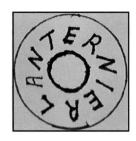

Mark 5, overglaze exporting or decorating mark in blue, "LANTERNIER" printed inside double circle without initial "A.," before 1890.

Mark 6, overglaze decorating mark in red, brown, or blue double circle, 1891 – 1914.

Mark 7, overglaze decorating mark in red and black, wreath and shield, after World War I.

Lanternier Factory Decorated Decorative China

Plate 547. Plate, 8¾" d; hand-painted blackberries; gold border overlaid with black floral designs and outlined in black; artist signed, "Martha." Lanternier Mark 1 with no white ware Mark. **$175.00 – 200.00.**

Plate 548. Cider pitcher, 9"d; hand-painted red berries with green leaves; gold trim; artist signed, but signature is not legible. "Limoges, France" Mark 6 and Lanternier Mark 1. **$350.00 – 400.00.**

Plate 549. Plate, 9½" d; inner border molded with scalloped designs in relief; orange, yellow, and lavender tulips make a colorful center decoration; gold trim. Lanternier Marks 1 and 4. **$150.00 – 175.00.**

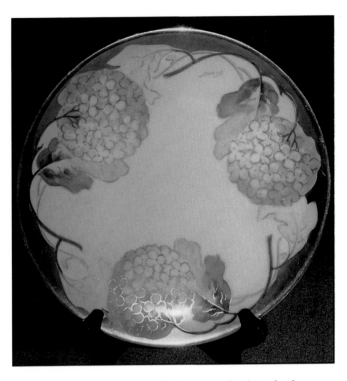

Plate 550. Plate, 8¾" d; large yellow roses accented with magenta; gold border; artist signed, "Duval." "Limoges, France" Mark 6 and Lanternier Mark 1. **$225.00 – 250.00.**

Plate 551. Plate, 8¾" d; hand-painted white hydrangeas enhanced with gold outlining and gold trim around border; artist signed, "Duval." "Limoges, France" Mark 6 and Lanternier Mark 1 with "Hand Painted" below Mark. **$175.00 – 225.00.**

Plate 552. Bouillon cup and saucer; hand-painted lavender flowers with green leaves; gold trim; artist signed, "Luc." "Limoges, France" Mark 6 and Lanternier Mark 1. **$150.00 – 175.00.**

Plate 553. Cup and saucer; red berries with gold and green leaves on a light green background; gold trim; artist signed, "Duval." Lanternier Mark 1 in red with no white ware mark. **$175.00 – 195.00 set.**

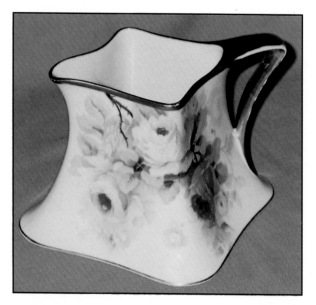

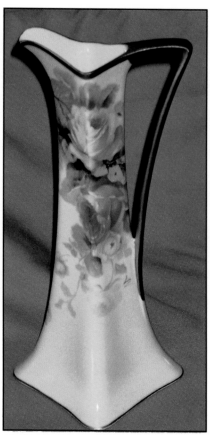

Plate 554. Cider or lemonade pitcher, 6" h, angular shape; hand-painted pink and yellow roses; gold trim; artist signed, "Luc." "Limoges, France" Mark 6 and Lanternier Mark 1. **$425.00 – 475.00** (mc).

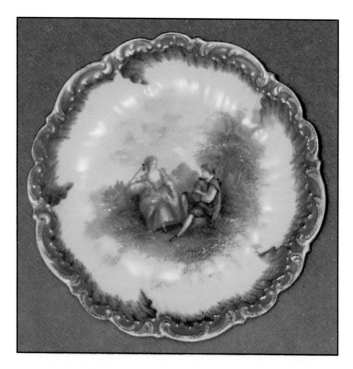

Plate 555. Tankard, 13" h, made in the same angular mold as the cider pitcher at left and decorated similarly; artist signed, "Luc." "Limoges, France" Mark 6 and Lanternier Mark 1. **$700.00 – 800.00.**

Plate 556. Plate, 9½"; figural pastoral scene of a couple in eighteenth century dress painted with a *mixtion* technique; brushed gold on border; artist signed, "Niox." Lanternier Marks 4 and 6. **$250.00 – 275.00.**

Plate 557. Plate matching preceding example, decorated with a different pastoral scene; artist signed, "Niox." Lanternier Marks 4 and 6. **$250.00 – 275.00.**

Lanternier Factory Decorated Table Wares

Plate 558. Divided dish, 10½" x 10", three sections with center handle; magenta flowers form a random pattern on a matte cream background accented with brushed gold on border. Lanternier Marks 4 and 6. **$350.00 – 400.00.**

Plate 559. Creamer, sugar bowl, cups and saucers, with tray; decoration is similar to that on the divided dish. Lanternier Mark 3 with no decorating mark. Tray, **$500.00 – 600.00;** creamer and sugar, **$300.00 – 350.00;** cup and saucer, **$100.00 – 125.00 set.**

Plate 560. Sauce tureen, small size for mustard or other condiments, with underplate; white and green floral design with magenta highlights; gold trim. Lanternier Marks 4 and 6. **$250.00 – 300.00.**

Plate 561. Fish set: platter, 22" l, and 12 serving plates, 9" d; scalloped shell border; transfer décor of natural colored fish and marine plants around outer borders. Lanternier Marks 4 and 6. **$1,800.00 – 2,000.00.**

Plate 562. Plate, 6¼" d; a large pink rose and a small yellow rose form pattern at base of plate with a stem of green leaves at top; gold trim. Lanternier Mark 4 and 6. **$25.00 – 30.00.**

Plate 563. Cup and saucer, large pink and white roses compose an inner border pattern; gold stenciled designs around outer border and interior top border of cup. Lanternier Marks 4 and 6. **$70.00 – 85.00.**

Plate 564. Chocolate pot, 10" h; sprays of pink and white flowers are scattered over surface; brushed gold trim. Lanternier Marks 4 and 6. **$400.00 – 450.00.**

Plate 565. Chocolate set: pot with a long handle, 6 cups and saucers, and tray; pink floral pattern in a garland design encircles top half of pieces between a gold band border and gold stenciled designs. Délinières & Co. Mark 3 and Lanternier Mark 1. **$1,000.00 – 1,200.00 set.**

Plate 566. Cup and saucer; small pink and white roses between gold bands form an inner border pattern. Lanternier Marks 4 and 6. **$50.00 – 60.00.**

Plate 567. Covered vegetable dish, 12" x 8"; pink and white floral transfer pattern placed randomly over body; gold trim. Lanternier Marks 4 and 6. **$200.00 – 250.00.**

Lanternier Non-Factory Decorated China

Plate 568. This compote and the three on the facing page are hand-painted with different flowers or fruit. Each is either artist signed "Annie M. Booth" or initialed "AMB," and dated 1895. A light pink finish surrounds the undecorated center of each with brushed gold around borders. Lanternier Mark 4. Compote decorated with catkins. **$375.00 – 425.00 each.**

Plate 569. Compote decorated with small purple berries.

Plate 570. Compote decorated with fir cones and needles.

Plate 571. Compote decorated with blackberries.

Plate 572. Plate, 9" d; a large pink rose with green leaves is painted over a light cream background; the border is painted in pink and green, accented with gold; artist initialed on back, "ff" in gold. Lanternier Mark 4. **$225.00 – 250.00.**

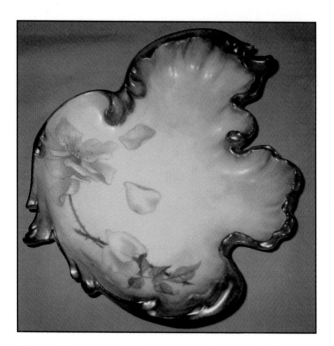

Plate 574. Chamber stick and candle snuffer; floral design on a matte cream ground; brushed gold on borders; artist initialed, "E. A. H." Lanternier Mark 4. **$300.00 – 350.00.**

Plate 573. Bowl, 8" l, irregular shape with heavily scalloped border; hand-painted pink flower with falling petals decorates one side; the border is painted like the preceding bowl and is signed by the same artist. Lanternier Mark 4. **$275.00 – 300.00.**

Plate 575. Butter dish, 7" d, with liner; transfer of a cherub on lid; matte cream finish with brushed gold trim. Lanternier Mark 4. **$275.00 – 325.00.**

Plate 576. Cake plate, shaped with a fluted and scalloped border, double-pierced handles, and molded shell designs; figural scene of a woman and two cherubs painted with the *mixtion* technique; gold enameled work and heavy gilding on handles and around border; artist initialed, "E. B. L." Lanternier Mark 4. **$500.00 – 550.00.**

Plate 577. Ewer, 10" h; graceful shape with scalloped spout and curved handle; hand-painted red and pink roses; a dark green finish above flowers extends to bottom of handle; small enameled gold flowers around spout; brushed gold on interior of spout. Lanternier Mark 4. **$650.00 – 750.00.**

Lanternier Dolls

Plate 578. Fashion doll made by Lanternier during the years of World War I. **$4,500.00 – 5,000.00.**

Plate 579. Fashion doll, 20" h, dressed in a dark wine velvet coat trimmed with lace. **$4,000.00 – 4,500.00.**

Jean Pouyat (JP)

The Pouyat family was one of the oldest French names connected with the Limoges porcelain industry. Jean Pouyat's grandfather had a faience factory in the 1760s at St. Yrieix. He also owned kaolin mines in that area in the late 1700s. Jean's father, François, operated a hard paste porcelain factory in Paris from the early 1800s until around 1840. Jean Pouyat established a company circa 1842 at Limoges. Jean died in 1849, and the business was carried on by his sons. About 1883, the company became known as La Céramique. The Pouyat and William Guérin companies were joined in 1912 (Meslin-Perrier and Monnerie, p. 29).

China manufactured by the Pouyat factory represents another of the most visible Limoges companies on the American antiques market. The firm carried on a large export trade with the United States during the late 1800s. Examples of Pouyat marked porcelain range from white wares and table china to factory decorated art objects and accessories. Double marks indicate that the items were factory decorated. Additional marks such as "Hand Painted" or "Peint et Doré a la main a Limoges" may appear with the marks. The company was particularly famous for its white wares or "blanks." Wood (p. 31) mentions that the company did not produce factory decorated dinner services until after 1890.

Some refinement to the Pouyat marks has been made based on information by Meslin-Perrier and Monnerie in *Le Manufacture De Porcelaine Pouyat, Limoges, 1835 – 1912*, 1994. The earliest mark attributed to the company dates circa 1851, according to Melin-Perrier and Monnerie, p. 28. See Mark 1 which incorporates the initials "J. P." over "L." Mark 3 which is the same as Mark 1 but with a line separating "J. P." and "L.," is noted by the authors to have been in use as early as 1862, used concurrently with Mark 1, although Mark 3 was not registered until 1875, and it was re-registered in 1891. Mark 5, which is the same as Mark 3 but with "FRANCE" added, was not registered until 1906. It is usual to assume that all marks with a country of origin date from 1891, based on our U. S. tariff law requirements. While Mark 5 was not registered until 1906, Meslin-Perrier and Monnerie conclude that the mark was used in 1902. They base that date on examples known to have been made in that year which were marked with our Mark 5. My supposition is that Mark 5 was used earlier than 1902, circa 1891, at least on exported china.

While the information on the registered Pouyat marks does not mention the same marks as overglaze decorating marks, we should be able to assume that the time periods would be the same. See Marks 2, 4, and 6 which are exactly the same as Marks 1, 3, and 5. A decorating mark composed of a green wreath entwined with pink ribbon encircling the name "J. Pouyat Limoges" printed in green was registered in 1906. The same mark, but with the name printed in gold, was also registered (see Mark 9). That mark was reserved for hand-decorated and richly decorated porcelain (Meslin-Perrier and Monnerie, p. 29). We show a variation of Mark 9, a green wreath without the pink ribbon but with gold letters. Mark 7, an overglaze decorating mark in red with "J. Pouyat Limoges" printed in a circular style, also does not have a registration date noted. Wood (p. 34), however, indicates that the mark was in use in 1900. The mark may have been used at the same time as Mark 6. The later wreath mark seems to have evolved from Mark 7. Marks 5, 8, and 9 are the most frequently seen Pouyat marks. When the Guérin-Pouyat firm became a part of Bawo & Dotter (Elite China) after World War I, the Pouyat marks continued to be used until the Bawo & Dotter company closed about 1932. (See Guérin and Bawo & Dotter.)

The first group of pictures is of decorative china made by the Pouyat factory which was either decorated at the factory or decorated by a Limoges artist. A number of pieces are found with a Pouyat white ware mark and an artist's signature, with no Pouyat or any other company's overglaze decorating mark. The names of various Limoges artists are found on china made by different factories, and usually the pieces also have some overglaze decorating mark. In instances where they do not, the pieces are shown under the company which made the china, such as Pouyat. Since the Pouyat company was famous for its blanks or white wares, it would not be unusual for Limoges painters to purchase and decorate white wares for themselves. It is also the case that the piece simply failed to get stamped with a decorating mark.

A large number of Pouyat white wares which were decorated by American china painters have been selected primarily to show the variety of shapes, applied and molded embellishments, and types of objects made by Pouyat, with the decoration actually being the second consideration. The Art Nouveau influence is certainly apparent in the shapes of the vases. Tankards fashioned with dragon-shaped handles, mask spouts, and jardinieres made with applied elephant head handles are also unique. See other Pouyat china in the chapter on Undecorated Limoges Porcelain to gain a better appreciation for the Pouyat blanks which also merit collection even though they have no painted decoration.

An advertisement for Pouyat China, distributed by Paroutaud and Watson in New York, in 1906 illustrates the company's decorating and white ware marks at that time.

Pouyat Ad and Marks

Mark 1, underglaze white ware mark in green, initials only, ca. 1851 – 1875.

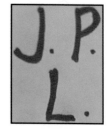

Mark 2, overglaze decorating mark in red, initials only, ca. 1851 – 1875.

Mark 3, underglaze white ware mark in green, initials underscored over "L.," ca. 1862 to early 1900s.

Mark 4, overglaze decorating mark in red, initials underscored over "L.," similar to Mark 2, ca. 1862 to early 1900s.

Mark 5, underglaze white ware mark in green with "FRANCE," ca. 1890 to 1932.

Mark 5a, underglaze white ware mark in green, like Mark 5, but with a patent date over the initials.

Mark 6, overglaze decorating mark in red, similar to Mark 4, but with "FRANCE," ca. after 1890, probably used for a short period.

Mark 7, overglaze decorating mark in red, name in a circle with "LIMOGES," ca. 1900 – 1906.

Mark 8, overglaze decorating mark, green wreath with uncolored ribbon and name printed in gold, ca. 1906 – 1932.

Mark 9, overglaze decorating mark, green wreath with pink ribbon and name printed in green or gold, ca. 1906 – 1932.

Pouyat Art Objects and Decorative China

Plate 580. Vase, 14" h; hand-painted figural décor of two semi-nude women; artist signed, "E. Furlaud." Pouyat Marks 5 and 9 with "Peint et Doré a la main a Limoges," printed in green. **$4,000.00 – 5,000.00.**

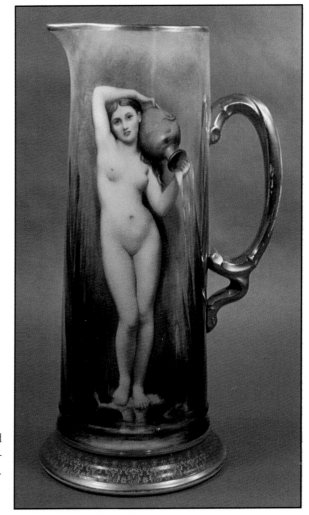

Plate 581. Portrait tankard, 13" h; hand-painted nude woman holding a water jug over left shoulder; heavily gilded handle. Pouyat Marks 5 and 9. **$3,000.00 – 3,500.00.**

Plate 582. Tankard, 12" h; hand-painted scene of a house located on the edge of a wooded river bank; a bridge is in the foreground; heavily gilded handle; artist signed, "Emile" (possibly Emile Pouyat). Pouyat Mark 5 with "Hand Painted" printed in blue. **$1,500.00 – 1,700.00.**

Plate 583. Tankard, 15" h; vividly painted mums in orange, pink, yellow, and white on a light yellow background with green highlights; gold trim; artist signed, "Duval." Pouyat Mark 5 with no decorating Mark. **$1,600.00 – 1,800.00.**

Plate 584. Tankard, 14½" h; dragon-shaped handle painted gold; large pink roses with green leaves on a pale green background; artist signed, but name is not legible. Pouyat Marks 5 and 9. **$1,800.00 – 2,000.00.**

Plate 585. Plate, 9" d; courtship scene with figures in eighteenth century dress; small pink roses on a light blue background around outer border. Pouyat Mark 5a with a patent date of "Dec. 6, 1898," and Mark 7. **$200.00 – 250.00.**

Plate 586. Vases, 12" h; figural scenes of eighteenth century couples in an outdoor setting by a lake painted by the *mixtion* method; the finish on the vases shades from a light blue to white; artist signed, "Héléne C." Pouyat Mark 1 on one vase and Pouyat Mark 5 on the other with no decorating mark, but signature indicates a French painter. **$2,500.00 – 3,000.00 pair.**

Plate 587. Plate, 7½" d; a postcard size winter scene of a house and a lake decorate center of plate. Pouyat Marks 1 and 2. **$225.00 – 250.00.**

Plate 588. Vase, 9" h; green monochrome décor of boats with masts; heavily gilded handles. Pouyat Marks 5 and 7. **$500.00 – 600.00.**

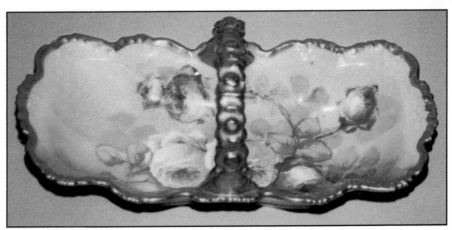

Plate 589. Basket, 9" x 5"; large pink and red roses painted on a shaded cream background; gilded border and handle; artist signed, "Duval." Pouyat Mark 5. **$425.00 – 475.00.**

Plate 590. Divided dish, three sections with scrolled handle, 13" d; gold paste flowers and leaves applied over a cobalt blue glaze; gilded handle. Pouyat Mark 3 with no white ware mark. **$500.00 – 600.00.**

Plate 591. Plate, 9" d; gold flowers and birds applied over a dark cobalt blue background; the small flowers are accented with a red-orange enamel. Pouyat Mark 3. **$250.00 – 300.00.**

Plate 592. Cake plate, 12" d; large white flowers on a shaded green background; gold trim; artist signed, "Duval." Pouyat Mark 5. **$425.00 – 475.00.**

Plate 593. Game bird plaques (see next photograph also), 18" d; wild ducks swimming in lake; artist signed, "Max." Pouyat Mark 5. **$1,200.00 – 1,400.00 pair.**

Plate 594. Matching game bird plaque; wild ducks in flight over lake.

Plate 595. Souvenir plates, 9¼" d; three plates commemorating the 1900 Exposition in Paris; transfer designs of different buildings. Pouyat Mark 5 with no decorating mark, but decoration was probably by a Paris studio; the first plate is titled, *Exposition Universelle de 1900 Vue General*. **$450.00 – 500.00 set.**

Plate 596. Souvenir plate titled, *Pavillion National des Etas Unis*.

Plate 597. Souvenir plate titled, *Palais Étrangers*.

Pouyat Factory Decorated Table Wares

Plate 598. Egg cup, 4" h; floral pattern composed of transfer outlines hand colored in rose, blue, gold, green, and bronze; gold luster trim. See other pieces from this early Pouyat dinner service in the next two photographs. Pouyat Marks 3 and 4. **$60.00 – 75.00.**

Plate 599. Dinner plate, 9¾" d. **$50.00 – 65.00.**

Plate 600. Tea set: covered sugar bowl, **$175.00 – 225.00;** tea pot, **$300.00 – 350.00;** creamer, **$150.00 – 175.00.**

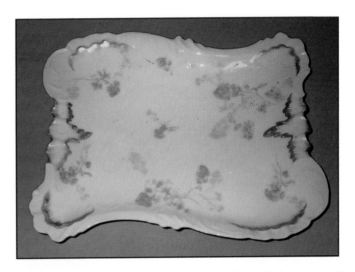

Plate 601. Platter, 14" x 8"; embossed designs on handles and border trimmed in gold. Pouyat Marks 3 and 4. **$350.00 – 400.00.**

Plate 602. Tray, 10½" x 8", irregular scalloped shape; small yellow flowers scattered over surface; scalloped designs on handles and inner border painted gold. Pouyat Marks 5 and 7. **$200.00 – 250.00.**

Plate 603. Plate, 10" d; deep cobalt blue border frames a white center which is decorated with gold stenciled *fleur-de-lis;* the *fleur-de-lis* also are overlaid on the border; heavy gold trim. Pouyat Mark 5 and a decorating mark for "Stewart Dry Goods, Louisville, Ky." **$125.00 – 150.00.**

Plate 604. Jam jar and underplate; cobalt blue enameled finish decorated with gold stenciled designs; heavily gilded handles and finial. Pouyat Marks 5 and 9. **$375.00 – 425.00 set**.

Plate 605. Cake plate, 13¾" d; a bouquet of pink flowers decorates center with similar flowers composing border; pattern is enhanced with white enameling and gold trim. Pouyat Mark 5 with a decorating mark for "Wanamaker's" (American retailer). **$250.00 – 275.00**.

Plate 606. Cake plate, 14" d, made in a mold very similar to the preceding plate, but with a border variation; a deep green glaze applied in a wide border around piece is embellished with gold stenciled flowers and scrolled designs; small pink floral garlands form an inner border around undecorated center; molded floral designs on handles and outer border painted gold. Pouyat Marks 5 and 9. **$250.00 – 275.00**.

Plate 607. Cup and saucer; red and lavender floral pattern. Pouyat Mark 5a with a patent date of "Dec. 1892," and Mark 7. **$75.00 – 90.00.**

Plate 608. Bowl, 10" l, with one handle; random pattern of small pink flowers. Pouyat Marks 5 and 7. **$100.00 – 120.00.**

Plate 609. Cake plate, 11" d; double-pierced handles; delicate pink and white flowers scattered over surface; brushed gold on border. Pouyat Marks 5 and 8. **$175.00 – 200.00.**

Plate 610. Ramekin and underplate; small gold flowers on a dark green background form a border pattern with an inner border of gold stenciled designs. Pouyat Marks 5 and 9 with "The Narbonne" printed in red. **$80.00 – 100.00.**

Plate 612. Breakfast set: plate, hot milk pot, tea pot, sugar bowl, cup and saucer, and egg cup; brightly colored birds and flowers form pattern with red borders and red outlining on handles and spouts. Pouyat Marks 5 and 8. **$400.00 – 450.00 set.**

Plate 611. Chocolate pot, 10" h; large orange poppies compose borders with a few flowers scattered over lower part of pot; heavy gold finish on handle and finial. Pouyat Marks 5 and 9. **$325.00 – 375.00.**

Plate 613. Sauce dish with attached underplate, 5" d; pink roses with enameled gold scroll designs and gold trim. Pouyat Mark 5 and decorating mark for American retailer, "Tilden Thumber, Providence, Rhode Island." **$150.00 – 175.00.**

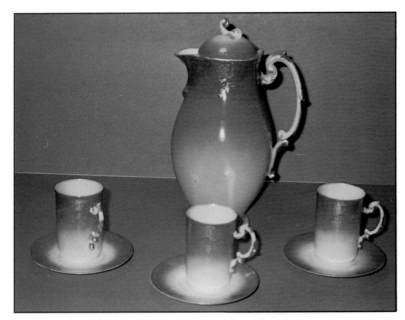

Plate 614. Chocolate set: pot with three cups and saucers; pieces are finished with a pompadour rose glaze shading to pale pink; gold stenciled designs around top borders; handles and finial trimmed in gold. Pouyat Marks 5 and 4. Chocolate pot, **$450.00 – 500.00;** cups and saucers, **$100.00 – 125.00.**

Plate 615. Fish set: plates, 8½" d; fish are portrayed in an underwater scene framed by a light green finish painted with gold designs. Pouyat Mark 5a with a patent date of "Dec. 6, 1898," and Mark 8. **$2,400.00 – 2,600.00 set.**

Plate 616. Platter to fish set, 22½" l.

Pouyat American Decorated White Wares

Paintings, Vases, and Jardinieres

Plate 617. Painting on porcelain, 16" d, framed, lion poised on edge of cliff; artist signed (illegible); the following painting is by the same artist. Pouyat Mark 5. **$2,500.00 – 3,000.00.**

Plate 618. Painting on porcelain, 15" x 12", framed, lion and lioness; artist signed (illegible); Pouyat Mark 5. **$3,000.00 – 3,500.00.**

Plate 620. Vase, 14" h; figural portrait of a woman in a white dress, pink roses are in the background; artist signed, "K. Ruybix." Pouyat Mark 5. **$2,200.00 – 2,500.00.**

Plate 619. Vase, 13" h; figural portrait of a woman holding a large jug under one arm with the other arm outstretched; artist initialed, "E. T. S. 1888." Pouyat Mark 3. **$1,400.00 – 1,600.00.**

Plate 621. Vase, 12" h; a semi-nude winged nymph kneels by water's edge; artist signed and dated, "L. Curran 1914." Pouyat Mark 5. **$1,200.00 – 1,400.00.**

Plate 622. Vase. 10½" h, dragon-shaped handles; a hand-painted scene entitled, "The Captive," protrays a tiger in chains held by three Arabs. A fourth man, dressed in red astride a camel, is in the background. A scene on the reverse side (not shown) focuses on the latter figure. The handles and lip of the vase are heavily gilded; artist signed, "E. Christie." Pouyat Mark 5. **$2,500.00 – 3,000.00.**

Plate 623. Vase, 13" h; scenic décor painted in greens and red-orange depicts steps leading to a terrace with trees and flowering bushes in the background; artist initialed and dated, "S. 1904." Pouyat Mark 5. **$1,200.00 – 1,400.00.**

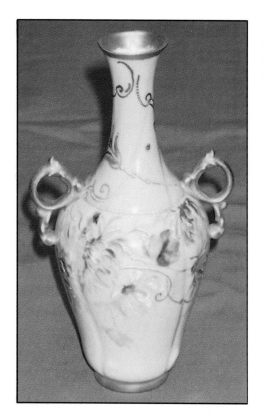

Plate 624. Vase, 9" h; large shaggy pink flowers accented with gold enameled designs and gold trim. Pouyat Mark 5. **$500.00 – 600.00.**

Plate 625. Reverse of Plate 624, decorated with flowers and a butterfly.

Plate 626. Vase, 14" h; hand-painted purple iris; artist signed on base, "A. Watts." Pouyat Mark 5. **$1,000.00 – 1,200.00.**

Plate 627. Vase, 11½" h, Art Nouveau style curved handles, see following two examples for the same mold; gold paste leaves and small flowers on a matte cream background; neck, handles, and base painted gold. Pouyat Mark 5. **$650.00 – 750.00.**

Plate 628. Vase, 10" h; violet flowers highlighted with white enamel; gold trim; artist initialed, "E. M. B." Pouyat Mark 5. **$600.00 – 700.00.**

Plate 629. Vase, 13" h; gold paste leaves and small flowers applied over a matte cream finish extend from neck to handles; large lavender flowers are painted on body of vase; handles and base painted gold. Pouyat Mark 5. **$700.00 – 800.00.**

Plate 630. Vase, 10¾" h; applied handles and openwork on pedestal base; lavender blue flowers painted on a light green background with a brighter green finish, accented with gold, on neck and base. Pouyat Mark 5. **$500.00 – 600.00.**

Plate 631. Vase, 10¾" h, serpent-shaped handles are heavily gilded; white lilies on a light green background cover body; handles, neck and base painted gold. Pouyat Mark 5. **$450.00 – 550.00.**

Plate 633. Vase, 9" h, handles extend from neck to body where they split into three sections; hand-painted blue birds; enameled gold scroll designs; red finish on neck and above base; handles, top of neck and base painted gold. Pouyat Mark 5. **$350.00 – 450.00.**

Plate 632. Vase, 10" h, vine-wrapped handles finished in gold; wine, pink, and yellow roses on a light blue ground; wine colored finish on neck and base. Pouyat Mark 5. **$550.00 – 650.00.**

Plate 634. Vase, 9" h, shaped like preceding vase; hand-painted pink flowers on a light cream background; handles and base painted gold. Pouyat Mark 5. **$400.00 – 500.00.**

Plate 635. Vase, 8½" h; hand-painted roses in yellow, pink, and white with orange highlights against a dark green background; handles and top of neck painted gold; artist signed, "LeRoy." Pouyat Mark 5. **$700.00 – 800.00.**

Plate 636. Vase, made in the unusual shape of a draw-string pouch; hand-painted flowers with gold trim; artist signed (illegible) and dated 1909. Pouyat Mark 5. **$175.00 – 225.00.**

Plate 637. Vase, 5¾" h; large white roses with smaller pink roses; green finish on neck. Pouyat Mark 5. **$150.00 – 175.00.**

Plate 639. Jardiniere, 9" x 12", elephant head handles heavily gilded; hand-painted pink roses; gold enameled leaves around neck. Pouyat Mark 5. **$2,000.00 – 2,200.00.**

Plate 638. Vase, 9" h; hand-painted pink dogwood with green leaves on a light cream background shading to dark green at base; interior of neck and handles painted gold. Pouyat Mark 5. **$325.00 – 375.00.**

Plate 640. Jardiniere, 12" x 14"; intricately twisted handles and highly scalloped pedestal base; hand-painted large white roses with brown and green leaves; pink roses on reverse (not shown); handles and borders painted gold. Pouyat Mark 5. **$2,400.00 – 2,600.00.**

Table Wares

Plate 641. Punch bowl, 12¾" h x 26" d, footed; hand-painted pink and red roses; gold trim. Pouyat Mark 5. **$1,200.00 – 1,400.00.**

Plate 642. Cider pitcher, 6¼" h; yellow flowers with green stems and leaves on a light pink background; neck and handle painted gold. Pouyat Mark 5. **$350.00 – 400.00.**

Plate 643. Chop plate, 18" x 14½"; clusters of multi-colored roses on a light blue background; gold trim. Pouyat Mark 5. **$450.00 – 500.00.**

Plate 644. Tea set: sugar bowl, tea pot, and creamer; note two-part design of handles and finials; pink roses accented with gold enameled designs and gold finish on handles and finials. Pouyat Mark 5. **$600.00 – 700.00 set.**

Plate 646. Candle holders, 16" h; pink and white roses with small blue flowers on a light pink background against a gold luster finish on neck and base. Pouyat Mark 5. **$400.00 – 500.00.**

Plate 645. Chocolate pot, 13" h; Art Deco angular-shaped finial and handle painted gold; pink and white roses painted at an angle under spout to complement shape of piece. Pouyat Mark 5a with a patent date of "April 2d 1907." **$550.00 – 650.00.**

Plate 647. Tray, 12½" x 9", ornately scrolled shape with pierced handles; hand-painted violets accented with enameled gold designs and gold trim. Pouyat Mark 5. **$300.00 – 350.00.**

Plate 648. Cider pitcher, molded beads on handle; hand-painted blackberries with green and yellow leaves and small white and pink flowers; gold trim. Pouyat Mark 5. **$550.00 – 650.00.**

Plate 649. Cider pitcher, red berries painted with light brown and green leaves; gold trim; artist signed, "Brinent." Pouyat Mark 5. **$400.00 – 450.00.**

Plate 650. Cake plate, 11½" d; blackberries with white blooms are highlighted by a dark green background; handles and rim painted gold; artist signed and dated, "M. R. Gray 1900." Pouyat Mark 5. **$350.00 – 400.00.**

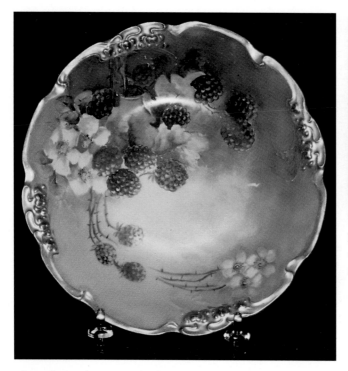

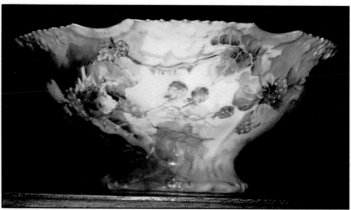

Plate 652. Fruit bowl, 5" h x 10" d, pedestal base; blackberries on a dark to light green background with rust highlights; artist signed, "A. Cote." Pouyat Mark 5. $500.00 – 550.00.

Plate 651. Plate, 10" d; blackberries with light pink blossoms painted on a tinted background; heavy gold trim. Pouyat Mark 5. $275.00 – 325.00.

Plate 653. Tea set; vines in relief are wrapped around handles; small blue flowers are painted against a multi-colored background with purple being predominant; gold trim. Pouyat Mark 5. $1,000.00 – 1,200.00 set.

Plate 654. Open sugar bowl and creamer; yellow and dark pink roses on a shaded light green background decorate exterior and also interior of sugar bowl; gold trim. Pouyat Mark 5. $250.00 – 300.00 set.

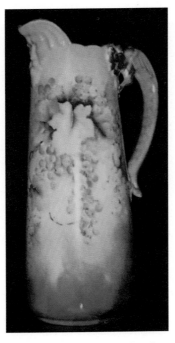

Plate 655. Chocolate pot, 10" h, delicate fluted designs around spout; hand-painted peach and red roses; gold trim. Pouyat Mark 5. **$250.00 – 275.00.**

Plate 656. Tankard, 11" h, dragon-shaped handle with "Man of the North" molded spout; hand-painted red currants; signed and dated, "Sara to Harry April 29, 1904." Pouyat Mark 5. **$425.00 – 475.00.**

Plate 657. Tankard, 10" h, drag-on-shaped handle painted a dull gold; hand-painted clusters of cherries; artist signed, "A. P. Nock." Pouyat Mark 5. **$500.00 – 600.00.**

Plate 658. Tankard, 14" h; dragon-shaped handle painted gold; hand-painted blackberries; dark blue-green finish at base; artist signed and dated, "J. DeWolf 1914." Pouyat Mark 5. **$800.00 – 900.00.**

Plate 659. Tankard, 13½" h, and six matching mugs, 5¼" h; purple and red grapes with green leaves; gold trim. Pouyat Mark 5. Tankard, **$600.00 – 700.00**; mugs, **$150.00 – 175.00 each.**

Plate 660. Tankard, 12" h, and five matching mugs; red and purple grapes on a tinted lavender background are visible on tankard; green and red grapes are visible on two of the mugs. Pouyat Mark 5. Tankard, **$500.00 – 600.00**; mugs, **$100.00 – 125.00 each.**

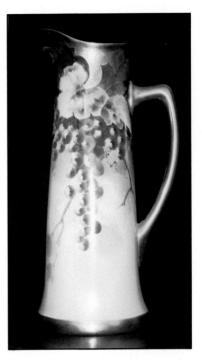

Plate 661. Tankard, 13" h; red cherries and green leaves against a brown background shading from light to dark; handle and border of neck painted gold. Pouyat Mark 5. **$700.00 – 800.00.**

Plate 662. Tankard, 15" h; red grapes with green leaves; gold scrolled design around spout; handle and base painted gold; artist signed, "F. Krieahe." Pouyat Mark 5. **$900.00 – 1,000.00.**

Plate 663. Mug, 5¾" h, dragon-shaped handle painted gold; red grapes painted in an Art Nouveau style on a pearl luster background. Pouyat Mark 5. **$200.00 – 225.00.**

Plate 664. Chalice, 10½" h; white and purple grapes framed with gold scroll designs; gold medallions at top and on base; dark wine-colored border; gold trim. Pouyat Mark 5. **$400.00 – 500.00.**

Plate 666. Pair of mugs, 5" h; portrait of a monk is painted on each mug against a dark brown background. Pouyat Mark 5. **$275.00 – 325.00 each.**

Plate 665. Tankard, 11" h, dragon-shaped handle and "Man of the North" molded spout are painted gold; large green leaves with clusters of red currants on a pale yellow to cream background decorate body; artist signed and dated on base, "Mem 09." Pouyat Mark 5. **$1,000.00 – 1,200.00.**

Plate 668. Tankard, 14¾" h; portrait of a monk pouring wine from a keg in a reserve on the front; white flowers and green leaves above portrait. Pouyat Mark 5. **$600.00 – 800.00.**

Plate 667. Tankard, 13" h; painting of a professor or clergyman holding a document, dressed in a brown robe and velvet beret; dark brown glaze; artist signed, "J. H. Schiwdler." Pouyat Mark 5. **$1,200.00 – 1,400.00.**

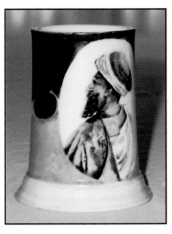

Plate 669. Mug, 5" h; portrait of an Arab. Pouyat Mark 5. **$325.00 – 375.00.**

Plate 670. Mug, 5½" h; painting of a man in a night cap uncorking a bottle of wine. Pouyat Mark 5. **$325.00 – 375.00.**

Plate 671. Mug, 6" h; portrait of a portly gentleman smoking a pipe and holding a glass of wine; artist signed, "Whitridge." Pouyat Mark 5. **$400.00 – 500.00.**

Martial Redon (MR)/LA Porcelain Limousine (PL)

The Redon name is an old one in the Limoges porcelain industry. Martial Redon was associated with Gibus from the mid 1850s until 1881. The name of the company was Gibus & Cie, however, until 1872 (d'Albis and Romanet, pp. 128, 129). That company manufactured art objects and decorative accessories. Mark 1 is incised, and Mark 2 is a stamped mark in red, incorporating Redon's initials. Pieces have been seen with both Marks 1 and 2, but examples which are obviously factory decorated have been found with only Mark 1. Very few examples, however, are found with the Gibus and Redon marks.

Redon took over the company in 1882. His white ware mark was like the red decorating mark of the earlier firm. A new decorating mark of "M. Redon Limoges" printed within a circle in red was put in use. White wares, table china, decorative accessories, and art objects were manufactured. Factory decorated pieces are not always double marked, however. Redon died in 1890, but the company and its marks were continued by Redon's son until about 1896 (d'Albis and Romanet, p. 130).

A few years later, in 1902, J. Redon joined the Barny & Rigoni company for a short time, until 1904. They instituted a new mark which included the name "M. Redon," taking advantage of the father's first name rather than the son's. Examples are rarely found in this country with any of those marks. When Redon left the company in 1904, Langle became a partner. See Barny & Rigoni under Other Limoges Factories.

About 1905 or 1906, new owners took charge and changed the factory name to La Porcelaine Limousine. This latest company implemented white ware marks which corresponded to the company's name, "PL," but they used the old Redon circular mark in red for their decorating mark. That company remained in business until the late 1930s. Some factory decorated china is found, but white wares painted by American china painters, especially dresser accessories, are more commonly seen.

Marks for the Martial Redon company are shown along with marks for his predecessor, Gibus & Cie, and his successor, La Porcelaine Limousine. Examples include pieces made by each of the factories. The specific mark is noted in each caption.

Gibus and Redon Marks

Mark 1, incised initials, ca. 1872 – 1881.

Mark 2, overglaze decorating mark in red, prior to 1882.

Martial Redon Marks

Mark 1, underglaze white ware mark in green without "FRANCE," ca. 1882 – 1890.

Mark 2, underglaze white ware mark in green with "FRANCE," ca. 1891 – 1896.

Mark 3, overglaze decorating mark in red or blue, sometimes accompanied by "Special" in a rectangle, in red, ca. 1882 – 1896.

Mark 4, overglaze decorating Mark in red, name written in script form with "HAND PAINTED," ca. 1882 – 1896.

M. Redon, Barny & Rigoni Mark

Barny, Rigoni, and Redon, ca. 1902 – 1904.

La Porcelaine Limousine Marks

Mark 1, underglaze white ware mark in green, initials underscored with "LIMOGES, FRANCE," ca. 1905 – late 1930s.

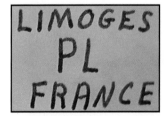

Mark 2, underglaze white ware mark in green, like Mark 1 without line, ca. 1905 – late 1930s.

Mark 3, underglaze white ware mark in green, with "LIMOGES" above initials and "FRANCE" below, ca. 1905 – late 1930s.

Mark 4, overglaze decorating mark in red, "M. REDON" in circle (used with one of the PL white ware marks), ca. 1905 – late 1930s.

Redon Decorative China

Plate 672. Vase, 6" h; pedestal base, applied handles painted gold; purple flowers with green leaves outlined in gold on a matte cream background. Gibus & Redon Marks 1 and 2. **$350.00 – 400.00.**

Plate 673. Vase, 8" h, handles shaped with flowers and branches in relief which are painted green with gold highlights; large pink flowers and green buds outlined in gold on an ivory matte background decorate body; sponged gold on neck and base. M. Redon Mark 1. **$650.00 – 750.00.**

Plate 674. Vase, 8" h, floral handles painted gold; hand-painted purple and yellow-gold dahlias with green leaves and buds on a white ground decorate front of vase; enameled gold scroll work frames flowers; turquoise finish on body with sponged gold around neck. M. Redon Mark 2. **$600.00 – 700.00.**

Plate 675. Urn, 3" x 4"; pale pink flowers and green leaves painted around body; gold trim on neck, lid, and base. M. Redon Mark 1. **$275.00 – 325.00.**

Plate 676. Vase (or letter holder), 6½" h; footed; hand-painted purple dahlias on a matte cream background; sponged gold on body; gilded feet. M. Redon Mark 1. **$350.00 – 400.00.**

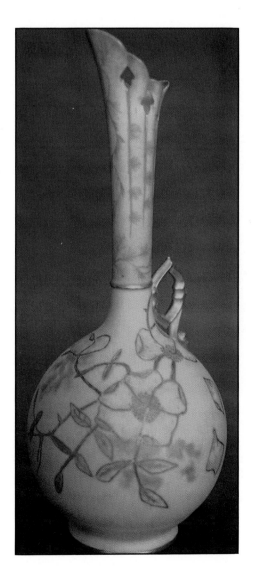

Plate 678. Plate 8¾" d; transfer décor of a cherub amidst clouds in center of plate; gold stenciled designs on outer border. M. Redon Marks 2 and 3. **$200.00 – 225.00.**

Plate 677. Ewer, 12½" h; openwork around neck; pastel blue flowers outlined in gold on a light cream background cover bulbous base; delicate branches and leaves painted in gold over a light pink finish on neck. M. Redon Mark 1. **$600.00 – 700.00.**

Plate 679. Plaque, 13½" d, heavily scalloped border with embossed designs; colorful scene of ducks on a pond with a terrace, flowering plants, and trees in the background. M. Redon Marks 2 and 4. **$800.00 – 900.00.**

Redon Table Wares

Plate 680. Bowl, 9" d; gold floral décor accented with white enamel painted on a cobalt blue background shading to light blue. M. Redon Marks 2 and 3. **$325.00 – 375.00.**

Plate 681. Demitasse cup and saucer; gold paste and white enameled flowers applied over a deep red finish; gold scrolled designs separate the flowers on the cup; interior of cup lined with gold. M. Redon Marks 2 and 3. **$250.00 – 275.00.**

Plate 682. Biscuit jar, 8" h; multi-colored floral spray across ribbed body; sponged gold around borders and on finial. M. Redon Marks 1 and 3. **$275.00 – 325.00.**

Plate 683. Chocolate pot, 9" h, scalloped shell and scroll designs around base; mixed flowers painted in orange, purple, yellow, and white on a light cream background; sponged gold around top border and spout; gilded handle and finial. M. Redon Mark 2. **$500.00 – 600.00 (mc).**

Plate 684. Demitasse cup and saucer, scalloped shell designs on base of cup; small purple flowers on a cream background form a pattern highlighted by gilded borders. M. Redon Mark 2. **$100.00 – 125.00.**

Plate 685. Plate, 8¾" d; hand-painted purple flowers in a circular design in center of plate; gold trim. M. Redon Mark 2. **$75.00 – 100.00.**

Plate 686. Plate, cup, and saucer; blue floral transfer pattern on a white body; brushed gold trim on cup handle. M. Redon Marks 2 and 3. Plate, **$50.00 – 60.00;** cup and saucer, **$70.00 – 80.00.**

Plate 687. Bowl, 10" x 7", scalloped oval shape; *mixtion* pattern of small flowers painted yellow with white enameled centers and light green leaves on a pale pink background; sponged gold highlights fluted designs around border. M. Redon Marks 2 and 3. **$140.00 – 165.00.**

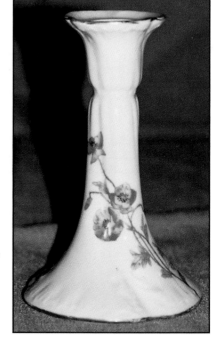

Plate 688. Candle holder, 5½" h; spray of orange poppies on a white body; gold trim. M. Redon Marks 2 and 3. **$85.00 – 100.00.**

Plate 690. Fish plate, 9" d, scalloped border with molded shell designs on inner border; a small fish swims above underwater plants; gold trim. M. Redon Marks 2 and 3. **$150.00 – 175.00.**

Plate 689. Candle holder, 7" h; hand-painted small purple flowers and green leaves on dark brown stems, on an ivory background, form a wrap-around design extending from base to upper part of body. M. Redon Marks 1 and 3. **$120.00 – 135.00.**

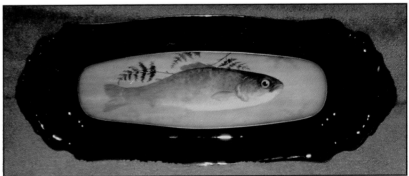

Plate 692. Platter to fish set (Plate 691).

Plate 691. Fish service (see Plate 692); plates (12), 9¾" d, and platter, 23½" l; a large fish in an underwater scene decorates center of pieces on a pale yellow shading to light blue ground with green vegetation above fish; dark cobalt blue border with gold trim frames center. La Porcelaine Limousine Mark 1 with no decorating mark, but set is factory decorated. **$3,000.00 – 3,500.00 set.**

Redon American Decorated White Wares

Plate 694. Vase, 6¼" h; figure of a cherub sitting on a chariot pulled by two white doves; gold trim. M. Redon Mark 1. **$350.00 – 400.00.**

Plate 693. Plate, 9" d; cherubs with golden hair painted in pale pink against a white background; gold trim on border extends toward center with scroll and leaf designs. M. Redon Mark 1. **$200.00 – 250.00.**

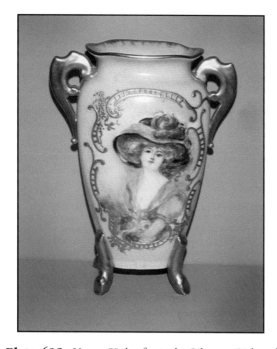

Plate 696. Vase, 10½" h, fancy handles shaped with sawtooth designs in relief; hand-painted white and pink mums on a pale blue background, accented with gold. M. Redon Mark 2. **$500.00 – 550.00.**

Plate 695. Vase, 8" h, footed; Gibson Girl style portrait of a woman wearing a large plumed hat; enameled gold scroll work frames portrait; handles and feet painted gold. Redon Mark 2. **$400.00 – 450.00.**

Plate 698. Vase, 14" h; hand-painted pink, yellow and white roses on a light green background; artist signed, "J. Cialard." La Porcelaine Limousine Mark 2. **$1,200.00 – 1,400.00.**

Plate 697. Vase, 9" h, canteen-shaped body; heavily gilded handles and feet incorporate flowers and branches; hand-painted winter scene; sponged gold around neck. Redon Mark 2. **$800.00 – 900.00.**

Plate 699. Ring tree and tray, 6" x 4"; hand-painted red berries and green leaves; gold trim. La Porcelaine Limousine Mark 2. **$120.00 – 140.00.**

Plate 700. Compote, 7½" d; abstract gold designs and small flowers painted around inner border and base; artist signed and dated, "Rucheler, 1914." La Porcelain Limousine Mark 1. **$225.00 – 275.00.**

Plate 701. Dresser set: tray, powder jar, hatpin holder, and hair receiver; hand-painted lavender flowers; gold trim. The tray is marked with La Porcelain Limousine Mark 2, and the other pieces have German marks. **$400.00 – 500.00 set.**

Lewis Straus & Sons

The Lewis Straus Company exported porcelain from Austria and Limoges to their New York based company from the 1890s until the mid 1920s. The Straus mark is found as an overglaze mark on factory decorated items. Often there is the white ware mark of the Limoges manufacturing company, such as Coiffe, but sometimes pieces are marked only with the Straus mark. It is possible that the manufacturing company decorated the china exclusively for the Straus firm. Alternatively, the Straus Company could have just chosen china, already decorated by various factories, to export. There may be some connection between the color of the Straus marks and whether the china was decorated exclusively for the company or not. The red, green, and gray marks may indicate decoration for Straus, and the blue mark may indicate non-exclusive decoration for the company. This is inconsequential, except it would be nice to know which factory, or Limoges studio, actually decorated the china. But as was probably intended by the exporters, the exported name remains associated with the china rather than the manufacturing or decorating companies. Blanks painted by American china painters are not found with a Straus mark. Pieces with the Straus marks are always professionally decorated. They are often hand-painted and signed by French artists. Examples range from highly decorative art objects to table wares.

Straus Marks

Overglaze exporting mark in blue, red, green, or gray, ca. 1890s – mid 1920s.

Overglaze exporting mark in red, a variation of Mark 1, with "New York," ca. 1890s – mid 1920s.

Straus Art Objects and Decorative China

Figural and Floral Themes

Plate 703. Relish dishes, 12" l; a pair of cherubs painted with the *mixtion* technique are shown in two poses with a light blue background around figures; scalloped border and embossed scroll designs painted gold. Coiffe Mark 2 and L. S. & S. Mark 1. **$425.00 – 475.00 each.**

Plate 702. Palace urn, 29" h; colorful hand-painted figural courtship décor: a man in a powdered wig is kneeling and playing a flute while a seated woman is attempting to place a garland of flowers on his head; artist signed, "Gayou." L. S. & S. Mark 1. **$5,500.00 – 6,500.00.**

Plate 704. Platter, 24" x 10", decorated with another cherub design enhanced by a frame of gold enameled leaves. Plates, 9" d (not shown), are also a part of this set. L. S. & S. Mark 1. **$800.00 – 900.00.**

Plate 705. Ewer, 11½" h; the same cherub decoration as the one on the top relish dish in Plate 703 is on this piece; gold enameled designs frame cherubs; small gold flowers are at base of design and on the neck; gold sponged work around spout; graceful scrolled handle heavily gilded. L. S. & S. Mark 1. **$650.00 – 750.00.**

Plate 706. Plate, 8" d, heavily scalloped border and fluted inner border painted gold; figural portrait of a woman in Victorian dress surrounded by a winter scene. Latrille Mark 1 and L. S. & S. Mark 1. **$225.00 – 275.00.**

Plate 707. Biscuit jar, 8" h; cameo figural courting scene portrays a couple in eighteenth century dress; elaborate gold scroll work frames reserve; red flowers and green leaves on body; gold trim. Laviolette Mark 1 and L. S. & S. Mark 1. **$400.00 – 500.00.**

Plate 708. Plate, 9" d, molded shell designs around inner border; transfer portrait touched with color shows the profile of a woman; red script beneath portrait is not legible, and it probably refers to the name of the person or original work on which the portrait is based. L. S. & S. Mark 1. **$125.00 – 145.00.**

Plate 709. Vase, 14" h x 11" w; outdoor scene of a woman holding a parasol, standing by a river; trees and buildings are in the background; a deep pink finish on neck and base; sponged gold on ornately shaped handles. L. S. & S. Mark 1. **$1,200.00 – 1,400.00.**

Plate 710. Charger, 12½" d, scrolled border design forms handles; a lavender and white floral reserve decorates center; fancy gold enameling and trim enhance the tinted pink and cream background. Granger Mark 2 and L. S. & S. Mark 1. **$400.00 – 500.00.**

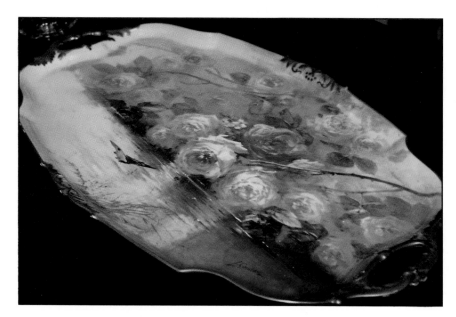

Plate 711. Tray, 33" x 19½" (extremely large size); vividly hand-painted pink and yellow roses reflected in bright blue water cover surface of piece; open handles and scalloped border painted gold; artist signed, "L. Coudert." L. S. & S. Mark 1. **$3,500.00 – 4,000.00**

Plate 712. Plate, 8" d; small pink and wine colored flowers form a random pattern around a reserve of white flowers framed with intricate gold enameled designs; brushed gold around border. L. S. & S. Mark 1. **$125.00 – 150.00.**

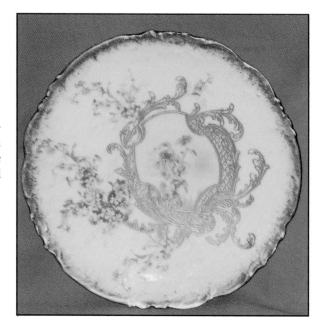

Plate 713. Relish dish, 12" l; small flowers enameled in blue, pink, and white scattered over surface; gold leaves and gold trim accent piece. Coiffe Mark 2 and L. S. & S. Mark 1. **$225.00 – 250.00.**

Animal, Game Bird, and Fish Themes

Plate 714. Plaque, 18" d; hand-painted hunting dog carrying a wild duck in his mouth. L. S. & S. Mark 1. **$500.00 – 600.00.**

Plate 715. Plaque, 18" d; matches preceding plate; this dog is carrying a rabbit. L. S. & S. Mark 1. **$500.00 – 600.00.**

Plate 716. Plaque, 13" d; two water fowl depicted in a marsh setting; gold trim. L. S. & S. Mark 1. **$350.00 – 375.00.**

Plate 717. Plate, 9½" d; colorful ring-neck pheasants in flight; gold trim; artist signed, "J. Morseys." Latrille Mark 1 and L. S. & S. Mark 1. **$275.00 – 300.00.**

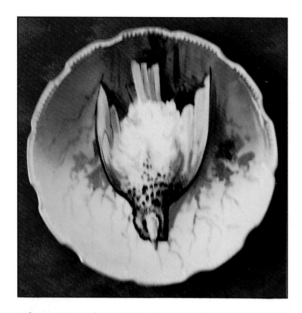

Plate 718. Plate, 9½" d; a dead game bird is painted against a dark brown shading to cream background; gold trim; artist signed, "Maxi." Latrille Mark 1 and L. S. & S. Mark 1. **$140.00 – 165.00.**

Plate 719. Plate, 9¾" d; turkey gobbler and hen painted on a cream and blue background; artist signed, "Melo." Latrille Mark 1 and L. S. & S. Mark 1. **$225.00 – 240.00.**

Plate 720. Plaque, 13" d; two game birds stand by water's bank; green plants and a pink iris are in the background; artist signed, "Max." L. S. & S. Mark 1. **$425.00 – 475.00.**

Plate 721. Plate 9" d; a fish floats on top of water; yellow flowers in the foreground; a wide etched gold border frames decoration; artist signed, "Tharard." L. S. & S. Mark 1. **$200.00 – 225.00.**

Plate 722. Plate, 9½" d; a fish is set against a dark shading to light green background; a white iris tinted with lavender is in the foreground; artist signed, "Bazanan." Coiffe Mark 3 and L. S. & S. Mark 1. **$175.00 – 200.00.**

Plate 723. Platter, 22½" l, 10" w, scalloped and beaded edge painted gold; a large fish on a green background is surrounded by water vegetation and shells; artist signed, "Melo." "Limoges, France" Mark 2 and L. S. & S. Mark 1. **$800.00 – 1,000.00.**

Plate 724. Fish service, plates, 9" d; a lake scene, painted in realistic blues and greens, features a large fish in the foreground of each piece; beaded border painted gold. Coiffe Mark 1 and L. S. & S. Mark 1. **$200.00 – 225.00 each.** (Serving pieces are in Plates 725 and 726.)

Plate 725. Gravy boat and underplate. $325.00 – 375.00.

Plate 726. Platter, 19" l. **$1,000.00 – 1,200.00.**

Miscellaneous Pieces and Decorations

Plate 727. Oyster plate, 8½" d, individual sections formed by lightly scalloped designs; wide gold border overlaid with blue enameled flowers; gold stenciled medallion in center. Coiffe Mark 2 and L. S. & S. Mark 1. **$250.00 – 275.00.**

Plate 728. Charger, 12" d, deeply fluted border; lilies of the valley decorate center and each section around border; gold trim. Laviolette Mark and L. S. & S. Mark 1. **$200.00 – 250.00.**

Plate 729. Asparagus platter, 9½" d, three sections; the bunch of asparagus in the center exhibits the intended use for the dish; gold enameled flowers and garlands around inner and outer borders and gold trim embellish the platter. Mavaleix Mark and L. S. & S. Mark 1. **$350.00 – 400.00.**

Plate 730. Pancake dish, burnished gold finish applied in a wide border around cover and underplate; pierced holes on cover are outlined in gold. Lanternier Mark 4 and L. S. & S. Mark 1. **$375.00 – 425.00.**

Tressemann & Vogt/Porcelain Gustave Vogt/Vogt & Dose (T. & V.)/Raynaud (R. & Co.)

The history of the Tressemann (sometimes spelled "Tressemanes") & Vogt Company can be traced to 1882, when the two became partners in the decorating and exporting business in Limoges. But the name Vogt had been connected with the Limoges porcelain industry for many years prior to the partnership with Tressemann. In the 1850s, John Vogt had founded a business in Limoges for exporting china to his New York based company which had been established in the 1840s. In the 1860s, John Vogt also opened decorating studios in Limoges and in New York. John Vogt's eldest son, Charles, took charge of the New York business, and the name of the company became Vogt & Dose, reflecting the association of John Vogt's nephew, Dose. In the early 1870s, John Vogt's son, Gustave, took over the Limoges operation. Subsequently, Tressemann became a partner, bringing an infusion of capital. Tressemann and Vogt began manufacturing their own china in 1891 (d'Albis and Romanet, p. 155). The Tressemann & Vogt partnership lasted sixteen years, until 1907. After that time, until about 1919, the company was known as "Porcelain Gustave Vogt." The company was sold to Martial Raynaud in 1919.

After Gustave Vogt's company was sold to Raynaud, his New York business continued in operation until 1931. That firm continued to sell imported china, and it also maintained the china decorating studio in New York (d'Albis and Romanet, pp. 155, 156). Gustave Vogt's son, Charles (called "Charly," to differentiate between him and his uncle), was sent as a young man from Limoges to New York to manage the decorating studio. He is noted to have traveled back to Limoges during the summers until 1929, where he chose designs for the studio (Vogt, 1995). Some examples of those designs are shown here as well as his shaving mug which was monogrammed and painted by a company artist. Charly Vogt also was a designer and artist at the studio, and some examples include his signature.

The pictures of the patterns, the shaving mug, and a portrait of John Vogt were furnished through the courtesy of Nathalie and Robert Vogt, the son of Charles (Charly) Vogt and great-grandson of John Vogt.

Although the New York based firm of Vogt and Dose decorated china made by the company in Limoges, no information has been found to indicate whether the New York studio marked its pieces with a specific decorating mark. We know that the New York studio was in operation long before and after the partnership of Tressemann & Vogt. We do not know, however, what, if any, marks were used, or if they simply used the same T. & V. Limoges marks. The Limoges factory may have double marked that part of the production which was sent to New York to be decorated. This latter supposition seems probable, because the few pieces found which have a "Vogt" signature have both a T. & V. white ware mark and a T. & V. decorating mark. D'Albis and

Romanet (p. 156) indicate that the Vogt and Dose company in New York closed about 1931 because the imported china from France and Germany was arriving already decorated, and "the situation of the decorators had become very precarious."

Numerous marks are associated with the T. & V. company, and although Tressemann was not a partner after 1907, marks with his initial appear to have been continued. Mark 1 seems to be perhaps the earliest mark. It is an exporting mark printed in blue and contains both partners' names. Mark 1a is similar, but it clearly shows the factory mark of Délinières & Co. (D. & Co.) and is on a D. & Co. pattern

Mark 2 is an early decorating mark. It is a "Bell" without "France," as part of the mark. Mark 3 is another decorating mark which is seldom seen. It is a rose or flower shape with "T. & V." and "FRANCE," and should date after 1891. Marks 1 – 3 were probably all used before the company manufactured any porcelain. The distinctive "Bell" mark changed design after 1907 when the company became "Porcelain Gustave Vogt" (see marks 14 – 16). The later "Bell" was continued by Vogt's successor, Raynaud, but Raynaud used his own initial, "R. & Co." over the "Bell" as a decorating mark. Some examples are found with the T. & V. white ware mark and Raynaud's Bell, but this only indicates that existing white ware stock was decorated by the later company. Such marks do not mean that Raynaud used the T. & V. white ware marks. Raynaud's white ware marks also incorporated his initial, "R." (see Raynaud marks in this chapter). Raynaud's version of the T. & V. Bell mark does not appear to have been used by the Raynaud company after the 1930s. When the Raynaud factory resumed production after World War II, ca. 1952, André Raynaud, Martial Raynaud's son, implemented different marks which did not incorporate any version of the T. & V. marks.

The white ware marks used by T. & V. are somewhat easier to date because none were used prior to 1891. Although mark 4a does not incorporate "France," it was still not used before 1891. Perhaps some other Limoges factory producing the china marked the pieces for T. & V., but there is no proof of this. Mark 4 was probably the first white ware mark used by the factory. A number of variations of the same mark are found (see marks 5 – 7). Mark 8 with "Déposé," is similar to the one shown by d'Albis and Romanet (p. 242) which they date after 1907 until 1919 when Raynaud took over the company. D'Albis and Romanet, however, also indicate that these same marks were continued by Raynaud. Examples, however, show that Raynaud also included his initials with the "Bell" mark or used his initials as a white ware mark as noted earlier. Thus, the Raynaud production after 1919 should not cause confusion for collectors because the marks clearly indicate the new owner.

Mark 9 is an overglaze decorating mark in purple with

"FRANCE." It is not seen often, and it may appear with the white ware mark of another factory. It should date after 1891. Decorating Mark 10 (red "Bell" with "LIMOGES") was found with white ware Mark 6, indicating a date of ca. 1900. Mark 11 (red "Bell" with "FRANCE") is the most commonly found T. & V. decorating Mark. It was probably used during the latter part of the 1891 – 1907 period.

Marks 12 – 15 are decorating marks which seem to have been used after 1907, after Tressemann ceased to be a partner. These marks are seldom found, however. Mark 16 is the most common decorating mark found for the 1907 – 1919 era. Sometimes Mark 16 is found with T. & V. white ware Marks 4 –7, rather than Mark 8. The explanation is that the white wares were not decorated until a later time, after the decorating marks had changed.

A large percentage of Limoges porcelain which is found on the American antique and collectible market carries the T. & V. marks. From the decoration, it is obvious that a lot of the production was also exported as blanks and decorated by American china painters. The T. & V. decorating mark can be found on china with the white ware marks of other Limoges' factories, indicating that the piece was decorated by T. & V., but not made by the company. The State china for President Benjamin Harrison was made and decorated by

Tressemann & Vogt in 1892. The back marks are 5a (white ware) and 10 (decorating mark in gold).

For collectors, the studio or factory decorated pieces are the most desirable. T. & V. plaques, which were hand-painted by American china painters as "paintings on porcelain," or punch bowls and tankards can be very valuable if the art work is exceptional and colorful, however. The factory and studio-decorated pieces are found more in the forms of table wares, such as pitchers, plates, biscuit jars, and accessories such as shaving mugs and dresser items as opposed to art objects or vases, urns, and jardinieres. Factory decoration included hand painting, the *mixtion* technique, and transfer applied designs. The table ware patterns are often very striking. They are usually bold in color with large designs, rather than small floral patterns in pastel colors. Extensive use of gold on the borders and white enamel highlights also enhanced many of the patterns.

The first set of pictures in this chapter is of table wares which are so finely decorated, many hand-painted and artist signed, that they are described as display china. Some of these pieces do not have a Tressemann & Vogt studio or factory decorating mark, but that can be inferred from the professional nature of the art work.

John Vogt

Charles Vogt's shaving mug. The mug is signed, "Laraque," and marked with T. & V. Mark 7. Charles was the son of Gustave Vogt and the grandson of John Vogt.

Table ware patterns designed by André Beyrand for Tressemann & Vogt. In the first picture, Beyrand's signature and fingerprints authenticate his original design. Notes, written in French on the designs and faintly visible in the pictures, were made by Charly Vogt. Beyrand was held in high esteem as an artist and designer. He worked for the Ahrenfeldt company and also designed for other Limoges factories. D'Albis and Romanet (p. 173) note that he was one of the best Limoges porcelain painters during the first half of the twentieth century.

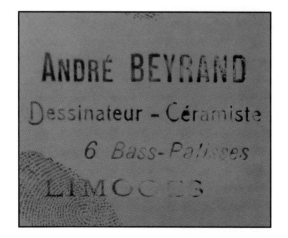

Mark 5a, underglaze white ware mark in green, initials with "FRANCE," ca. 1892 – 1907.

Mark 5b, underglaze white ware mark in green, like Mark 5a, except with "SOUVENIR." This particular mark is found on items decorated with famous people or commemorative events.

Mark 5c, underglaze white ware mark in green, like Marks 5 and 5a, but with a patent date and design name, which may vary.

Mark 5d, underglaze white ware Mark in green with "FRANCE" printed over the rectangle with the "T. & V." initials and "Pat'd April 2d 1889." Note that the patent date is earlier than when the company began manufacturing porcelain in 1891. But this and other examples with patent dates prior to 1891 indicate that Tressemann & Vogt patented their designs and/or shapes before the time of production.

Mark 6, underglaze white ware mark in green, initials with "FRANCE, DÉPOSÉ," ca. 1892 – 1907, probably about 1900.

Mark 7, underglaze white ware Mark in green, initials with "LIMOGES, FRANCE," ca. 1892 – 1907, probably latter part of period.

Mark 7a, underglaze white ware mark in green, like Mark 7 but printed with a date which varies; 1917 is shown in this example.

Mark 7b, underglaze white ware mark in green, like Mark 7, but printed with a patent date and design name, which vary. "Patd Feby 26 1901" and "Century" printed on example of mark.

Mark 8, underglaze white ware mark in green, initials with "LIMOGES, FRANCE, DÉPOSÉ, ca. 1907 – 1919.

Mark 9, overglaze decorating mark in purple, bell with "FRANCE," ca. 1892 – 1907, early part of period.

Mark 10, overglaze decorating mark in red or gold, bell with "LIMOGES," ca. 1892 – 1907, probably about 1900.

Mark 11, overglaze decorating Mark in red, brown, or gold, bell with "FRANCE," ca. 1892 – 1907, latter part of period.

Mark 12, overglaze decorating mark in purple with "FRENCH CHINA" over initials, and "LIMOGES," ca. 1907 – 1919, rarely seen.

Mark 13, overglaze decorating mark in red or purple, "CHINA" printed over initials and "FRANCE" below, ca. 1907 – 1919, rarely seen.

Mark 14, overglaze decorating mark in green with "French China" printed below Bell in a banner; design name in center which may vary, ca. 1907 – 1919, rarely seen.

Mark 15, overglaze decorating mark in purple, "HAND PAINTED" printed inside double circle around bell.

Mark 16, overglaze decorating mark in purple with "LIMOGES" printed above Bell, ca. 1907 – 1919.

Mark 16a, overglaze decorating mark in purple, like Mark 16, but with "DÉCORÉ PAR" printed over Bell, ca. 1907 – 1919.

Mark 16b, overglaze decorating mark in purple, like Mark 16, but accompanied with a banner printed with "Hand Painted," ca. 1907 – 1919.

Raynaud Marks

Mark 1, underglaze white ware mark in green, initials underscored with "LIMOGES, FRANCE," ca. 1920s – 1930s.

Mark 2, overglaze decorating mark in purple, "R & C LIMOGES" over T&V Bell with "FRANCE," ca. 1920s – 1930s.

Tressemann & Vogt Factory and Studio
Decorated Porcelain
Display China

Plate 731. Plate, 8½" d; a pair of cherubs, one reclining, decorate center; a heavy application of gold highlights the embossed floral and scroll designs. "Limoges, France" Mark 6 and T. & V. Mark 11. **$200.00 – 250.00**.

Plate 732. Chocolate pot, 10" h; cherubs, one standing, wearing a blue drape, and the other kneeling, wearing a pink gown; small gold stenciled *fleur-de-lis* around border of spout and lid; handle and finial painted gold. T. & V. Marks 4 and 10. **$700.00 – 800.00**.

Plate 733. Chocolate pot, 10" h; gold paste flowers and light green leaves cover body; the gold handle is accented with a pattern of green lines. T. & V. Mark 5a with no decorating mark, but art work is of factory or studio origin. **$550.00 – 650.00**.

Plate 734. Plate, 9" d; hand-painted roses on a white background are surrounded by an irregularly-shaped etched gold frame covering the remainder of the surface. T. & V. Mark 5a with no decorating mark, but art work is of factory or studio origin. **$325.00 – 375.00.**

Plate 735. Charger, 14¾" d; a spray of hand-painted roses on a dark brown shading to light cream background decorates right half of plate; gold trim; artist signed, "Damet." T. & V. Marks 8 and 16b. **$500.00 – 600.00.**

Plate 736. Chocolate pot, 10" h; pink floral spray with green leaves on an orange background covers body; a wide band of gold around the middle breaks the design. T. & V. Mark 2 in gold, rare mark. **$700.00 – 800.00.**

Plate 737. Cider pitcher, 8" d; large red and pink roses on a light green background; gold trim. T. & V. Marks 7 and 16. **$425.00 – 475.00.**

Plate 738. Chocolate set: chocolate pot, cups and saucers (6), and tray; fancy handles curl over the tops of the cups; reserves of hand-painted roses framed in gold on front of pieces; small floral designs accent borders; gold embellishments on pieces, as well as gilded handles and trim, enhance the decoration; artist signed, "Magne" on each piece; T. & V. Marks 7 and 11 with "All Over Hand Painted" printed within a banner in red. **$2,500.00 – 3,000.00 set.**

Plate 739. Cider pitcher, 6½" h; hand-painted lavender and pink flowers on an off-white background; gold trim. T. & V. Marks 7 and 15. **$450.00 – 550.00.**

Plate 740. Cider pitcher, 7" h; similar pink and lavender floral design as on pitcher above; molded scrolled designs around neck and base and handle painted gold. T. & V. Marks 5a and 15. **$550.00 – 650.00.**

Plate 741. Demitasse pot, 7½" h; sprays of pink roses on a white background are accented by a deep green glaze extending in a scrolled design from neck to handle and around base of spout; gold enameled designs outline the green finish; finial and handle painted gold. T. & V. Mark 5c with a patent date of "Dec. 22d 1896" and a design name of "Venice." There is no decorating mark, but the art work is factory or studio. **$550.00 – 650.00.**

Plate 742. Tankard, 15½" h; light and dark pink roses in a large spray design cover front of piece; a dark green finish extends from neck to top handle and from bottom of handle to base with a wide band of white background in the middle; scalloped work around base and handle painted gold; artist signed, "Fiseier." T. & V. Marks 7 and 16b. **$1,200.00 – 1,400.00.**

Plate 743. Tankard, 15" h; large red and pink roses on a light to dark green background; handle with applied flower and curling stem is painted gold. T. & V. Marks 7 and 16. **$1,400.00 – 1,600.00.**

Plate 744. Tankard, 15½" h; same form as preceding piece; small white flowers and large green leaves decorate top and middle of piece; embossed leaves around base outlined in gold; floral design on handle and rim base painted gold. T. & V. Marks 7 and 16. **$1,200.00 – 1,400.00.**

Plate 745. Tankard, 15½" h; purple and yellow pansies scattered over a white background; rim of neck, handle, and scalloped work around base painted gold. T. & V. Marks 7 and 16. **$1,300.00 – 1,500.00.**

Plate 746. Pitcher, 6½" h; hand-painted figural semi-nudes on a deep pink background are portrayed in an Art Deco style on both sides of pitcher; woman draped in blue gazing at a compact. T. & V. Mark 11 with "FRANCE," underglaze in green. **$400.00 – 450.00.**

Plate 747. Reverse of pitcher in Plate 746: seated figure, draped in yellow around waist, putting on an earring.

Plate 748. Tobacco jar; wine and pink roses, accented with small white flowers decorate lid and body; dark olive green finish on lower part of jar and lid; applied pipe on lid painted gold; artist signed, "Leroy." T. & V. Marks 7 and 16. **$400.00 – 500.00**

Table Wares Decorated with Game and Fish Themes

Plate 749. Game service: platter, 18¼" l x 12¼" w, and twelve serving plates, 9¼" d; game birds in natural settings decorate all pieces; a light blue glaze on borders is accented with an irregular, gold painted inner border that frames the center patterns. This plate and two others, as well as the platter, are shown in this and the following two photographs. Coiffe Mark 2 and T. & V. Mark 11. **$3,500.00 – 3,800.00 set.**

Plate 750. Two plates from game service.

Plate 751. Platter from game service.

Plate 752. Game service: platter, 18" l, with twelve serving plates; different game birds, framed with gold scrolled designs, decorate the top of each plate; brushed gold trim; the platter is decorated with a pair of wild ducks in the center; all pieces are artist signed, "Genamaud." Two plates from set. T. & V. Marks 8 and 16. **$3,800.00 – 4,000.00 set.**

Plate 753. Two plates from game service in Plate 752.

Plate 754. Platter from game service in Plate 752.

Plate 755. Fish plates, 9" d; a river scene with a large fish in the foreground covers the surface of the plates; realistic coloring of water and sky. T. & V. Mark 10 in gold, no white ware mark. **$225.00 – 250.00 each**.

Plate 756. Oyster plate, 10" d; a deep pompadour rose glaze outlines sections of the plate; gold stippling accents space between sections; embossed scrolled designs highlighted in gold. T. & V. Marks 8 and 16. **$300.00 – 325.00.**

Table Ware Patterns

Plate 757. Shaving mug, 4" h; a white rose with small blue flowers on a white background; gold trim. T. & V. Mark 7 with a decorating mark for Marshall Field (American department store). **$200.00 – 250.00**.

Plate 758. Pitcher, 6" h; floral pattern tinted with a deep pink and accented with yellow enamel; gold stenciled designs around handle; gold trim. T. & V. Marks 4a with "Marguerite Pat'd. July 1st 86" overglaze mark in red; note "Marguerite" is a shape design, not a pattern name. **$75.00 – 100.00.**

Plate 759. Tea set: tea pot, 7" h, covered sugar, and creamer; delicate blue floral sprays over surface of pieces; gold trim. T. & V. Marks 5d and 13. **$400.00 – 450.00 set.**

Plate 760. Daisy pattern; this is a very popular transfer design consisting of large white daisies and green leaves. Variations of the Daisy pattern include different colors highlighting the flowers, such as orange, apple green, and turquoise as shown in this and the following eight examples; there are other different floral patterns which were decorated in a similar fashion. The flowers are usually highlighted with white enamel. These patterns are often on the distinctive white wares which have embossed designs around the scalloped borders and are heavily gilded. This bowl, 8½" d, has no any coloring around the pattern. T. & V. Mark 16. **$75.00 – 100.00.**

Plate 761. Tea pot, 9½" from spout to handle; Daisy pattern. **$275.00 – 325.00**.

Plate 762. Pudding set: bowl, 7½" d, 3" h, and underplate, 12½" d; Daisy pattern. T. & V. Mark 10 on bowl and Mark 16 on underplate. **$400.00 – 450.00 set.**

Plate 763. Plate, 8¼" d; Daisy pattern on apple green background. T. & V. Mark 6 and "HAND PAINTED." **$70.00 – 85.00.**

Plate 764. Nappy, 6" d; Daisy pattern on apple green background. T. & V. Marks 8 and 16. **$150.00 – 175.00.**

Plate 765. Chamberstick; Daisy pattern on a turquoise background. T. & V. Marks 6 and 16. **$225.00 – 275.00.**

Plate 766. Plate, 7" d; Daisy pattern on an orange background. T. & V. Marks 8 and 16. **$50.00 – 65.00.**

Plate 767. Sugar bowls: covered and footed bowl, 3½" h; bowl with pedestal base, 5½" h; open bowl, 5½" l; Daisy pattern decorates all three bowls on an orange background. T. & V. Mark 16 on each. Covered bowls, **$175.00 – 195.00 each;** open bowl, **$125.00 – 140.00.**

Plate 768. Compote, 11½" h, 7½" d; Daisy pattern on an orange background decorates the exterior and interior of piece; gold trim on borders and scalloped work on base. T. & V. Mark 16 with "NEW PAL 1887" printed under mark. It is not clear, except for the date, what this particular mark indicates. **$500.00 – 600.00.**

Plate 769. Plate, 8¼" d; Daffodil pattern on an apple green background; gold trim. T. & V. Marks 6 and 11. **$70.00 – 85.00.**

Plate 770. Bowl, 8½" d; White Rose pattern on an apple green background. T. & V. Mark 2. **$100.00 – 125.00.**

Plate 771. Bowl, 8¼" d, footed; Mistletoe pattern; brushed gold trim. T. & V. Mark 16. **$225.00 – 275.00.**

Plate 772. Plate, 8½" d; Dogwood pattern on a dark green background with a light pink tint to flowers. T. & V. Marks 6 and 11. **$70.00 – 85.00.**

Plate 773. Punch bowl, 4½" h x 9" d; Dogwood pattern of pink and white blossoms on a dark green background decorates exterior and interior of bowl. T. & V. Marks 6 and 10. **$600.00 – 700.00.**

Plate 774. Cracker jar, 6" h x 8" w, and underplate, 8¼" d; large pink roses with green leaves form a random pattern; gold trim. T. & V. Marks 7 and 11. **$425.00 – 475.00 set.**

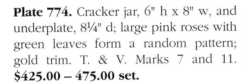

Plate 775. Charger, 12" d; Red Clover pattern on an orange background; scalloped border highlighted with gold; T. & V. Marks 8 and 11. **$225.00 – 275.00.**

Plate 776. Candle holders, 6" h; wine, pink, and yellow roses; brushed gold trim. T. & V. Marks 8 and 16. **$220.00 – 245.00 pair.**

Plate 777. Cup and saucer, 3½" h; large wine, pink, and yellow roses almost cover surface of cup; large pink roses on left side of saucer; brushed gold trim. T. & V. Marks 7 and 11. **$80.00 – 100.00 set.**

Plate 778. Powder box, 5½" d; Poppy pattern in multi-colors. T. & V. Marks 5a and 11. **$250.00 – 300.00.**

Plate 779. Tile, 8" d; Poppy pattern in center framed with a gold inner border; embossed border designs undecorated. T. & V. Marks 5b and 11. **$120.00 – 140.00.**

Plate 780. Bowl, 7" d; Art Nouveau style floral pattern composed of pink, yellow, and white flowers with green stems and leaves; apple green finish around border; gold highlights. Coiffe Mark 2 and T. & V. Mark 11. **$60.00 – 75.00.**

Plate 781. Holly pattern; the following pictures are of eleven pieces decorated with holly leaves and red berries on a dark green background with handles, finials, and borders painted gold. The last three pieces are of different renditions of the pattern with either another color background or the design placed on a white background. Unless otherwise noted, all pieces are marked with T. & V. Marks 2 and 5a. Cup and saucer, with pattern also on the interior of the cup. **$100.00 – 125.00.**

Plate 782. Bouillon cup and saucer. **$150.00 – 175.00 set.**

Plate 783. Creamers, in two shapes. **$125.00 – 150.00 each.**

Plate 784. Bowl, 8" d. **$120.00 – 140.00.**

Plate 785. Chocolate pot, 10½" h. **$500.00 – 600.00.**

Plate 786. Punch bowl, 4½" h x 9" d; T. & V. Marks 8 and 16b. **$600.00 – 700.00**

Plate 787. Pair of chambersticks, saucers with brass holders and handles. **$200.00 – 225.00 each.**

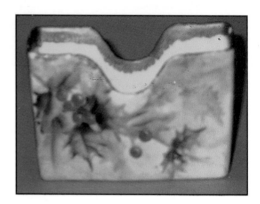

Plate 789. Card holder, 1½" h x 4" d; no background finish; brushed gold trim. T. & V. Mark 8 with no white ware mark. **$100.00 – 125.00.**

Plate 788. Powder bowl or jar, 6" d (large size), T. & V. Marks 7 and 16. **$375.00 – 425.00.**

Plate 790. Chamberstick, 6" d; holly pattern on a white background; gold trim. T. & V. Mark 5b with no decorating mark. **$150.00 – 175.00.**

Plate 791. Celery dish, 13" l, light blue-green background around pattern on outer border. **$125.00 – 150.00.**

Plate 792. Cups and saucers, clusters of blue flowers compose a border pattern with a lightly smudged coloring; gold stenciled designs around interior border. T. & V. Marks 5a and 11. **$75.00 – 95.00.**

Plate 793. Pieces matching preceding pattern: dinner plate, **$65.00 – 80.00;** butter pat, **$25.00 – 30.00;** fruit bowl, **$25.00 – 30.00.**

Plate 794. Platters from set: 12",
$225.00 – 250.00; 14", $250.00 –
275.00; 19", $400.00 – 450.00.

Plate 795. Cake plate, Cornflower pattern forms
an inner border around well of plate; gold outlining on handles. T. & V. Mark 12, no white ware
mark. **$125.00 – 150.00.**

Plate 796. Sugar bowl, 5¼" h x 7¾" d; another
version of a Cornflower pattern in a spray
arrangement; gold trim. T. & V. Marks 4a and 12
with importing mark of "W. W. Beveridge, Washington, D. C." **$120.00 – 145.00.**

Plate 797. Butter tub, 4½" d, and drainer; the blue Cornflower pattern decorates interior of tub with a reverse color of white flowers on a blue background on the drainer and exterior; gold trim. T. & V. Mark 4a. **$175.00 – 200.00.**

Plate 798. Bowl, 10" d; garlands of small pink roses form a border and center pattern. Coiffe Mark 2 and T. & V. Mark 2. **$60.00 – 75.00.**

Plate 799. Pudding set: serving bowl, 9½" d; baking liner, 7" d; underplate, 11" d; pink tinted inner border with small pink roses forming a garland around center and scattered across underplate; scrolled edges of border undecorated except for small touches of gold. T. & V. Marks 5a and 11. **$425.00 – 475.00 set.**

Plate 800. Punch bowl and punch cups (8 in set), 6¼" h x 14" d, on a 3" h separate base; similar floral pattern and design as pudding set, but with an apple green finish on outer borders. T. & V. Marks 8 and 16. **$2,000.00 – 2,400.00 set.**

Plate 801. Mug, 5½" h; reserves of pink roses framed with gold scroll designs are on front and back of mug; gold trim. T. & V. Marks 7 and 16. **$150.00 – 175.00.**

Plate 802. Covered bon bon dish, 5" square; hand-painted pink roses decorate four sections of lid which are separated by a molded ribbon design with a bow in relief in the center; smaller flowers are around edge of lid, brushed gold trim. T. & V. Mark 9 with exporting mark of "J. Mc. D. & S." printed in purple over Mark (see this mark under Other Limoges Companies Without Examples). **$150.00 – 175.00.**

Plate 803. Butter pat, 3" d; gold stenciled border pattern of small *fleur-de-lis*. T. & V. Marks 7 and 16. **$25.00 – 30.00.**

Plate 804. Luncheon place setting decorated with a gold stenciled medallion in the center with a gold line border around the wells of the pieces; scalloped outer borders painted gold. T. & V. Mark 16. Luncheon plate, **$45.00 – 60.00;** bread & butter plate, **$35.00 – 45.00;** cup and saucer, **$70.00 – 80.00.**

Plate 805. Pudding set: bowl, 3½" h, 10" d, and underplate, 12½" d; clusters of small white flowers with light green leaves form a random pattern over surface; gold trim. T. & V. Marks 5a and 11. **$400.00 – 450.00 set.**

Plate 807. Leaf dish, 8" d; a wide cobalt blue finish highlights the white center; gold stenciled designs decorate center and are also overlaid on the cobalt border; T. & V. Marks 4a and an illegible imported mark. **$150.00 – 200.00.**

Plate 806. Plate, 9" d, octagonal shape; a silver metal border encases plate around outer and inner borders with an apple green glaze between the silver bands forming an Art Deco design. T. & V. Mark 8 with "DÉPOSÉ" printed above initials instead of below "FRANCE," and "Higgins & Seiter, New York" importing mark. There is no information regarding who applied the silver. This type of metal work on porcelain was popular during the early 1900s, on both American and European porcelain. **$175.00 – 225.00.**

Plate 808. Plate, 5" d; an etched gold inner border encircles the undecorated center and highlights the bright green finish which surrounds it; outer border painted gold. "Limoges, France" Mark 6 and T. & V. Mark 14. **$40.00 – 45.00.**

Plate 809. Souvenir china made for and marked in purple, "The National Remembrance Shop, Washington, D. C.," with Raynaud Mark 1 or T. & V. Mark 7 or 9. The china is decorated with the seal of the United States; gold stenciled designs around the borders; gold trim. These pieces show the transition of the Tressemann & Vogt marks to its successor, Raynaud. Open sugar and creamer, **$375.00 – 425.00 set**.

Plate 810. Tea set: tea pot, 5" h; 7" w; open sugar bowl, 5" h; creamer, 4½" h. **$500.00 – 600.00 set.**

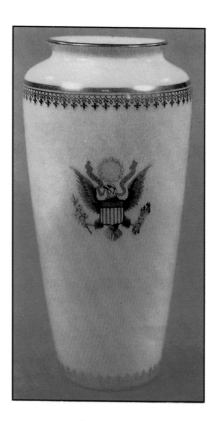

Plate 811. Vase, 7½" h. $250.00 – 275.00.

T. & V. Non-Factory Decorated White Wares

Paintings on Porcelain

Plate 813. Painting on porcelain, 16" l x 14" w; reclining nude figure in an Art Nouveau style. T. & V. Mark 7. $3,500.00 – 4,000.00.

Plate 812. Painting on porcelain, 14" l x 7" w; figural portraits of two partially nude women surrounded by a wispy drape and clouds, artist signed (illegible). T. & V. Mark 7. $3,000.00 – 3,500.00.

Plate 814. Painting on porcelain, 8" l x 6" w; figural scene of woman and cherub on a pier. T. & V. Mark 5a. **$2,000.00 – 2,400.00.**

Plate 815. Painting on porcelain, 9" x 12"; hand-painted red, pink, and white roses. T. & V. Mark 7. **$1,400.00 – 1,600.00.**

Plate 816. Painting on porcelain, 13" x 15½"; hand-painted white daffodils. T. & V. Mark 7. **$1,800.00 – 2,000.00.**

Table Wares with Portrait and Figural Themes

Plate 817. Plate, 9" d; profile of a woman with long golden hair, dressed in an orange gown, hand painted in an Art Nouveau style. T. & V. Mark 8. **$600.00 – 800.00.**

Plate 818. Plate, 9" d; profile of a woman with an elaborate hair style, dressed in a white gown; background matches preceding portrait with orange flowers added to the foreground. T. & V. Mark 8. **$600.00 – 800.00.**

Plate 819. Plate, 9" d, reticulated border; a little girl in a light yellow dress, holding a long blue ribbon over her head, is painted in the center; gold trim. T. & V. Mark 5a. **$175.00 – 200.00.**

Plate 820. Tray, 16½" l; portrait of a reclining nude holding a little girl with long brown hair; artist signed, "Grace E. R. Chapman." T. & V. Mark 7. **$325.00 – 375.00.**

Plate 821. Chocolate pot, 11" h; portrait of a cherub perched on a garden wall; a deep wine finish on top of pot is overlaid with gold designs; spout, finial, and base painted gold. T. & V. Mark 5a. **$700.00 – 800.00.**

Plate 822. Tray, 8" x 11"; transfer portraits of Martha and George Washington on either side of their home. "Washington's Home Mt. Vernon, Va." is printed at the bottom of the tray. This piece was professionally decorated as a souvenir item, but there is no mark to identify the decorating firm. T. & V. Mark 7. **$225.00 – 275.00.**

Plate 823. Mug, 5" h; hand-painted figure of an innkeeper. T. & V. Mark 7. **$275.00 – 325.00.**

Plate 824. Tankard, 14½" h; figural portrait of a monk drinking wine, painted in brown tones with embossed designs on body outlined in gold. Combined with gold scroll designs. T. & V. Mark 7. **$800.00 – 1,000.00.**

Table Wares with Floral and Fruit Themes

Plate 825. Tea strainer, pink roses with green leaves; gold trim; artist initialed, "M. O. M." T. & V. Mark 7. **$125.00 – 150.00.**

Plate 826. Biscuit jar, 4½" h; a spray of large flowers painted a light pink with green leaves on a cream background decorates jar; brushed gold trim. T. & V. Mark 5d with a patent date of "April 24, 1889." **$250.00 – 300.00.**

Plate 828. Butter tub with drainer; hand-painted yellow flowers; gold trim. T. & V. Mark 7. **$120.00 – 140.00.**

Plate 827. Biscuit jar, 7" h; gold enameled scroll designs, accented with light blue, on a light cream background. T. & V. Mark 5d with a patent date of "April 2d 1889." **$275.00 – 325.00.**

Plate 829. Candle holders, 5½" h; yellow daisies painted on base; gold trim. T. & V. Mark 7. **$120.00 – 140.00 pair.**

Plate 830. Divided seafood dish; two fish are painted on the larger section, and lemons are painted on the smaller section, indicating where to place each. Scrolled edges and handle are heavily gilded; artist signed, "E. Keil." T. & V. Mark 8. **$300.00 – 350.00.**

Plate 831. Cake plate, 10½" d; large roses painted in pale yellows and pinks; gold trim. T. & V. Mark 5, but with "LIMOGES" printed above rectangle. **$120.00 – 145.00.**

Plate 832. Cup and saucer; the saucer is a large size, 7" d; yellow pansies accented with gold scroll designs; fancy handle, designed with openwork, painted gold. T. & V. Mark 5a. **$125.00 – 150.00.**

Plate 834. Whiskey jug, 7" h; hand-painted birds; dark brown finish on bottom half; gold trim. T. & V. Mark 7. **$350.00 – 400.00.**

Plate 833. Plate, 9" d; reticulated border; large white flowers with yellow centers cover two-thirds of plate; gold trim. T. & V. Mark 4. **$120.00 – 140.00.**

Plate 835. Whiskey jug, 6" h; hand-painted red cherries. T. & V. Mark 7. **$300.00 – 350.00** (without lid).

Plate 836. Whiskey jug, 7" h; multi-colored roses on a pastel background; gold trim. T. & V. Mark 7. **$500.00 – 600.00.**

Plate 837. Cider pitcher, 6" h; hand-painted red cherries with green leaves on a dark to light brown background; handle painted gold; artist signed, "J. Edith MacNaughton." T. & V. Mark 7. **$350.00 – 400.00.**

Plate 838. Tankard, 15½" h, an applied leaf and curling vine decorate handle in an Art Nouveau style; purple grapes on a light green to blue background; gold trim; artist signed on base, "F. Paxton 1905." T. & V. Mark 7. **$900.00 – 1,100.00.**

Plate 839. Tankard, 14" h, and four mugs, 4" h; hand-painted blackberries and flowers; a deep rose finish on base and handle of pieces; gold trim; artist signed, "S. Posey." T. & V. Mark 4b. Tankard, **$1,000.00 – 1,200.00;** mugs, **$125.00 – 150.00 each.**

Plate 840. Condensed milk container and underplate; hand-painted raspberries; gold trim. T. & V. Mark 7. **$450.00 – 500.00 set.**

Plate 841. Tankard, 14½" h; blackberries painted on a pastel background; gold trim on handle and base. T. & V. Mark 7. **$550.00 – 650.00.**

Plate 843. Bowl, 9" d, three applied feet; blackberries, flowers, and green leaves are painted on the interior and exterior; gold trim. T. & V. Mark 7. **$350.00 – 400.00.**

Plate 842. Divided dish, 12" d; blackberries and flowers on a light green background; scrolled handle painted gold. T. & V. Mark 7. **$375.00 – 425.00.**

Plate 844. Tankard, 14½" h; blackberries painted on a light green background changing to a grape color on bottom half and on handle. T. & V. Mark 7. **$600.00 – 800.00.**

Plate 845. Charger, 17" d; pink and yellow roses painted on a dark pink background shading to white; gold trim. T. & V. Mark 7. **$600.00 – 700.00.**

Plate 846. Tray, 18½" d, irregular border trimmed in gold; red and yellow roses with green leaves on a gray to green background. T. & V. Mark 7. **$800.00 – 900.00.**

Plate 847. Charger, 13" d, scalloped edge; partially ripe apples decorate left side of piece. T. & V. Mark 7. **$425.00 – 475.00.**

Plate 848. Tray, 11½" d; large red apples with green leaves. T. & V. Mark 7. **$375.00 – 425.00.**

Plate 849. Punch bowl, 6½" h, 16" d; hand-painted purple, pink, and green grapes; border and feet painted gold. T. & V. Mark 7. **$1,600.00 – 1,800.00 set**.

Plate 850. Punch bowl, 16" d, with footed base; large red roses and light green leaves on a light green background; foot of bowl unpainted; feet of base painted gold. T. & V. Mark 5a on both pieces. **$2,500.00 – 2,700.00.**

Plate 851. Punch bowl, 13" d, on separate base; vividly painted yellow, pink, and red roses on a pastel background; bottom foot of bowl and base have a dark green finish. T. & V. Mark 8. **$2,800.00 – 3,000.00.**

Jardinieres and Vases

Plate 852. Ferner, 3½" h x 7" w, footed; stylized floral designs on a gold background are painted in an Art Deco style around top border; knob feet painted gold. T. & V. Mark 7. **$150.00 – 200.00.**

Plate 853. Jardiniere, 11½" d; sailboats decorate middle of piece between gold bands; a black finish painted under neck and around base. T. & V. Mark 7. **$325.00 – 375.00.**

Plate 854. Vase, 8" h x 13½" d, rare shape in a very large size; large pink roses painted in an Art Nouveau style; gold finish on neck; artist signed, "Vera Gray." T. & V. Mark 7. **$1,600.00 – 1,800.00.**

Plate 855. Jardiniere, 11½" h x 11" w, footed; handles fitted with rings; light pink roses painted on a large reserve on the front; a light blue finish, highlighted with gold, surrounds reserve. T. & V. Mark 5a. **$1,500.00 – 2,000.00.**

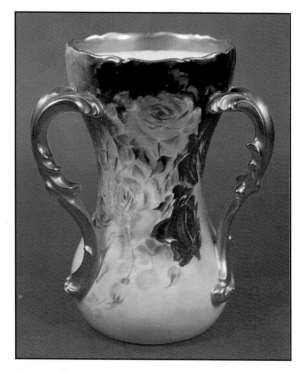

Plate 856. Loving cup vase, 7" h, three scrolled handles painted gold; pink and red roses; artist initialed on base, "M. E. J." T. & V. Mark 8. **$400.00 – 450.00.**

Plate 857. Vase, 6½" h; pink flowers painted on a light green background; gold trim. T. & V. Mark 7. **$225.00 – 275.00.**

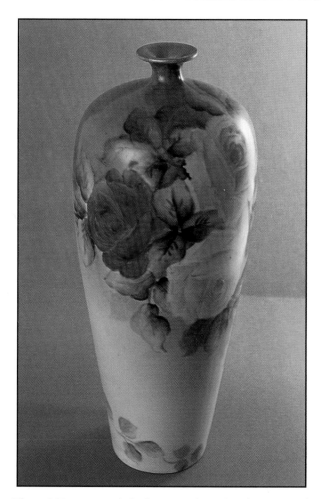

Plate 859. Vase, 14" h; white, dark pink, and yellow roses on a pastel background; inscribed, "To Mother From Eva July 30 1905." T. & V. Mark 7. **$900.00 – 1,100.00.**

Plate 858. Vase, 14" h; large pink and red roses with green leaves on a pale to dark green background. T. & V. Mark 7. **$1,200.00 – 1,400.00.**

Plate 860. Vase, 16" h; light and dark pink roses cover surface; gold border around neck; artist signed, "L. Haste." T. & V. Mark 7. **$1,400.00 – 1,600.00.**

Plate 861. Vase, 18" h; pink and white iris on a light gray background with a darker finish on the neck. T. & V. Mark 7. **$1,600.00 – 1,800.00.**

Plate 862. Vase, 8½" h, on pedestal base, rare figural mold with gilded handles made in the shape of Trojan heads; pink and white flowers are highlighted by white enameled designs; gold trim. T. & V. Mark 5a. **$1,000.00 – 1,200.00.**

Accessory Items

Plate 864. Tobacco jar, 6" h, with applied pipe on lid; large orange poppies painted on a rust-orange background; pipe painted gold. T. & V. Mark 7. **$325.00 – 375.00.**

Plate 863. Humidor, 8" h, with a match-stick holder on top of lid; white flowers painted on a brown background. T. & V. Mark 7. **$300.00 – 350.00.**

Plate 865. Humidor, 5½" h; vivid red-orange flowers on a matte cream background; sponged gold trim. T. & V. Mark 7. **$400.00 – 500.00.**

Plate 866. Mustache mug; small blue flowers; gold trim; artist signed and dated, "Kastin Dec. 25, 1919." T. & V. Mark 7. **$225.00 – 275.00.**

Plate 868. Powder box, 4½" d; cherubs painted on a pale blue ground. T. & V. Mark 5a. **$275.00 – 325.00.**

Plate 867. Shaving mug, 3½" h; "John McCaffrey" painted in gold on front; gold trim. T. & V. Mark 7. **$150.00 – 175.00.**

Plate 869. Hand mirror, 9" l, 5" d; lavender and white flowers painted on back of mirror. T. & V. Mark 5a. **$250.00 – 300.00.**

Plate 870. Picture frame, 9" h x 6½" w, deeply scalloped border with embossed designs outlined in gold; small violet flowers painted around opening. T. & V. Mark 5a. **$375.00 – 425.00.**

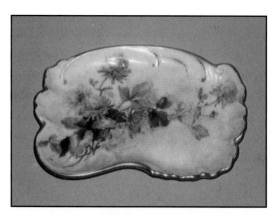

Plate 871. Pin tray, 5" l; pink and white flowers; gold trim. T. & V. Mark 7. **$50.00 – 60.00.**

Plate 872. Paperweight, 5½" l x 3" w, with molded quill in the center; small white flowers accented with gold are painted on either side of quill. T. & V. Mark 5a. **$150.00 – 175.00.**

Plate 873. Powder box, 5½" d; a garland of pink roses and green leaves encircles a reserve which is monogrammed "EMH" in gold; pastel blue finish. T. & V. Mark 7. **$275.00 – 325.00.**

Other Limoges Companies

Barny & Rigoni

A porcelain factory was established by Barny and Rigoni about 1894. The company used a Mark of "LIMOGES, FRANCE" printed within a flag. In 1902, J. Redon, son of Martial Redon, joined the firm. At that time the marks of the factory changed to include the Redon name, reflecting the father's initial "M.," rather than his son's (see Mark 2). Redon left the company in 1904 and was replaced by Langle (see Marks 3 and 4). That partnership also was short lived. New owners changed the name of the business to La Porcelaine Limousine (see that company under Martial Redon). La Porcelaine Limousine incorporated the old Redon decorating mark with their own white ware mark instead of continuing any of the Barny and Rigoni marks. Very few examples are found with any of the marks associated with the Barny and Rigoni company. The pieces shown here are highly decorated. Barny & Rigoni also sold undecorated porcelain (see one example in the chapter on undecorated white wares). The figural charger shown in Plate 874 could also be non-factory decorated, although the art work is professional.

Barny & Rigoni Marks and Examples

Mark 1, "Limoges, France" printed in flag design, ca. 1894 – 1902.

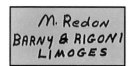

Mark 2, ca. 1902 – 1904.

Mark 3, underglaze white ware mark in green, ca. 1904 – 1906.

Mark 4, overglaze decorating mark, ca. 1904 – 1906.

Plate 874. Charger, 12" d; portrait of a semi-nude woman with a cherub on her shoulder, seated on a river bank with trees in the background. Barny & Rigoni Mark 1. **$1,200.00 – 1,400.00.**

Plate 875. Plate, 9½"; wild ducks in flight are painted in brilliant colors; orange and white flowers in the foreground; the wide border has a black finish overlaid with a gold diaper floral pattern; pink roses are scattered around border; artist signed, "Luc." Barny & Rigoni Mark 1. **$275.00 – 325.00.**

Plate 876. Plate, 9½" d; this plate matches the preceding in border decoration; game birds in center; artist signed, "Luc." Barny & Rigoni Mark 1. **$275.00 – 325.00.**

Jean Boyer (J. B.)

The Jean Boyer factory was in production in Limoges from about 1919 until the mid 1930s. Marks include a white ware mark and two versions of a decorating mark. A variation of Mark 2 is found without the banner and printed in gold. Table wares and decorative china were made by the company. Relatively few examples are found in the United States.

Jean Boyer Marks and Examples

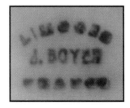

Mark 1, underglaze white ware mark in green, ca. 1919 – mid 1930s.

Mark 2, overglaze decorating mark in blue, ca. 1919 – mid 1930s.

Plate 877. Coffee pot, 11" h; multi-colored geometric pattern, in an Art Deco style, forms top border of pot and base of lid; gold spout and handle. Jean Boyer Marks 1 and 2. **$325.00 – 375.00.**

Plate 878. Game bird plate, 9½" d; colorful bird painted on a sepia background in center; scalloped border trimmed in gold; artist signed, "Max." Jean Boyer Mark 1 and variation of Mark 2 (without banner and in gold). **$225.00 – 250.00.**

Plate 879. Game bird plate, 9½" d; cockatoo on a sepia background, matching preceding plate and marked the same. **$225.00 – 250.00.**

Demartial & Tallandier (D. T.)/Gustave Demartial (G. D. & Co.)

Art objects were the special focus of this company which was in operation from 1868 until 1883. Figures, vases, and ornamental table wares were superbly decorated and marked with the owners' initials in red. Although the company made porcelain, no white ware mark is noted for the firm. D'Albis and Romanet (p. 168) note that Demartial & Tallandier actually characterized themselves as "décorateurs." Evidently, they considered themselves artists first over manufacturers.

Gustave Demartial was the only owner of the company after 1883. A white ware Mark of "G. D. & Co." over "Limoges" is noted by d'Albis and Romanet (p. 256) as being used until 1893. There is some confusion over this particular mark as Lesur and Tardy (p. 113) show the same mark for G. Demartine & Cie. The Demartine mark should be "G. D. & Cie.," I believe.

Demartial & Tallandier/Gustave Demartial Marks and Examples

Gustave Demartial mark, underglaze white ware mark, "G. D. & Co." over "LIMOGES," ca. 1883 – 1893.

Demartial & Tallandier mark, overglaze decorating mark in red, initials, "D & T" over "L," ca. 1868 – 1884.

Plate 880. Pair of figures, 13" h on pedestal bases decorated with white flowers in relief.; finely sculptured figures of two women dressed in gowns enameled in a high glaze olive green, accented with yellow flowers and a bright green trim. Demartial & Tallandier mark in red. **$5,000.00 – 6,000.00 pair.**

Plate 881. Vase, 9" h, squared handles taper from neck to top of body; gold paste flowers, leaves, and a bird applied on a cream background. The mark on this vase is "G. D. & Co." over "L" with "Déposé." This varies slightly from the mark shown for Gustave Demartial, but this piece will be attributed to that company until information may prove otherwise. **$450.00 – 550.00.**

G. Demartine & Cie. (G. D. & Cie.)

The Demartine factory was in business during the late 1800s to early 1900s. The company was also known as "Avenir China." The decorating mark incorporates that name. The postcard below from the early 1900s shows an advertisement for the company with its trademark. Table wares and decorative items are found with the Demartine marks. The white ware mark reflects the initials of the owner. The decorating mark is sometimes found on the white wares made by other Limoges factories.

Postcard advertising Avenir China with the company's trademark and a street scene in Limoges.

Demartine Marks and Examples

Mark 1, underglaze white ware mark in green, initials with "Limoges, France," ca. after 1891 to early 1900s.

Mark 2, overglaze decorating mark in blue-green with "Avenir" printed inside a circle, ca. after 1891 to early 1900s.

Plate 882. Berry bowl, 5¼" d; red-orange flowers with green leaves; gold trim. Demartine Mark 1 and J. Mc. D. & S. exporting mark. **$15.00 – 18.00.**

Plate 883. Clam plate, 8½" d; a small pink rose decorates each section with a small blue flower separating sections; gold trim. Coiffe Mark 3 and Demartine Mark 2. **$175.00 – 195.00.**

Plate 884. Plate, 6" d; hand-painted walnuts and green leaves; gold border outlined by a thin black band; artist signed, "Chamel." Coiffe Mark 3 and Demartine Mark 2. **$125.00 – 145.00.**

Plate 885. Plate, 6" d; hand-painted green apples with a similar ground and border as the preceding piece and marked the same, but with a different artist's signature, "Planehay." (The last letters are not clear, so the name may be spelled differently.) **$125.00 – 145.00.**

Fontanille & Marraud (F. M.)

Established during the 1930s, this company is still in operation. The firm was known earlier as Porcelaine Artistique. Gift and souvenir objects were produced as well as artistic wares and miniatures. One example of souvenir ware is shown here. See the chapter on Limoges Minatures for miniatures made by Fontanille & Marraud.

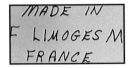

Mark 1, after 1935.

Mark 2, "Porcelaine Artistique," after 1935.

Mark 3, "Porcelaine Artistique," with "Barbotine" and "Grand Feu," after 1935.

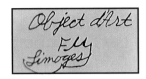

Mark 4, "Object d'Art," after 1935.

Plate 886. Trinket box, 4½" d; souvenir item decorated with the Eiffel Tower. Fontanille & Marraud Mark 4. **$200.00 – 225.00.**

André Giraud

André Giraud was in business in Limoges during the 1920s. He became associated with Brousseau during the 1930s. The company produced white wares and decorative accessories. Few examples are seen, and those are always blanks decorated by American china painters.

André Giraud Mark

Underglaze white ware mark in green, ca. 1920s.

Plate 887. Humidor, 5" h, with applied pipe; hand-painted pine cones, non-factory decoration. Giraud mark. **$300.00 – 350.00.**

Oscar Gutherz

Oscar Gutherz and his brother Edgar were involved in the porcelain business in Austria around 1899. Pieces seen with the Limoges Gutherz mark usually do not carry any white ware mark. The Austrian company was especially know for its hand-painted decorations, and the work on examples with the Limoges mark is also very well executed. The company appears to have been only a decorating studio in Limoges during the late 1800s. Two versions of an overglaze decorating mark are shown here.

Oscar Gutherz Marks

Mark 1, overglaze decorating mark in red, doughnut shape, ca. late 1800s.

Mark 2, overglaze decorating mark in red, triangular shape, ca. late 1800s.

Plate 888. Oyster plate; marine vegetation painted in red-orange and green surrounds the individual sections which are outlined in black. Gutherz Mark 2, no white ware mark. **$250.00 – 300.00.**

Plate 889. Platters and a serving bowl from a set of dinner ware; gold stenciled designs and white enameled flowers overlaid on a cobalt blue border; gold medallions form the center pattern on a white background; gold trim. Pouyat Mark 3 and Gutherz Mark 1. Serving bowl, **$200.00 – 250.00;** platters, 12" to 19", **$300.00 – 700.00 each** depending on size.

Plate 890. Coffee pot, 10" h; small purple and blue flowers, painted in the *mixtion* manner, form a floral branch on body and lid; gold trim on spout and finial. Gutherz Mark 1, no white ware mark. **$325.00 – 375.00.**

Hinrichs & Co.

This company was a New York-based importer of Limoges porcelain. The mark includes the initials "H. & C." and is a red overglaze decorating mark. Those same initials are sometimes found as an underglaze white ware mark. In my second edition, I noted that it might be attributed to Hinrichs, but no information has been found to confirm that. See the "H. & C." white ware mark in the chapter, Limoges Marks Without Examples.

Hinrichs & Co. Mark

Hinrichs & Co. mark, overglaze decorating/importer mark in red; "LIMOGES FRANCE" printed over a shield containing the initials "H & C" with "DÉPOSÉ" below, early 1900s.

Plate 891. Cup and saucer; gold paste floral pattern highlighted with a deep rose color; gold sponged work on handle. "DÉPOSÉ" printed underglaze in green and Hinrichs & Co. mark. **$100.00 – 125.00.**

Latrille Frères

Founded in 1899, Latrille Frères operated until 1913. The company was located in an old abbey which had been used earlier as a porcelain factory by the Latrille brothers' father (d'Albis and Romanet, pp. 92; 240). J. Granger is noted to have been associated with the company from 1908 until 1913 (d'Albis and Romanet, p. 92). In my first edition, the white ware mark used by Latrille Frères was listed as an unidentified Limoges mark. The "Old Abbey" decorating mark shown here was attributed to H. Créange, for according to Lesur and Tardy (1967, p. 111), Créange used the mark. The mark, however, probably refers to the mark found on pieces exported or sold by Créange, for he was listed as a *negociant*, and not actually a manufacturer (see Créange in the chapter Limoges Marks Without Examples). The "Old Abbey" mark has also been associated with J. Granger. That

"Old Abbey" mark, however, is a different version from the one used by Latrille Frères. See J. Granger under Mavaleix/Granger in this chapter.

China found with the "Old Abbey" mark which is attributed to Latrille Frères (Mark 3) usually has Mark 1 as the white ware mark. Mark 1, however, is also found alone on non-factory decorated porcelain or with the decorating mark of some other Limoges factory. Mark 2 appears to be an early decorating mark for the company. It was probably used prior to Granger's association with the company. The mark was found on a piece of china originally exported to England, thus it is possible that Mark 2 was not used on china exported to America. Mark 3 is another overglaze decorating mark, and it is sometimes found without a white ware mark.

Latrille Frères Marks

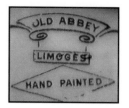

Mark 1, underglaze white ware mark in green, star with "LIMOGES FRANCE," ca. 1899 – 1913.

Mark 2, overglaze decorating mark in red, ca. 1899 – 1908, probably toward end of period.

Mark 3, overglaze decorating mark in green, "OLD ABBEY," ca. 1908 – 1913.

Latrille Frères Factory Decorated China

Plate 892. Plaque, 10" d; sailboat scene signed by "Duval." Latrille Frères Marks 1 and 3 (without "Hand Painted"). **$325.00 – 375.00.**

Plate 893. Small dish, 5½" d; brightly painted yellow and pink flowers with green leaves; gold trim; artist signed, "Max." Coiffe Mark 3 and Latrille Frères Mark 3. **$100.00 – 125.00.**

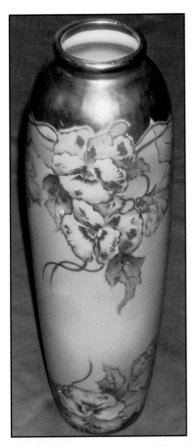

Plate 895. Plate, 8¼" d; hand-painted white grapes with green and white leaves; gold trim; artist signed "Duval." Latrille Frères Marks 1 and 3. **$220.00 – 240.00.**

Plate 894. Vase, 15" h; Art Nouveau floral design of lavender tinted pansies on a light yellow to cream background; neck and top of vase painted gold. Mavaleix Mark and Latrille Frères Mark 3. **$1,400.00 – 1,600.00.**

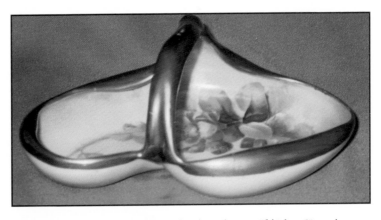

Plate 897. Bon-bon dish in a basket shape, 7½" l x 5" w; large pink flowers painted on interior; heavy gold trim. Latrille Frères Mark 3, no white ware mark. **$220.00 – 240.00.**

Plate 896. Plate, 8¼" d; red poinsettias with light and dark green leaves; gold trim; artist signed, "Lamour." Latrille Frères Marks 1 and 3. **$175.00 – 200.00.**

Plate 898. Waste bowl, 5" d; pink and white roses; brushed gold around border. Latrill Frères Mark 2, no white ware mark. **$65.00 – 75.00.**

Plate 899. Covered sugar bowl and creamer; pink flowers and green leaves with curling vines painted in an Art Nouveau fashion; gold trim. Latrille Frères Mark 3, no white ware mark. **$325.00 – 375.00 set.**

Plate 900. Biscuit jar, 7" square; pink roses decorate body; embossed leaf designs on feet and around handles painted gold. "Limoges, France" Mark 6 and Latrille Frères Mark 3. **$325.00 – 375.00.**

Latrille Frères Non-Factory Decorated China

Plate 901. Ferner, 5" h x 8¾" w, footed; purple, pink, and yellow flowers painted on a white background; gold trim. Latrille Frères Mark 1. **$375.00 – 425.00.**

Plate 902. Vase, 14" h; ornately shaped handles are painted gold; large white flowers accented with leaves in shades of green and brown painted on an ivory background. Latrille Frères Mark 1. **$700.00 – 800.00.**

Plate 903. Vase, 12½" h; intricate twisted handles; shaggy purple and pink flowers painted on middle of body, outlined by scrolled designs; a gold net is painted around the neck. Latrille Frères Mark 1. **$650.00 – 750.00.**

Laviolette

This factory was in business from 1896 – 1905 (d'Albis and Romanet, p. 240). No decorating mark is documented for the company. Examples either have a decorating mark used by another Limoges company or no decorating mark at all. Those without a decorating mark appear to have been decorated by American china painters. It is possible, as discussed earlier under Coiffe, that the white ware company actually was responsible for the decoration of china bearing the overglaze decorating marks of exporting firms such as Leonard and Straus, for example. The two items shown here each have the overglaze exporting mark in blue of P. H. Leonard. For other examples of Laviolette white wares which are shown under a decorator or exporter mark, see the Laviolette entry in the Index.

Laviolette Mark

Underglaze white ware mark in green, arrow with "LIMOGES, FRANCE," ca. 1896 – 1905.

Plate 904. Bowl, 12" d; scalloped and fluted border heavily decorated in gold; gold stenciled medallion in center. Laviolette mark and P. H. Leonard Mark 1 in blue. **$225.00 – 250.00.**

Plate 905. Charger, 12½" d; octagonal shape; small dark red flowers and light blue-green leaves form a pattern over surface; a wide blue band across the top of the piece adds an unusual touch. Laviolette mark and P. H. Leonard mark in blue. **$250.00 – 275.00.**

Lazeyras, Rosenfeld & Lehman (L. R. & L.)

From all indications, this company was a decorating firm. Lazeyras, Rosenfeld & Lehman appears to be the successor to the Th. Lazeyras decorating studio, ca. 1920s. The marks are found on very decorative china, most with figural or portrait subjects. Game bird plates and fish services are also found with L. R. & L. marks. These marks usually appear alone, without any accompanying white ware mark. Two

other marks are attributed to this company because the style of the marks and the initials are the same, except the last "L" is missing. The marks probably reflect the time when the third partner, Lehman, was not associated with the company. The particular pieces with those Marks (see Marks 4 and 5) have the white ware mark used by J. Granger, ca. 1922 – 1938. Thus the L. R. marks would have to be after 1922.

Mark 1, overglaze decorating mark in red or blue, ca. 1920s.

Mark 2, overglaze decorating mark in red, crown and oval with initials and "PORCELAINE LIMOGES, FRANCE," ca. 1920s.

Mark 3, overglaze decorating mark in gray or green, crown with initials, ca. 1920s.

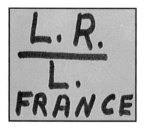

Mark 4, overglaze decorating mark in blue, "L. R." over "L" with "FRANCE," after 1922.

Mark 5, overglaze decorating mark in blue, "L. R." with "LIMOGES, FRANCE," after 1922.

Lazeyras, Rosenfeld & Lehman Examples

Plate 906. Charger, 15½" d; street scene with figures in eighteenth century dress; heavily gilded rococo border; artist signed, but not legible. L. R. & L. Mark 2. **$1,800.00 – 2,000.00.**

Plate 907. Decorative plaque, 12" d; cavalier seated on a bench and pouring a glass of wine; gold trim; artist signed, but not legible. L. R. & L. Mark 3. **$800.00 – 1,200.00.**

Plate 908. Decorative plate, 10" d; figural scene of a robed woman standing and petting a cat perched on a stool; gold trim; artist signed, "Muville." L. R. & L. Mark 2. **$400.00 – 500.00.**

Plate 909. Plaque, 12" d; portrait of a woman with golden brown hair dressed in a flowing pink gown; artist signed, "Triple." L. R. & L. Mark 3. **$1,400.00 – 1,600.00.**

Plate 910. Plaque, 13" d; portrait of a woman in a white cape and cap; gold trim; artist signed, "Dubois." L. R. & L. Mark 2 with "Purigan Mai" printed on back, possibly referring to name of woman. **$1,000.00 – 1,200.00.**

Plate 911. Plaque, 14" d; figural scene of a woman sitting on a fence surrounding a pond with swans, a man is behind her; artist signed, "Muville." L. R. & L. Mark 3. **$1,600.00 – 1,800.00.**

Plate 912. Plaque, 14" d; figural scene of a man and two women; the man is extending his hand over the wall to one of the women; artist signed, "Muville." L. R. & L. Mark 2. **$1,600.00 – 1,800.00.**

Plate 913. Plate, 10½" d; courtship scene of couple seated in a garden; artist signed, "Valentine." L. R. & L. Mark 2. **$550.00 – 650.00.**

Plate 914. Plaque, 15½" d; courtship scene of a couple strolling down a garden path in eighteenth century dress; gold trim; artist signed, "Muville." L. R. & L. Mark 2. **$1,800.00 – 2,000.00.**

Plate 915. Bowl, 6" d; two cherubs, one reading a book, decorate center; stenciled gold floral designs around border; gold trim. V. F. Mark underglaze and L. R. & L. Mark 4. **$75.00 – 100.00.**

Plate 916. Plate, 9" d; dark and light pink flowers with light green leaves outlined in gold on a green background are placed around border; a gold stenciled medallion is in the center; heavily gilded fluted rim. L. R. & L. Mark 2. **$140.00 – 165.00.**

Plate 917. Plate, 8½" d; hand-painted purple plums; gold trim; artist signed, "Alix." Coiffe Mark 3 and L. R. & L. Mark 3 with "Hand Painted" printed over Mark. **$200.00 – 225.00.**

Plate 918. Fish set: serving plates, 9½" d (10 in set); sauce boat and under-plate (not shown); platter, 18" l (see Plate 919); small fish with underwater vegetation on pale pink background; fancy scalloped and floral designs enameled in gold decorate upper part of pieces. Granger Mark 2 and L. R. & L. Marks 4 and 5. **$2,800.00 – 3,000.00 set.**

Plate 919. Platter of fish set in Plate 918.

Plate 920. Handled plate, 9½" d; pair of wild ducks in flight; heavily gilded border; Coiffe Mark 2 and L. R. & L. Mark 2. **$250.00 – 275.00.**

Plate 921. Game bird platter, 18" l x 12" w, from a service for 12 (different birds are painted on each serving plate, not shown). The platter portrays birds in flight with a scenic view of hunters in a boat; ornately scalloped and gilded inner border with wine glazed outer border; artist signed, "Dubois." L. R. & L. Mark 1. Platter, **$1,200.00 – 1,400.00.**

André Le Gentile

An Eiffel Tower mark was used as a decorating mark by André Le Gentile. Lesur and Tardy (p. 132) show that the mark was registered in 1889. The examples here have a Pouyat white ware mark from the 1876 – 1890 period. The decoration on the china is a *mixtion* type similar to designs used by Charles Field Haviland in the 1880s.

Le Gentile Mark

Le Gentile mark, overglaze decorating mark in red; Eiffel Tower with "LIMOGES" printed beneath, ca. 1889.

Plate 922. Compote, 9" d; floral pattern composed of pink tinted flowers and dark gray-brown leaves; brushed gold trims borders and handles. Pouyat Mark 3 and Le Gentile mark. **$325.00 – 375.00.**

Plate 923. Tureen and underplate matching compote in Plate 922. **$600.00 – 700.00 set.**

P. H. Leonard (PHL)

This firm was based in New York City. It imported porcelain from Germany and Limoges during the 1890s until the years of World War I. The Leonard mark was used instead of a Limoges factory decorating mark, and it can be found with the white ware marks of several Limoges companies. The Leonard mark can also be found on china without any white ware mark. It is likely that the white ware company also decorated the china, but perhaps according to specific designs of Leonard. All examples appear to be factory decorated and not American hand-painted blanks. Two new marks are shown for this company.

P. H. Leonard Marks

Mark 1, overglaze exporting mark in red, blue, or gray, ca. 1890s – 1914.

Mark 2, overglaze exporting mark in red; "LEONARD" printed within a shield with "LIMOGES" underneath, ca. 1890s – 1914.

Mark 3, overglaze exporting mark in red; "PHL" initials over "L," ca. 1890s – 1914.

P. H. Leonard Examples

Plate 924. Butter pat; a stem with two pink flowers and green leaves compose pattern; brushed gold around border. Coiffe Mark 1 and Leonard Mark 2. **$25.00 – 30.00.**

Plate 925. Plate, 6¾" square with molded shell designs in each corner; pattern is composed of different types of multi-colored floral sprays. Leonard Mark 3, no white ware mark. **$35.00 – 45.00.**

Plate 926. Tray, 17" x 15½", leaf-shaped handles painted gold; a pair of cherubs decorates center; small flowers scattered over surface; brushed gold on outer border. T. & V. Mark 7 and Leonard Mark 1. **$700.00 – 800.00.**

Plate 927. Celery tray, 12" l x 5" w; scalloped and fluted border decorated in gold; dainty multi-colored floral sprays around inner border on a pale to dark pink background. Lanternier Mark 4 and Leonard Mark 1. **$225.00 – 250.00.**

Plate 928. Celery tray, 12" l x 6" w; heavily embossed designs on border painted gold; a gold stenciled medallion is in center of dish. Leonard Mark 3. **$225.00 – 250.00.**

Plate 929. Celery tray, 13" l x 5½" w; a reserve on right side of dish is hand painted with a marsh scene featuring two cranes; red and green leaves outlined in gold frame reserve. Leonard Mark 1. **$350.00 – 400.00.**

L. W. Levy & Co. (IMPERIAL)

According to the Kovels (1973, p. 40), this New York-based company used two different marks. One mark included the initial, "L" (for Levy), but the other letter, "D," is ambiguous. I have shown this mark under Unidentified Marks in earlier editions. The "Imperial" mark is found more frequently, and collectors often refer to china with that mark as "Imperial Limoges." The marks are overglaze and are found on highly decorative wares. Pieces are often artist signed. Lehner (p. 261) lists a Levy Brothers China Company located in New York City during the late 1930s and 1940s. The company both imported and decorated china. Several more Imperial examples have been found since my last edition was published. Based on the decoration and marks, the time period seems earlier than the 1930s, but probably not as early as the late 1800s. Examples were probably made and decorated after World War I, through the 1920s.

Levy Marks

Mark 1, overglaze decorating mark in red, post World War I – 1920s.

Mark 2, a variation of Mark 1 with "LIMOGES, FRANCE" printed beneath it in red or blue, ca. post World War I – 1920s.

Mark 3, overglaze decorating mark in red of a crescent shape printed with the initials "L. D. & Co." and "LIMOGES, FRANCE" printed beneath it, post World War I – 1920s.

Plate 930. Plate, 9½" d; hand-painted mythological figural scene: women dancing in clouds while men play musical instruments; cherubs in the background; a wide gold etched border frames painting; artist signed, "A. Sanstre." "Limoges, France" Mark 6 and Levy Mark 1. **$700.00 – 900.00.**

Plate 931. Plaque, 15¼" d; tea garden scene featuring figures in eighteenth century dress, accented in vivid colors; border painted gold; artist signed, "Muville." Levy Mark 3. **$1,800.00 – 2,000.00.**

Plate 932. Plaque, 11¼" d; colorful scene of a woman seated on a garden bench and holding a closed parasol; artist signed, "Luz." Levy Mark 2. **$700.00 – 800.00.**

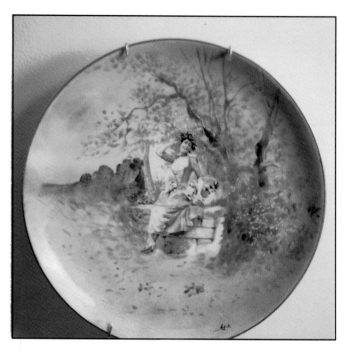

Plate 933. Plaque, 11¼" d; decorated similarly to Plate 932, but with a different girl, seated on a garden wall; artist signed, "Luz." Levy Mark 2. **$700.00 – 800.00.**

Plate 934. Plate, 8½" d; multi-colored mums painted on a blue background; gold trim; artist signed, "J. Murray." Coiffe Mark 3 and Levy Mark 2. **$200.00 – 225.00.**

Plate 935. Plate, 8½" d; a pair of fish swim above green plants and pink flowers. Pouyat Mark 5 and Levy Mark 2. **$175.00 – 225.00.**

Plate 936. Charger, 11½" d; game birds painted against a rust-orange background; pink flowers in the foreground; artist signed, "Puisoyes" (or Puisoyer). Levy Mark 1. **$300.00 – 350.00.**

S. Maas (S. M.)

Few examples are found with the mark used by Maas. The overglaze mark in red or blue incorporates his initials. The company seems to have been a decorating studio rather than a manufacturer and was active during the 1890s. White ware marks of other Limoges factories are found with his decorating mark, and his mark is also found without any white ware mark.

Maas Mark and Examples

Overglaze mark in red or blue, ca. 1890s.

Plate 937. Divided dish, 11½" x 12", scrolled handle painted gold; gold paste flowers and small light pink roses decorated inner border with a pompadour rose glaze on outer border; gold trim. Maas mark with no white ware mark. **$450.00 – 550.00.**

Plate 938. Divided dish, 12" d, scrolled handle painted gold; each section is decorated with Paris scenes in a *mixtion* style; the reserves are framed with gold scrolled designs; floral clusters and a light blue finish around inner border add to the decoration. Maas mark. **$600.00 – 700.00.**

Macy

An overglaze mark in gold and black has the letters "M A C Y" printed around a star shape with "LIMOGES" printed above the mark and "FRANCE" printed beneath it. This appears to be a mark used on Limoges china made for Macy's, the New York department store. There is no white ware mark, but the pattern on the example is very similar to one by Vignaud Frères (see this chapter).

Macy Mark

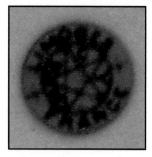

Overglaze importing mark in gold and black, ca. 1920s – 1930s.

Plate 939. Serving bowls, from a set of table ware decorated with a transfer border pattern of small pink rose garlands on the inner border and a yellow outer border accented with gold scrolled designs. Macy mark. **$60.00 – 75.00 each.**

Charles Martin (CM)

Charles Martin was the successor to the Nivet Company during the 1880s. Martin was associated with several different people until about 1920 when Duché joined the company. White wares, table china, and art objects were produced until about the mid 1930s. The decorating marks for the company are similar to one white ware mark, a triangle with a "CM" monogram, see Marks 2 and 3. These marks appear to date from the early 1900s until the factory closed. Another white ware mark is attributed to Martin, see Mark 1. This mark is probably after 1891. It was used during the same period as decorating Mark 3 because pieces are found with both marks. The decorating mark may have either "DÉCOR" or "DÉPOSÉ" printed on one side of the triangle. "MARTIN" over "FRANCE" is sometimes found as an overglaze mark as well.

Martin Marks

Mark 1, underglaze white ware mark in green, bird flying between banners with "LIMOGES, FRANCE," after 1891.

Mark 2, underglaze white ware mark in green, "CM" monogram in triangle, probably used after Mark 1, ca. early 1900s to mid 1930s.

Mark 3, overglaze decorating mark in blue or green, "CM" monogram in triangle with "LIMOGES, FRANCE," and either "DÉCOR," or "DÉPOSÉ," ca. early 1900s to mid 1930s.

Martin Factory Decorated China

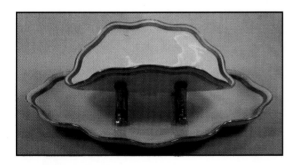

Plate 940. Asparagus dish, 9" l x 6" w, with underplate, 13" l; scalloped outer borders trimmed in gold with gold bands around inner borders; applied feet finished in gold. Martin Marks 1 and 3 (without "Décor" or "Déposé"). $450.00 – 500.00.

Plate 941. Plate, 8" d; a variety of different green leaves forms a pattern extending from the outer border to inside the well of the plate; brushed gold around outer border. Martin Marks 1 and 3. $60.00 – 85.00.

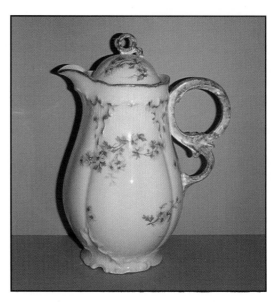

Plate 943. Chocolate pot, 10" h, "Q" shaped handle and finial; pink floral transfer pattern; gold-sponged work on handle and finial. Martin Marks 1 and 3. **$350.00 – 400.00.**

Plate 942. Plate, 8¾" d; dainty multi-colored flowers decorate center and border, overlaid with gold enameled designs. Martin Marks 1 and 3. **$75.00 – 100.00.**

Martin Non-Factory Decorated China

Plate 945. Egg cup tray (see Plate 946); hand-painted blue flowers decorate each section which is designed to hold an egg; handle and deeply scalloped rim painted gold. Martin Mark 1. **$500.00 – 600.00 set.**

Plate 944. Tray, 11¾" d; purple grapes and gold leaves painted in an Art Nouveau style; artist signed, "M. Wigginton." Martin mark similar to Mark 2 but with "DÉPOSÉ" at the base of the triangle. **$400.00 – 500.00.**

Plate 946. Tray from Plate 945 with egg cups.

Plate 947. Pitcher, 9" h; hand-painted white water lilies on a light green background; handle and neck painted gold. Martin Mark 1. **$225.00 – 275.00.**

Plate 948. Pitcher, 9" h; hand-painted red currants with green leaves. Martin Mark 1. **$350.00 – 400.00.**

P. M. Mavaleix (PM de M)/J. Granger (GM)

Paul Maurice Mavaleix was associated with Balleroy and Mandavy during the early 1900s. From 1908, he was in business by himself until about 1914. After World War I, ca. 1920, J. Granger joined his company (d'Albis and Romanet, p. 170). There has been some confusion about Mavaleix's white ware mark. The mark consists of a monogram incorporating the letters "PM DE M," which stand for Mavaleix's full name. The letter P, however, seems to be a B, but actually there is just a fancy loop between the P and the M. Relatively few examples are found with this mark. Most are white wares which have been decorated by other factories or studios. No overglaze decorating mark has been attributed to the company.

J. Granger became head of the Mavaleix factory from about 1922. Granger had been associated with Latrille Frères from 1908 – 1913 (see Latrille Frères). The white ware monogram mark used by Granger after he took over the Mavaleix company includes an "M" for Mavaleix. An "Old Abbey" mark is found as an overglaze decorating mark with Granger's white ware mark. When he was at the Latrille Frères factory, a different version of an "Old Abbey" mark was used as a decorating mark there. Pieces with the Granger white ware marks usually have a decorating mark of another factory or studio, or are examples of blanks decorated by American china painters. The business was in operation until about 1938.

Mavaleix/Granger Marks

Mavaleix underglaze white ware mark in green, "PM DE M" monogram with "LIMOGES, FRANCE," ca. 1908 – 1914.

Granger Mark 1, underglaze white ware mark in green, "GM" monogram with "LIMOGES FRANCE," ca. 1922 – 1938.

Granger Mark 2, underglaze white ware mark in green, GM monogram with "FRANCE, DÉPOSÉ," ca. 1922 – 1938.

Granger Mark 3, overglaze decorating mark in black and gold, crossed swords and a wreath with "Old Abbey Limoges" printed beneath. "MADE IN FRANCE" may or may not appear with the mark, ca. 1922 – 1938.

Plate 949. Charger, 11" d; large yellow and pink roses painted on a light cream background; gold trim; artist signed, "Moly." Mavaleix mark and "Limoges, France" Mark 9 in black. **$400.00 – 500.00.**

Plate 950. Plate, 10" d; small pink roses in gold reserves punctuate black and gold bands around outer border; very small pink and green floral designs around inner border; two thin blue lines encircle well and accentuate pattern; gold trim. Granger Marks 1 and 3. **$50.00 – 60.00.**

P. Merlin-Lemas (PML)

This company manufactured and decorated porcelain in Limoges during the 1920s. Only the white ware mark for this factory is shown by other references. The decorating mark includes the name of the company. Few examples are found.

Merlin-Lemas Marks and Examples

Mark 1, underglaze white ware mark in green, ca. 1920s.

Mark 2, overglaze decorating mark in red, "CHATEAU DES P. M. LEMAS," ca. 1920s.

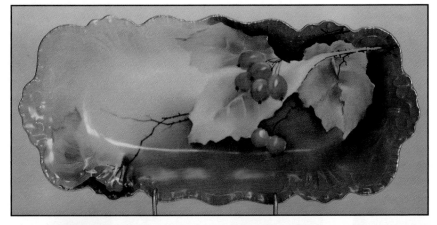

Plate 951. Celery dish, 12" x 5¾" d; red currants and large green leaves are painted against a burnt-orange background shading to yellow; artist signed, "Lapin." Pouyat Mark 5 and Merlin-Lemas Mark 2. **$225.00 – 275.00.**

Plate 952. Portrait plate, 9½" d, mounted in a gilded metal footed compote; portrait of Madame Pompadour decorates center; elaborate decoration in gold surrounds portrait; artist signed, "G. Kow." Merlin-Lemas Marks 1 and 2. **$1,400.00 – 1,600.00.**

Pairpoint

The Pairpoint Glass Company of New Bedford, Massachusetts, decorated Limoges white wares during the early 1900s. A special mark, "Pairpoint Limoges, " is found on examples expertly and richly decorated by artists of that company. No Limoges white ware mark has been found in conjunction with the Pairpoint decorating mark, thus the Limoges manufacturer remains unknown. Perhaps the company purchased blanks from various Limoges companies as did other American decorating studios.

Pairpoint Mark and Examples

Overglaze decorating mark in green for American decorating company, early 1900s.

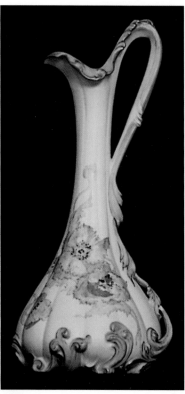

Plate 953. Pitcher, 16" h; an Art Nouveau shape is apparent in the relief work on the handle and base; hand-painted pink and lavender flowers on a cream body; a bright green finish accented with gold decorates handle, neck, and base. Pairpoint mark. **$2,200.00 – 2,700.00.**

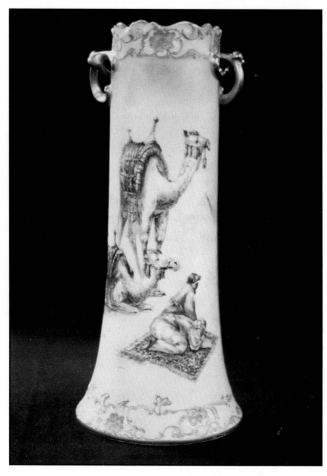

Plate 954. Vase, 14" h, ring-shaped handles; desert scene featuring camels and a figure kneeling on a prayer rug; artist signed, "Steffin." Pairpoint mark. **$3,000.00 – 3,500.00.**

Plate 955. Vase, 13" h, double-pierced handles on either side of neck; blue monochrome hand-painted windmill scene with a figure and animals in the foreground. Pairpoint mark with "Delft," indicating type of decoration. **$2,000.00 – 2,500.00.**

Paroutaud Frères Non-Factory Decorated Examples

Plate 962. Covered sugar and creamer; colorful hand-painted Oriental décor; artist signed on base, "R. Hail." Paroutaud Frères Mark 2. **$250.00 – 300.00.**

Plate 963. Toast tray, green leaves and gold vines painted in Art Nouveau style; artist signed, "Valdior." Paroutaud Frères Mark 2. **$100.00 – 125.00.**

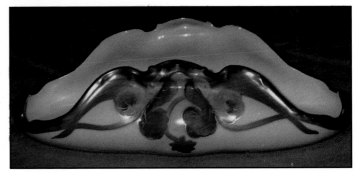

Plate 964. Cup and saucer; small blue flowers painted around borders; light blue finish on body; gold trim. Paroutaud Frères Mark 1. **$70.00 – 95.00.**

Plate 965. Pitcher, 8" h, and four mugs, 3½" h; Art Nouveau floral design accented with gold bands; handles and tops of pieces painted gold. Paroutaud Frères Mark 2. **$400.00 – 500.00 set.**

Plate 966. Jardiniere, 7½" h x 11" d; footed, with griffin-shaped handles; large pink flowers and green leaves outlined in gold; pearlized finish on the interior; heavy gold trim. Paroutaud Frères Mark 2. **$1,000.00 – 1,200.00.**

Paul Pastaud (Porcelaines d'Art)

This Limoges decorating studio was founded in 1911 by Joseph Pastaud who died in 1927. The business was carried on by Paul Pastaud until 1954 and by Jean Pastaud from 1954 until 1986. At that time, Richard Lenoir became the owner, but the Pastaud name was retained, becoming Pastaud S. A., and subsequently, from 1995 – 1998, Pastaud, S. A. (Inc.). The original buildings of the studio in Limoges were destroyed in 1998 in order for a new high rise to be erected. The company was rebuilt in the new *Espace Porcelaine* museum.

Pastaud specialized in very rich decorations which included cobalt blue and extensive use of gold. Historically, roses have been associated with decoration on Limoges porcelain, and thus the term, "Rose de Limoges," was coined. Pastaud became famed for its own renditions of rose décor. In Plate 967 is a photograph of the original plate decorated with a "Rose d Limoges" which was used in Pastaud's advertising during the 1930s. A framed platter in Plate 968 illustrates another version of the "Rose de Limoges." The company also filled specialty orders for famous people, including a dinner service made for President Franklin D. Roosevelt during the 1930s. A plate from that service is shown in Plate 969.

Several marks were used by the company over the years. One of those reflects the time in the 1930s when the firm decided to sell directly to their customers to lower costs. A page of Pastaud letterhead also includes this notation of selling directly to their clients. Information on the Pastaud Company, including marks, letterhead, and several examples were furnished by Raymonde Limoges. No values are noted for the Rose de Limoges pieces or the Roosevelt plate since these are not available on the American market.

Pastaud Marks

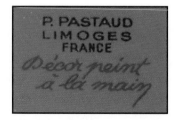

Mark 1, overglaze decorating mark in green with "Décor peint a la main" (hand painted) in red, ca. 1925.

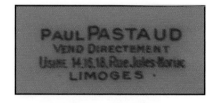

Mark 2, overglaze decorating mark in blue with notation that the company sells directly *vend directement,* and the street address, ca. 1930s.

Mark 3, overglaze decorating mark in gold, ca. 1950s.

Mark 4, overglaze decorating mark in black, ca. 1950s.

Mark 5, overglaze decorating mark in red, ca. 1950s – 1986.

Mark 6, overglaze decorating mark in black, ca. 1986 – 1995.

Pastaud Examples

Plate 967. "Rose de Limoges," original plate used in Pastaud's advertising in the 1930s. Pastaud Mark 2.

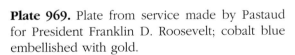
Plate 968. Framed platter, decorated with Pastaud's hand-painted roses.

Plate 969. Plate from service made by Pastaud for President Franklin D. Roosevelt; cobalt blue embellished with gold.

Plate 970. Goose knife rest; head and top of goose painted gold; there were other animals in this series including a cat, dog, bird, rabbit, and squirrel; note the streamlined shape, typical of the Art Deco style popular when these were made about 1925. Pastaud Mark 1. **$100.00 – 125.00.**

Plate 971. Candle holders; simple gold trim in another modern shape. Pastaud Mark 1. **$150.00 – 175.00 pair.**

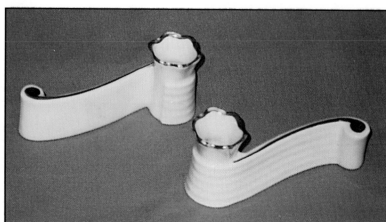

Plate 972. Ash tray, shaped like a club from a suit of cards; gold trim on white with gold stenciled designs and a medallion in the center. Pastaud Mark 4. **$35.00 – 45.00.**

Plate 973. Vase, 12" h; large gold paste flowers, stems, and leaves highlighted with turquoise enameled beading in the form of small flowers and studding the center of the larger gold blossoms; artist signed, "H. Joie." "Limoges, France" Mark 6 and Pastaud Mark 3. **$1,800.00 – 2,000.00.**

Plate 974. Vase, 12" h, a large reserve of hand-painted pink roses with one yellow bloom decorates front of vase; a dark cobalt blue finish covers body and is overlaid with small enameled flowers; artist signed, "Leroussaud." Pastaud Mark 5. **$2,200.00 – 2,500.00.**

Plate 975. Reverse of Plate 974; irises painted in gold.

Plainemaison

The Plainemaison Company was in business from the 1890s until about 1910. Few examples are found with the factory's mark. I had noted in earlier editions that evidently the company only manufactured white wares because examples always appear to have been painted by American china painters or French decorating studios. From correspondence with a descendant of the Plainemaison family, however, it seems that the company did have its own decorating studio, but did not export much of its production. Plainemaison (1995) noted that some examples made by the company bore the exporting mark used by Blakeman & Henderson. He noted that the Plainemaison company also sold blanks to exporters, but could not say that the Plainemaison factory actually decorated the china with the Blakeman & Henderson marks. The printed mark shown here was registered in 1895. The company also used an incised mark of "P FRS" (Plainemaison, 1999). Examples shown here, however, are marked only with the printed white ware mark used by Plainemaison.

Plainemaison Mark and Examples

Underglaze white ware mark in green, three stars with "LIMOGES, FRANCE," ca. 1890s – 1910.

Plate 976. Pair of candle holders, 7" h; small pink flowers with green leaves painted around base; tops painted gold; non-factory decoration. Plainemaison mark. **$225.00 – 250.00 pair.**

Plate 977. Dresser tray, 11" x 8"; hand-painted pink flowers arranged in a garland around middle; non-factory decoration. Plainemaison mark. **$225.00 – 250.00.**

Plate 978. Candle holder, 9" h; Art Nouveau design of purple grapes and gold leaves; artist signed, "Arles." This same decoration is shown with different white ware marks, exemplifying how American china painters purchased different blanks which they decorated with the same designs; non-factory decoration. Plainemaison mark. **$125.00 – 150.00.**

Porcelaine Pallas

This company was a decorating firm in Limoges between 1926 and 1950. Few examples are found. The piece shown here is a transfer pattern called "Gold Pheasant." The name of the pattern is printed with the mark. This same design was shown in the second edition on a dresser tray marked with a monogram of an unidentified company, "AJ&Co." There does not seem to be any connection between the two, except perhaps the time period which is probably the same.

Porcelaine Pallas Mark

Overglaze decorating mark in green, ca. 1926 – 1950.

Plate 979. Bowl, 3" h, 8" square; Gold Pheasant pattern featuring the bird in the center with transfers of small multi-colored flowers scattered over surface; gold trim. **$120.00 – 145.00.**

Royal China

The mark, "Royal China Limoges," printed with a crown, is found as an overglaze decorating mark in red. This mark is attributed by the Kovels (1973, p. 41) to the Royal China Decorating Company in New York. Another "Royal China" mark could possible be attributed to the same company, but based on the source of one set of china with this other "Royal China" mark, I have not included it here, but rather under Unidentified Companies and Examples. One example with the Royal China mark shown here was found on a blank made by the Gérard, Duffraisseix & Morel Company and another example (not shown) had a Granger white ware mark. Thus the time period for this "Royal China" mark spans the early 1900s to the 1920s.

Royal China Mark

Royal China, overglaze decorating mark in red, ca. early 1900s – 1920s.

Plate 980. Inkwell holder; white flowers with green leaves on a white background; gold trim around borders combined with gold sponged work. GDM Mark 2 and Royal China mark. **$150.00 – 175.00.**

Leon Sazerat and Blondeau (LS)

Leon Sazerat began his career in the Limoges porcelain industry during the 1850s. He was associated with Blondeau from the early 1880s. Mark 1 is found on white ware, and Mark 3 is on factory decorated china. Both of these marks seem to reflect the time of the company after Sazerat's death, however, in 1891. Mark 1 includes "FRANCE" (used after 1891), and Mark 3 includes the names of Blondeau's part-ners after Sazerat died, Pichonnier and Duboucheron (d' Albis and Romanet, p. 132). That later company remained in business until the late 1890s. Mark 2 would have been used prior to 1891. Few examples are found with any of the marks. Pieces appear to be professionally decorated, although there is not always an overglaze decorating mark.

Sazerat Marks and Examples

Mark 1, underglaze white ware mark in green with "FRANCE," ca. after 1891 – late 1890s. The same mark without "FRANCE," before 1891.

Mark 2, overglaze decorating mark in red, name printed inside double circle with a star in the middle, before 1891.

Mark 3, overglaze decorating mark in red with "BLONDEAU, PICHONNIER, and DUBOUCHERON," after 1891 – late 1890s.

Plate 981. Cup and saucer; gold enameled leaves with white enameled flowers on a shaded dark to light rust-colored background; handle touched with sponged gold. Sazerat Marks 1 and 3. **$125.00 – 150.00.**

Plate 982. Plate, 7½" d, delicately fluted border; large pink roses highlighted with white enamel; gold trim. Sazerat Mark 1 with no decorating mark. **$75.00 – 100.00.**

Plate 983. Coffee pot, 8" h; a spray of lavender flowers with green leaves on white body; handle, spout, and finial sponged with gold. Sazerat Marks 1 and 3. **$400.00 – 450.00.**

Camille Tharaud (CT)

This company was established after World War I, about 1920. The Tharaud factory remained in business actually until the late 1960s, but it was during the 1920s and 1930s that the production gained renown. A variety of art objects was made, and the company became famous for its "Grand Feu" technique of firing porcelain at extremely high temperatures (d'Albis and Romanet, pp. 208, 209). A pair of busts are illustrated.

C. Tharaud Marks

Tharaud, C., Mark 1, "CT" monogram, ca. 1920s.

Tharaud, Mark 2, "C THARAUD" printed in monogram form, ca. 1920s.

Plate 984. Bust of a young boy in bisque mounted on a cobalt blue stand, 15" h; this piece is based on the original sculpture by C. Houdon, and that name is impressed on the back of the piece. C. Tharaud Mark 2 in gold and impressed. **$1,200.00 – 1,500.00.**

Plate 985. Bust of a young girl, companion to the boy. C. Tharaud Mark 2 in gold. **$1,200.00 – 1,500.00.**

Touze, Lemaître Frères & Blancher (T. L. B.)

This business was formed after World War I, succeeding an older Touze factory originally established in 1868 (d' Albis and Romanet, p. 172). The T. L. B. factory was in production until the late 1930s. Pieces made by the factory are not often seen. The mark is unusual because it is in the form of a chicken. A mark of "Limoges, France, Unique" was also used by the company. Mark 1 incorporates only the initials of Jean-Baptiste Touze while Mark 2 reflects the names of the other partners.

Touze, Lemaître Frères & Blancher Marks

Mark 1, underglaze white ware mark in green; initials "J. B. T. & Cie," ca. 1920s – 1930s.

Mark 2, overglaze mark in black; initials "T. L. B.," ca. 1920s – 1930s.

Plate 986. Plate; hand-painted scene of deer, lake, and mountains; artist signed, "Arvy." Touze Mark 1. **$225.00 – 275.00.**

Plate 987. Coffee set: covered sugar, coffee pot, covered creamer, and cup and saucer; Art Deco shape; large yellow-orange roses form an overall pattern; spouts, finials, handles, and outlines of front and back panels painted silver. TLB Mark 2. Coffee set, **$400.00 – 500.00;** cup and saucer, **$60.00 – 75.00.**

Union Céramique (U. C.)

Table wares are usually the primary type of china found with the marks of Union Céramique. One example shown here, however, shows that the firm also made dolls. The company was in business from about 1909 until 1938. Both a white ware and a decorating mark were used by the factory.

Union Céramique Marks and Examples

Mark 1, underglaze white ware mark in green, ca. 1909 – 1938.

Mark 2, overglaze decorating mark in red or green, ca. 1909 – 1938.

Plate 988. Plate, 7¼" d; dinner ware pattern decorated with a gold stenciled border. U. C. Mark 1 and a decorating mark for Marshall Field, American department store. **$15.00 – 18.00.**

Plate 989. Plate, 9¼" d; dinner ware pattern composed of a floral transfer border design distinguished by small insets of pink roses on a white background. Union Céramique Marks 1 and 2. **$45.00 – 55.00.**

Plate 990. Doll, 6" h, window display model; marked, "U. C." over "FRANCE" in a rectangle. **$400.00 – 500.00.**

Union Porcelainiere

Several individuals owned this factory between 1928 and 1940. Only one mark is documented for Union Porcelainiere. Few examples are seen, but the one shown here is factory decorated.

Union Porcelainiere Mark and Example

Underglaze white ware mark in green, ca. 1928 – 1940.

Plate 991. Plate from dinner service; pattern of small red roses around outer border and single blooms scattered around inner border; scalloped border and well of plate outlined in red. Union Porcelainiere mark. **$45.00 – 55.00.**

Vignaud Frères

Established in 1911, Vignaud Frères remained in operation until 1938. White wares and factory decorated table china were produced.

Vignaud Marks

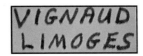

Mark 1, underglaze white ware mark in green, after 1911 – 1938.

Mark 2, overglaze decorating mark in green, fancy "V" with vine and "LIMOGES," ca. 1911 – 1938.

Mark 3, underglaze white ware mark in green, "FRANCE, VIGNAUD, LIMOGES," ca. 1938 and after.

Plate 992. Open vegetable bowl, 9¾" l x 7½" w; beaded work on handles painted gold; yellow inner border with small red and white floral designs; gold trim. Vignaud Marks 2 and 3. **$100.00 – 120.00.**

Plate 993. Mug, 5½" h; hand-painted red cherries; gold trim. Vignaud Mark 1, non-factory decoration. **$150.00 – 175.00.**

Vultury Frères

The mark used by Vultury Frères is that of a bird with "Limoges/France." Note that this is not the same bird mark as "Limoges, France" Mark 6 (see following chapter on Unidentified Limoges Marks and Examples). The Vultury factory was in business from about 1887 until 1904. Examples are rarely seen, and no decorating mark is noted for the company. The fish service shown here, however, is profes-sionally decorated and carries the blue exporting mark of L. Straus & Sons. I have noted elsewhere that examples with Straus or some other American importers may have actually been decorated by the white ware factory. Therefore, I have placed this set here to give an example of the company's production.

Vultury Frères Mark and Examples

Underglaze white ware mark in green, ca. 1887 – 1904.

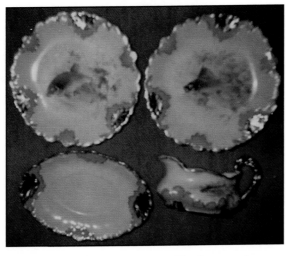

Plate 995. Platter to set in Plate 994, 23½" l x 10½" w.

Plate 994. Fish set: twelve plates, 8¾" d, sauce boat and under-plate; fish décor highlighted by borders painted with designs in green and gold. Vultury Frères mark and L. S. & S. mark in blue. **$2,800.00 – 3,000.00 set.**

Unidentified Limoges Marks and Examples

A & D

These initials are found as an overglaze decorating mark in either green or red. The decorating studio is unidentified. From examples, the mark appears to have been in use during the late 1890s through the early 1900s.

A & D Mark and Examples

Overglaze decorating mark in green or red, ca. late 1890s to early 1900s.

Plate 996. Plate, 9½" d; a deep wine inner border is overlaid with gold stenciled designs and broken by three floral reserves painted in bright colors; a gold medallion decorates the center; gold stenciled patterns around well and outer border. A & D mark in green. **$70.00 – 95.00.**

Plate 997. Chocolate pot, 12" h, and two cups and saucers; large dark pink roses around top half of chocolate pot with a bright pink finish above flowers; small roses and green garlands below a gold band decorate lower half of pot; cups and saucers are decorated similarly; braided handles and finial painted gold. Coiffe Mark 3 and A & D mark in green. Chocolate pot, **$500.00 – 600.00;** cups and saucers, **$100.00 – 125.00 each.**

AJCO

These initials appear as a fancy monogram in an overglaze decorating mark in blue. The studio is unidentified. The example and type of mark indicate a time period of the 1930s or later. The same pattern shown for this company is on a bowl decorated by Porcelaine Pallas who was in business during the late 1920s and 1930s as well (see Other Limoges Companies and Examples).

AJCO Mark and Example

Unidentified decorating studio, overglaze monogram mark in blue, ca. 1930s or later.

Plate 998. Dresser tray, 10½" l; Gold Pheasant pattern with multi-colored small flowers lightly highlighted with white enamel. "Limoges, France" Mark 6 and AJCO mark. **$200.00 – 225.00.**

Authentique

"AUTHENTIQUE" is a rather ambiguous mark found printed under "LIMOGES, FRANCE." It appears as an overglaze stamp. The decoration of the example with this mark suggests a time no earlier than the 1920s.

Authentique Mark and Example

Overglaze decorating mark in green, ca. 1920s

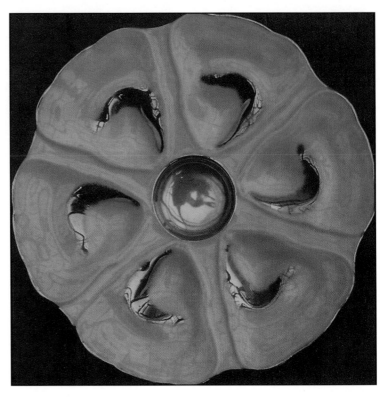

Plate 999. Oyster plate; each section is highlighted with a splash of gold luster which also decorates the center sauce dip and the outer border. Authentique mark. **$175.00 – 200.00.**

A V

These initials are found as an impressed mark without any identifying white ware or decorating mark. The mark could possibly be that of Aragon and Vultury who operated in Limoges during the 1880s. The Moss Rose pattern which is on the examples was popular during that era.

A V Mark

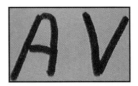

Impressed mark, unidentified factory, possibly Aragon and Vultury, ca. 1880s.

Plate 1005. Covered box, 5½" l; orange, yellow, and black circular designs are featured on a green background divided by abstract white lines in an Art Deco style. Serpaut mark and B. S. mark. **$350.00 – 400.00.**

Beaux-Arts

This mark was found as a decorating stamp on an example decorated in an Art Nouveau floral style, placing the mark ca. early 1900s.

Beaux-Arts Mark and Examples

Overglaze decorating mark in green with "FRENCH CHINA," ca. 1900.

Plate 1006. Covered box, 6" l, oval shape; white roses with curling vines decorate body and lid. Beaux-Arts. **$225.00 – 275.00.**

C. H.

These initials with the seal of Limoges are found as an underglaze white ware mark. This mark has not been identified, but it is interesting to note that the decorating mark used by Bawo & Dotter was the same seal or arms of Limoges. An example with the C. H. mark also had a Bawo & Dotter decorating mark. No information has surfaced to indicate if Bawo and Dotter took over a factory which used such a seal, with Bawo and Dotter subsequently adapting it as a decorating mark. The example shown in Plate 1007 is marked with P. H. Leonard's exporting mark in blue. The C. H. mark should be ca. 1880s or to 1890.

C. H. Mark and Example

Underglaze white ware mark in green with Arms of Limoges and "Déposé," ca. 1880s-1890.

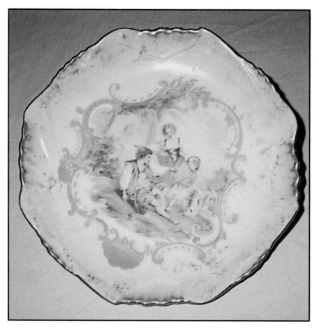

Plate 1007. Plate, 9" d; courting scene framed by scroll and shell designs painted gold. C. H. mark. **$250.00 – 275.00.**

CMC or GMC

A monogram mark with these initials (unclear if first letter is a C or a G) is an underglaze white ware mark in green. The time period for the mark is after 1890 until 1914.

Underglaze white ware mark in green, ca. after 1890 – 1914.

Plate 1008. Chocolate pot, 11" h; yellow flowers within gold bands form a center design around the middle of the pot; finial and handle painted gold. CMC or GMC mark. **$400.00 – 500.00.**

C R A

These initials with three *fleur-de-lis* and "Fabrique En France" were found as an overglaze decorating or exporting mark printed in blue. The mark was on an example with the white ware mark of the Laviolette Limoges factory. Because the CRA mark does not incorporate the word "France," it may be a mark used by a Paris decorating studio.

C R A Mark and Example

Overglaze decorating or exporting mark in blue, ca. early 1900s.

Plate 1009. Biscuit jar; pink flowers with yellow centers accented with red are painted by the *mixtion* method on the front of jar; smaller flowers decorate lid; fluted shapes around top of jar painted gold. Laviolette mark and C R A mark. **$325.00 – 375.00.**

C. V. & Cie.

A quite elaborate mark, incorporating a globe and a star with "Limoges Déposé" and these initials, is an overglaze decorating stamp found on a tea set. There is no white ware mark. The shape of the pieces as well as the decoration are similar to Haviland china made during the 1880s.

C. V. & Cie. Mark

Overglaze decorating mark in red; "C. V. & Cie." is printed under mark, ca. 1880s.

Plate 1010. Tea set; small birds, butterflies, and dragonflies distinguish this floral pattern; gold outlining accents most of the pieces. C. V. & Cie. mark. Tea plate, **$40.00 – 50.00;** cup & saucer, **$60.00 – 75.00;** waste bowl, **$35.00 – 45.00;** cake plate, **$150.00 – 175.00;** creamer, **$75.00 – 100.00;** tea pot, **$225.00 – 275.00;** covered sugar bowl, **$125.00 – 150.00.**

Plate 1011. Vase, 12" h; figural scene portraying a small boy, dressed in plaids, looking through a telescope; brightly colored flowers and palm trees complete the decoration. C. V. & Cie. mark. **$600.00 – 700.00.**

Chateau De St. Cloud

This overglaze decorating mark was found on La Porcelaine Limousine blanks, indicating that the mark is after 1905.

Chateau De St. Cloud Mark and Examples

Overglaze decorating mark in red, ca. after 1905.

Plate 1012. Pair of cabinet plates, 8½" d; transfer courting scenes of figures in eighteenth century dress decorate the center of each piece; a wine border overlaid with gold stenciled designs frames the decoration. La Porcelaine Limousine Mark 1 and Chateau De St. Cloud mark. **$150.00 – 175.00 each.**

Plate 1013. Plate, decorated with a scene similar to the one in Plate 1012.

E. G. D. & Co.

These unidentified initials and "Couleurs Feu De Four," "Inalterables" are an overglaze decorating mark in green. The mark is on an example of Gérard, Dufrasseix & Morel white ware decorated with a flow-blue type floral décor. The mark should have been in use during the 1890s.

E. G. D. & Co. Mark and Examples

Overglaze decorating mark in green, ca. 1890s.

Plate 1014. Platter, 12" l; cobalt blue floral pattern scattered over surface; sponged gold and gold outlining decorates border and mold shapes of piece. GDM Mark 2 and E. G. D. & Co. mark. **$250.00 – 275.00.**

Plate 1015. Covered vegetable dish, 11" l, with the same pattern as Plate 1014. **$325.00 – 375.00.**

Florale

A wreath with "Florale" printed within is found as an overglaze decorating mark in green. The mark is on a Balleroy blank, placing the time of the mark around the 1920s.

Florale Mark and Example

Overglaze decorating mark in green, ca. 1920s.

Plate 1016. Demitasse cup and saucer; yellow geometric designs around inner border; gold trim. Balleroy Mark 1 and Florale mark. **$50.00 – 65.00 set.**

G. D.

An impressed mark with these initials has been found on several examples. No white ware or decorating mark is on the piece shown, but a D. & Co. early decorating mark on another example raised the question if perhaps "G. D." stood for Guéry & Délinièrs, predecessor of Délinières & Co. The mark will remain under "Unidentified" until more information is found. The shape of the pieces as well as the decoration indicates the mark is from 1870s – 1880.

G. D. Mark

Impressed initials, ca. 1870s – 1880s.

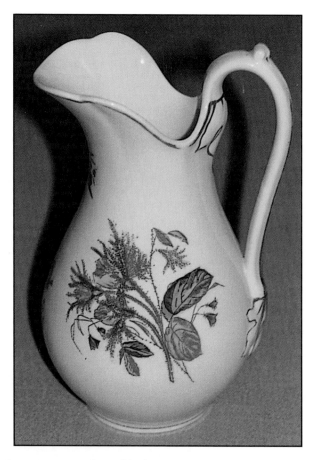

Plate 1017. Pitcher 8½" h; Moss Rose pattern, brightly colored over transfer, decorates sides and front of piece; molded leaf designs at top and base of handle outlined in gold. G. D. mark. **$275.00 – 325.00.**

L. B. H.

An overglaze red decorating mark incorporates these initials. The few examples seen have been on Coiffe blanks.

L. B. H. Mark and Example

Overglaze decorating mark in red, unidentified studio, ca. 1890s.

Plate 1018. Plate, 8½" d; a small rose spray in the center of the plate is enclosed by a floral garland; gold trim accents outer border. Coiffe Mark 2 and LBH mark. **$75.00 – 100.00.**

Limoges Art Porcelaine Co.

An example made by A. Lanternier carries an overglaze decorating mark of this company. The decoration is very fine, but no other pieces have come to my attention to help identify the mark more specifically.

Limoges Art Porcelaine Co. Mark and Example

Overglaze decorating mark in green, early 1900s.

Plate 1019. Pancake dish, 9½" d; large pink and white roses painted on a shaded blue background; artist signed, "Habemert." Lanternier Mark 4 and Limoges Art Porcelaine Co. mark. **$1,000.00 – 1,200.00.**

"Limoges, France" Marks

"Limoges, France," with or without some symbol, is found as a mark on many examples of Limoges porcelain. The majority of these marks are underglaze white ware stamps, but the companies who used those marks are unidentified. Often there is an identified company's decorating mark with the "Limoges, France" mark which can help indicate the time period when these several factories were in business. Most of the pieces shown here do not have an overglaze decorating or exporting mark, however. Nearly all of the examples exhibit factory decoration. "Limoges, France" Mark 6, however, is one which is often found on American hand-painted blanks. A few of the unidentified marks do not have an example in this chapter, but a reference is noted in the caption of the mark for an example shown under the company of the decorating or exporting mark.

"Limoges, France" Mark 1

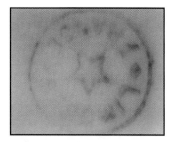

Mark 1, underglaze white ware mark in green, star in a circle, ca. after 1891.

Plate 1020. Cake plate, 10" d; fluted border with beaded work finished in gold; a gold stenciled medallion is in center on a cream background. "Limoges, France" Mark 1 and A. Klingenberg Mark 2. **$225.00 – 250.00.**

"Limoges, France" Mark 2

Mark 2, underglaze white ware mark in green with "LIMOGES" printed over a straight line with "FRANCE" below line, ca. after 1891.

Plate 1021. Plate; vividly painted fish scene; magenta flowers and leaves in the foreground; sea gulls against a blue sky in the background; gold trim. "Limoges, France" Mark 2 and a fake Sèvres mark. **$200.00 – 225.00.**

Plate 1022. Server, 12" l, mounted on a footed gilded metal base with applied bird and branch at top of dish; red flowers with blue ribbon on a shaded pink background painted over a heavily embossed body design; artist signed, "EP." "Limoges, France" Mark 2 without a decorating mark, but piece exhibits professional French decoration. **$700.00 – 900.00.**

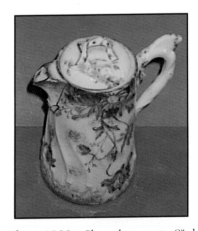

Plate 1023. Chocolate pot, 8" h; orange and yellow floral sprays form a large design over body and lid, accented with sponged gold. "Limoges, France" Mark 2. **$400.00 – 450.00.**

Plate 1024. Inkwell and pen holder, 6½" l, with insert; multi-colored flowers painted in a reserve on the front; a dark green glaze on body; gold accents unpainted handles. "Limoges, France" Mark 2. **$250.00 – 325.00.**

"Limoges, France" Mark 3

Mark 3, underglaze white ware mark in green, banner shape, after 1891.

Plate 1025. Cup and saucer; sprays of purple flowers with light green leaves on a white background; border finished with a pink glaze; handle and trim painted gold. "Limoges, France" Mark 3. **$75.00 – 95.00.**

Plate 1026. Coffee set matching pattern on cup and saucer in Plate 1025. Coffee pot, **$450.00 – 500.00**; creamer, **$125.00 - 150.00**; covered sugar bowl, **$150.00 – 175.00.**

"Limoges, France" Mark 4

Mark 4, underglaze white ware mark in green, crescent shape, ca. after 1891.

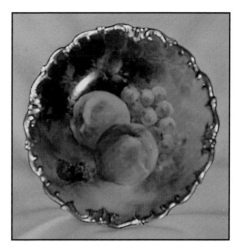

Plate 1027. Plate, 10½" d; heavily scalloped border painted gold; hand-painted fruit; artist signed, "Rosier." "Limoges, France" Mark 4. **$250.00 – 275.00.**

Plate 1028. Plaque, 10½" d; harbor scene portraying a woman standing in front of a sea wall; a child has her arms and legs wrapped around her; gold trim. "Limoges, France" Mark 4. **$600.00 – 700.00.**

Plate 1029. Pitcher, 5¼" h x 6" w, dolphin-shaped handle; hand-painted red currants; gold trim. "Limoges, France" Mark 4 and Blakeman & Henderson Mark 2. **$175.00 – 200.00.**

"Limoges, France" Mark 5

(See example under "Authentique" at the beginning of this section).

Mark 5, underglaze white ware mark in green with "LIMOGES" printed in a crescent shape over "FRANCE," after 1891.

"Limoges, France" Mark 6 and Examples

Mark 6, underglaze white ware mark in green (and overglaze in red), "LIMOGES" printed over "FRANCE," after 1891.

Plate 1030. Plate, 10" square, open ring shapes on each corner; hand-painted blackberries and pink flowers on a pastel tinted background; gold trim. "Limoges, France" Mark 6. **$300.00 – 350.00.**

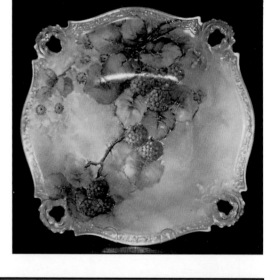

Plate 1031. Plate, 8" d; hand-painted red berries and white flowers framed by a clover-shaped gold border; artist signed, "Luc." "Limoges, France" Mark 6. **$175.00 – 225.00.**

Plate 1032. Vase, 9" h, dragon-shaped handles; Oriental scene of a fisherman and his net painted in gold. "Limoges, France" Mark 6. **$500.00 – 600.00.**

"Limoges, France" Mark 7

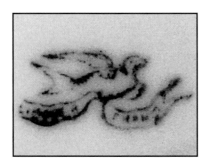

Mark 7, underglaze white ware mark in green, bird with banner, ca. after 1891.

Plate 1033. Demitasse cup and saucer, small pink flowers and enameled gold scrolled designs decorate top half of pieces against a light lavender-pink background; gold trim. Klingenberg Mark 9 and "Limoges, France" Mark 7 with an overglaze decorating mark in red which is illegible. **$75.00 – 100.00.**

"Limoges, France" Mark 8 and Example

Mark 8, overglaze decorating or exporting mark in blue, "LIMOGES, FRANCE," printed within an oval shape, ca. after 1891.

Plate 1034. Charger, 14" d; court scene with a gentleman preparing to be barbered or shaved; artist signed, "Dubois." "Limoges, France" Mark 8. **$2,000.00 – 2,200.00.**

"Limoges, France" Mark 9

(See example under "Mavaleix" in the preceding section, Other Limoges Companies and Examples)

Mark 9, overglaze decorating mark in gray, bees, and hive, after 1908.

"Limoges, France" Mark 10

(See example under "Bawo & Dotter" in the first section on Major Limoges Companies)

Mark 10, underglaze white ware mark in green, three small stars over an anchor, ca. 1870s – 1880s.

"Limoges, France" Mark 11

Mark 11, overglaze decorating mark in dark gray, a crown over a banner printed with "LIMOGES" over "FRANCE."

Plate 1035. Plate, molded shell designs around border have a dark pink finish; a red-orange finish with a scenic lake background decorates center. "Limoges, France" Mark 11. **$200.00 – 225.00.**

P. et Fils

This mark might have been used by "Perrigault et Fils." That company was in business between 1897 and 1914 (Lesur and Tardy, p. 142). The mark is an overglaze decorating stamp in red.

P. et Fils Mark and Example

Overglaze decorating mark in red, ca. early 1900s.

Plate 1036. Chocolate pot, 9" h; one panel on the front of the pot is hand-painted with a lake scene; gold enameled flowers on an ivory background decorate other panels; embossed leaf designs on lid and base painted a deep green, accented with gold; handle and spout painted gold. P. et Fils mark. **$450.00 – 550.00.**

Royal China

"ROYAL CHINA" and "22 Karat" printed with a coat of arms in a gold seal mark are found on the following examples. This mark is unidentified. It is possible that it was a mark used by the Royal China Decorating Company of New York (see Other Limoges Companies and Examples). But another mark in red accompanies the gold seal which states "Limoges French Decoration Hand Painted." Other examples have been seen with this mark, and they all are heavily decorated with gold. "Hand Painted" refers to color touch-up work to the transfers and stenciled designs. This type of decoration was popular after World War I through the 1920s.

Royal China Mark and Examples

Overglaze decorating seal mark in gold, after 1914 – 1920s.

The seven pieces shown here are from a set of dinner ware complete with many serving pieces. Only a sample can be included, but the decoration speaks for itself. Colorful mythological, courtship, classical, and pastoral scenes are richly embellished with etched gold borders and stenciled work which exposes part of the body of the pieces. There are different scenes on each piece.

Plate 1037. Plate, cherub, and two women. Royal China mark. **$200.00 – 250.00.**

Plate 1038. Plate, reclining maiden with angel. **$200.00 – 250.00.**

Plate 1039. Plate, three women with a man playing a musical instrument. **$200.00 – 250.00.**

Plate 1040. Cup and saucer, three women and cherub decorate saucer with a similar but different scene on the interior of the cup. **$200.00 – 250.00.**

Plate 1041. Tea pot on a trivet, **$400.00 – 500.00 set.**

Plate 1042. Platter, courtship scene with a French chateau in the background. **$800.00 – 1,000.00.**

Plate 1043. Square tray, classical figural scene of a woman showing a baby to another woman and a shepherd. **$500.00 – 600.00.**

S & S

These initials represent an underglaze white ware mark used after 1891.

S & S Mark and Example

Underglaze white ware mark in green, initials over "L" and "France."

Plate 1044. Platter, 14" l; yellow, blue, and brown flowers form a large and small spray decoration at the top and base of piece; gold trim and brushed gold accents. S & S mark and L. S. & S. exporting mark. **$325.00 – 375.00.**

SW

A monogram with these initials framed within a wreath, with "BIARRITZ" printed above, is an unidentified decorating mark.

SW Mark and Examples

Overglaze decorating mark in red, after 1891.

Plate 1045. Plate, 10½" d; hand-painted hunting dog with a game bird in his mouth; artist signed, "Dusay." SW mark. **$275.00 – 325.00.**

Plate 1046. Plaque, 10" d; courtship scene of couple in a garden setting; artist signed, "Lancy." SW mark. **$800.00 – 1,000.00.**

V. F.

These initials with "FRANCE" are surrounded by small stars to form a white ware mark. This is not a mark used by Vignaud Frères.

V. F. Mark and Example

Underglaze white ware mark in green, unidentified factory, early 1890s.

Plate 1047. Candle holders; large scrolls on bases are painted green; gold outlining accents designs around base; necks painted gold. V. F. mark. **$225.00 – 275.00 pair.**

Ambiguous Symbols

Several unidentified marks are illustrated here which incorporate some symbol in the mark rather than an initial. They are all overglaze decorating marks.

Symbol Mark 1 and Examples

Symbol Mark 1, overglaze decorating mark in red with "LIMOGES FRANCE," late 1800s to early 1900s.

Plate 1048. Plaque, 15" d; vividly painted figural scene of a woman holding a baby dressed in a christening robe with a man and woman admiring the child; artist signed, "E. Furlaud." Symbol Mark 1. **$2,200.00 – 2,500.00.**

Plate 1049. Plaque, 15" d; figural scene of a woman in a wedding gown seated on a garden bench with a man and woman in attendance. Note the colors and garden scene backgrounds are similar in this and the preceding plaque. Both have the same mark, but this piece is artist signed, "Muville." Symbol Mark 1. **$2,200.00 – 2,500.00.**

Symbol Mark 2

This unidentified mark is composed of the silhouette of a horse and rider. It is an overglaze decorating mark. "LIMOGES FRENCH DECORATION HAND PAINTED WARRANTED 22 CARAT GOLD" is printed beneath the mark. This is the same notation printed with the Royal China mark shown earlier in this chapter. That mark, though, does not have "22 Carat Gold" printed with the mark, rather "22 Karat" is part of the Royal China gold seal mark. Note the spelling of "Karat" and "Carat." The former is usually considered the European version and the latter the American version. This horse and rider mark as well as the Royal China mark may also be connected to the Royal China Decorating Company of New York City (see Other Limoges Companies). The decoration on the example with the horse and rider mark is not as lavish as the china shown for the Royal China mark. The decoration on this piece is similar to that used by American china companies during the late 1920s and early 1930s.

Symbol Mark 2

Symbol Mark 2, silhouette of horse and rider, overglaze decorating mark, ca. 1920s – 1930s.

Plate 1050. Plate; 10" d; overall etched gold finish with a center reserve decorated with a transfer courtship scene. Symbol Mark 2. **$50.00 – 60.00.**

Symbol Mark 3

An overglaze gold stamp with the figure of a prancing horse is an unidentified decorating mark. "LIMOGES FRANCE" is printed beneath the mark in red.

Symbol Mark 3 and Example

Symbol Mark 3, gold stamp impressed with the figure of a prancing horse, ca. 1920s and after.

Plate 1051. Plate, 10¾" d; the pattern is composed of a wide green border overlaid with gold stenciled designs between etched gold bands. Symbol Mark 3. **$100.00 – 125.00.**

Undecorated Limoges Porcelain

Blanks, or undecorated porcelain, are interesting examples of Limoges porcelain and merit consideration and collectibility. The majority of the Limoges factories which exported to the United States prior to World War I did a large business with this undecorated white ware. The china painting era was in full swing in the United States, and there was a large market for fine porcelain to decorate. Fortunately, some of those blanks failed to get painted. Such pieces are quite collectible. The details of the mold and workmanship of the potter are more visible on blanks. Several pieces have been selected for this section to illustrate more closely the fine quality of Limoges porcelain. A number of factories are represented. One of the most popular white wares is the Ranson pattern made by the Haviland Company. Some pieces are included. One point of interest about that china is that, except for one piece, all have Frank Haviland's mark (see Frank Haviland under Haviland & Co.

in the section on Major Limoges Companies).

An ad from a catalog in 1919 for Thayer & Chandler shows this company sold white ware in Chicago, where china painting was a large business before and after World War I. Another ad for the company describes how china was prepared for gold encrusted decoration. It states that:

"Background is etched into the china through the glaze, leaving the design in relief. Just apply gold over the pattern and the background in a solid mass with medium large square shading brush. Use either straight Roman gold or two parts Roman to one part Liquid Bright Gold, or straight Liquid Bright Gold. Burnish as usual with spun glass burnisher or burnishing sand. No burnishing necessary when straight Liquid Bright Gold is used."

Plate 1052. Vase, 9½" h, 8" w; elegantly scalloped handles and neck. Pouyat Mark 5. **$350.00 – 400.00.**

Plate 1053. Tankard, 14¾" h; scalloped neck, dragon-shaped handle. Pouyat Mark 5. **$450.00 – 500.00.**

Plate 1054. Tankard, 10½" h; completely plain with no embossed designs. Pouyat Mark 5. **$150.00 – 175.00.**

Plate 1055. Tankard, 10" h; lightly embossed design around base and on handle. Délineières & Co. (D. & Co.) Mark 3. **$250.00 – 300.00.**

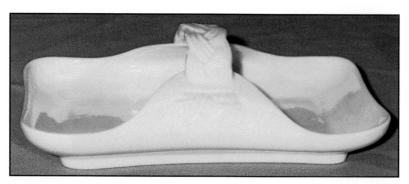

Plate 1057. Basket, 8" l x 5" w; braided handle on a rectangular shape. Haviland & Co. Mark 8. **$300.00 – 350.00.**

Plate 1056. Basket, 2" h x 5" w; Oriental design with bamboo-shaped handles and feet. A. Giraud mark. **$100.00 – 125.00.**

Plate 1058. Basket, 5½" h x 6" w; scalloped designs in relief decorate base. Pouyat Mark 5. **$150.00 – 175.00.**

Plate 1059. Talcum shaker, 5" h; three feet with delicate scroll work at top of feet. La Porcelaine Limousine Mark 1. **$75.00 – 100.00.**

Plate 1060. Coffee set: creamer, covered sugar, coffee pot; triangular shape; braided rope handles and finials; applied rope and knot designs on body. Haviland & Co. Mark 9. **$500.00 – 600.00 set.**

Plate 1061. Invalid feeder; lightly scalloped design on top of feeder. Haviland & Co. Mark 9. **$175.00 – 225.00.**

Plate 1062. Candle holders, 8" h; square shape. Bernardaud & Co. Mark 2. **$100.00 – 150.00 pair.**

Plate 1063. Wash basin and pitcher, six-sided; Bernardaud & Co. Mark 1. **$600.00 – 800.00 set.**

Plate 1064. Platter, 14" l, 9½" w; embossed designs around inner border. Barny & Rigoni Mark 3. **$125.00 – 150.00.**

Plate 1065. Tea pot, 5½" h x 7" w; embossed designs on handle extending onto body. Pouyat Mark 5. **$225.00 – 275.00.**

Plate 1066. Mustard tureen, braided handles on each side; ring designs form handle of lid. Charles Field Haviland Mark 2. **$150.00 – 175.00.**

Plate 1067. Haviland's popular Ranson design is shown in the following five photographs. The first four items were made by Haviland, but they were marked for Frank Haviland (Mark 1). For some reason, these pieces were never decorated. Cup and saucer, **$40.00 – 50.00.**

Plate 1068. Creamer, **$60.00 – 75.00;** covered sugar, **$75.00 – 100.00.**

Plate 1069. Celery dish, **$70.00 – 85.00.**

Plate 1070. Covered butter dish, **$200.00 – 250.00.**

Plate 1071. Covered vegetable, H. & Co. Mark 11. **$150.00 – 175.00.**

Limoges Porcelain Decorated by Professional American Art Studios

China painting was a vocation as well as an avocation for American women and men during the late 1800s through the 1920s. Professional art studios were in business during that era. Many of these were located in Chicago, with Pickard perhaps the most well known. Others, however, were also busy purchasing undecorated white wares, made by various Limoges and other European porcelain factories, to be decorated and sold commercially. Today these pieces are first collected according to a particular artist or decorating firm with the company which made the blank being of secondary importance. For that reason, unless the item is unusual or the mold unique, Limoges collectors rarely concentrate on these examples. Thus, I have included only a sample of Limoges blanks which were decorated by American professional art studios. Values, in general, are high, often quite a bit more than French decorated Limoges. To learn more about many American art studios and china painters, see Alan Reed's very informative book, *Collector's Encyclopedia of Pickard China,* which includes other Chicago art studios and artists as well as Pickard.

Limoges Porcelain Decorated by Professional American Art Studios

Plate 1072. Cup and saucer; red and green flowers form wide border accented with gold stenciled designs. C. J. Ahrenfeldt Mark 4 and "R-B Boston" printed in a red black, decorating studio. **$100.00 – 125.00.**

Plate 1073. Tankard, 12" h; red roses on a dark green ground. T. & V. Mark 7 with "D'Arcy's Hand Painted," decorating mark in red, a Kalamazoo, Michigan art studio, operating ca. 1910. **$800.00 – 1,000.00.**

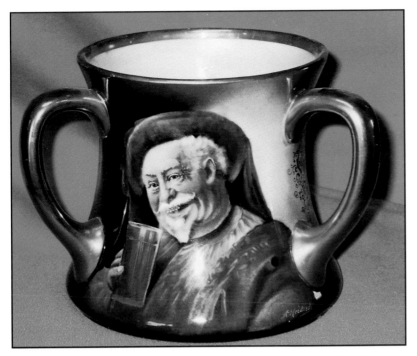

Plate 1074. Loving cup, 6" h, 3 handles; portrait of Falstaff; artist signed, "Heidrich." Guérin Mark 3 and trademark of "E. W. Donath," a Chicago art studio from 1906 – 1928. **$900.00 – 1,100.00.**

Plate 1075. Tankard, 15" h; portrait of Falstaff by "Heidrich," matching Loving Cup. Pouyat Mark 5 and the "E. W. Donath" decorating mark. **$1,400.00 – 1,600.00.**

Plate 1076. Vase, 14" h; nude figural portrait of woman, with a feather boa, painted on a reserve on the front; gold etched finish surrounds reserve; artist signed, "Osborne," a Chicago artist, ca. 1913 – 1918. Bernardaud Mark 1. **$1,800.00 – 2,000.00.**

Plate 1077. Plate, 8½" d; brilliantly colored leaves painted on a white background; outer border decorated with enameled flowers and beaded designs; artist signed, but the name is not legible. Délinières & Co. Mark 3 and a "Pickard" decorating mark, early 1900s. **$200.00 – 250.00.**

Plate 1079. Cake plate; bright orange flowers painted over gold and black borders frame a single orange flower with gold leaves. T. & V. mark with a 1908 patent mark and a Pickard decorating mark. **$300.00 – 350.00.**

Plate 1078. Cup and saucer; dark pink, purple, and white flowers; gold borders outlined in black. Guérin Mark 3 with a "Pickard" decorating mark. **$120.00 – 140.00.**

Plate 1080. Bowl; orange poppies and white daisies; artist signed, "Yescheck," a Pickard artist. T. & V. Mark 7 with a patent date of "February 26th 1901," and a Pickard decorating mark. **$400.00 – 600.00.**

Plate 1081. Vase; colorful pheasant in an etched gold frame surrounded by multi-colored flowers. T. & V. Mark 7 with "1917" printed as part of mark, and a Pickard decorating mark. **$800.00 – 1,000.00.**

Plate 1082. Painting on porcelain, 15½" l; desert scene, an Arab is kneeling on a prayer rug in front of a pair of camels; artist signed, "Weiss," a Pickard artist. Guérin Mark 3 and a Pickard mark, ca. 1903 – 1905. **$3,500.00 – 4,000.00.**

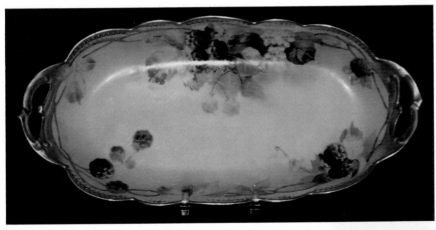

Plate 1083. Celery dish, 13" l; hand-painted blackberries; Klingenberg Mark 6 and a Pickard decorating mark. **$400.00 – 500.00.**

Plate 1084. Dresser set; hand-painted purple flowers on a light yellow-green background. Bawo & Dotter (Elite) Mark 5 and a Pickard decorating mark. Tray, **$400.00 – 500.00;** covered powder jars, **$300.00 – 400.00 each;** hair receiver, **$200.00 – 300.00.**

Plate 1085. Tankards: left, 10½" h; red currants; artist signed, "Blaha;" right, 11½" h; pink, white, and red roses; artist signed, "E. Challinor." T. & V. Mark 7 and Pickard decorating marks. **$1,000.00 – 1,200.00 each.**

Plate 1086. Vase; pale pink flowers on branches. Guérin Mark 3 and the Ravenwood decorating studio mark which was used by the Sinclair Glass Co. of Corning, New York, ca. 1900 – 1910. **$300.00 – 350.00.**

Plate 1087. Plate, 8½" d; hand-painted boat scene; artist signed, "F. Caky." Haviland & Co. Mark 12 and a Stouffer decorating mark, a Chicago art studio. **$325.00 – 375.00.**

Plate 1089. Punch bowl, 10" h x 14" d, on a separate 4½" pedestal base; etched gold décor covers top half of bowl; gilded base. Délinières & Co. Mark 3 with a "White's Art Co. Chicago Hand Painted" decorating mark, ca. 1914 – 1923. **$2,500.00 – 3,000.00.**

Plate 1088. Tankard, 12½" h; Falstaff figural portrait. Délinières & Co. Mark 3 and an over-glaze mark in red for, "E. Thorne's Na Studio Chicago Opera House." **$800.00 – 1,000.00.**

Limoges Companies Without Examples

In the first and second editions, a number of marks were shown without any example. Most of these marks represent companies which either exported little, if any, porcelain to the United States, or were companies which began business after World War II, the arbitrary cut-off date for the era covered by my book. Those companies are listed in this section along with the marks they used, if known. Both identified and non-identified companies are included. In addition, some American importer marks are shown. Some of those do have examples in the preceding chapters. Be sure to consult the Index to Companies if you cannot find a particular mark. Please note that the marks shown in the previous chapters and in this section do not exhaust the number of Limoges marks for factories, decorating studios, importers, or exporters. The marks covered in this book are chiefly from the 1870s through the 1930s.

François Alluaud II

After the death of his father in 1799, François Alluaud II, took over the operation of the historical Alluaud factory which had been established after the end of the French Revolution, ca. 1798. The Alluaud company became the largest in Limoges during the first half of the nineteenth century. A variety of decorative objects were manufactured. Additionally, the company sold its white wares to other factories and decorators. A large export business was conducted with other European countries and the United States. The business remained directly in the Alluaud family until about 1876, when it was taken over by Charles Field Haviland. Marked examples of the Alluaud company are rarely found in this country although a few marks were used which are shown here (see Charles Field Haviland).

Mark 1, "FA," ca. before 1876.

Mark 2, "AF," ca. before 1876.

Mark 3, "AF" monogram, ca. before 1876.

Aluminite

René Frugier was the owner of a porcelain factory which was known by the name of "Aluminite." This word refers to the special porcelain cookware the company manufactured. The company was established about 1900. It survived World War I and II, but it was eventually taken over by the Haviland Company about 1964 (d'Albis and Romanet, p. 152). A variety of marks was used, but dating is inexact. Most reflect the period of the 1920s. Few examples are found in this country. The mark shown here incorporates the initials of René Frugier, but the "G" is unexplained.

"FRG, Limoges, France,"
ca. 1920s.

Henri Ardant

The Ardant company was noted for its artistic production which seems not to have been geared to export to the United States. A distinctive "bird on a branch" mark was used by the company which was in business from about 1859 until the early 1880s.

Bird on a branch, ca. 1859 to early 1880s.

B. H.

These initials printed inside a small shield compose an underglaze white ware mark. This is not the mark used by H. Balleroy. Very few pieces have been seen with this stamp. From examples, the mark was in use during the 1920s.

Underglaze white ware mark in green, unidentified factory, ca. 1920s.

H. Balleroy

Henri Balleroy was associated with Mandavy and Mavaleix from about 1901 until 1908. In 1908, Henri and his brother, Antoine, formed a company. They manufactured decorative accessories and table wares. In the first edition, two other marks were attributed to this firm. Later research indicates that those are the marks of other factories (see B. H. above and Blakeman & Henderson under Major Limoges Companies).

The white ware mark is "B & Cie," which should not be confused with the Bernardaud mark, "B. & Co." The only decorating mark noted for Balleroy is Mark 2, shown below, which includes the Balleroy name.

Mark 1, underglaze white ware mark in green, ca. 1908 – late 1930s.

Mark 2, overglaze decorating mark, ca. 1908 – late 1930s.

George Bassett

The George Bassett company was a New York-based importing firm. Factories in Limoges and Austria produced table wares designed for the American market and stamped them with the Bassett mark. Pieces do not have a white ware mark, but were decorated at the factory which produced them. From examples, the time period for this firm would be the late 1800s until World War I, coinciding with the time when several American businesses were engaged in the porcelain importing trade in both Limoges and Austria. Bassett china is not particularly scarce, but it is also not particularly collectible. Examples are not in the form of art objects or decorative accessories. Rather, floral transfer patterned table china is found which is of interest primarily if one is attempting to match a particular pattern. Value for Bassett china, however, should be in a comparable category with other dinner ware patterns of the same era.

Overglaze import mark in red or green, ca. late 1800s – 1914.

Boisbertrand

A banner mark was used by the Boisbertrand company which operated from about 1884 until the late 1930s. Boisbertrand was associated with several different people during those years. Lack of examples with the factory's mark indicates that the production was not geared to export to the United States.

"LIMOGES" printed inside banner, ca. late 1920s.

Burley & Tyrell

"B T Co." was the importing mark used by the Chicago-based Burley & Tyrell Company. Burley & Tyrell imported Limoges and other European porcelain. The porcelain was decorated by the manufacturing company, and the Burley and Tyrell mark may appear with a white ware mark of some Limoges factory or alone. The firm was in business around 1912 in Germany (Röntgen, p. 389), thus the pre World War I years should reflect a similar time period for the company's Limoges mark.

Overglaze importing mark in green, "B T & Co.," pre World War I.

C. et J.

These initials are the basis for an overglaze decorating mark in red. The studio is unidentified.

Overglaze decorating mark in red, ca. late 1800s – 1914.

Chabrol Frères and Poirer

This Limoges company was in business from about 1917 until the late 1930s.

Wings and star mark, ca. 1920s.

Chapus & Ses Fils

A white ware mark with the initials, "M L," was used by this factory between 1928 and 1933. An overglaze decorating of "Astral Limoges" was also used (d'Albis and Romanet p. 238). An example sent to me by a collector of a factory decorated dinner ware pattern was marked only with the white ware mark and an overglaze mark of "Limoges France."

Mark 1, underglaze mark of "Limoges France."

Chauffraisse, Rougerie & Co.

"L. Hermitage" with initials, "C R," for Chauffraisse and Rougerie, compose a mark used by the factory during the late 1920s. The company was in business only from 1925 to the mid 1930s.

"L. Hermitage" mark with "CR," ca. late 1920s.

Comte D'Artois

An overglaze mark composed of a crown and "Comte D'Artois" was used by an unidentified company as a stamp on Limoges porcelain. The mark is usually found without any other mark, but one example had an importing mark for "Gimbel Brothers, Limoges" (see that mark in this chapter). It is possible that Gimbel Brothers may be the source of the "Comte D'Artois" mark. Relatively few examples are seen, but the mark was probably in use from the 1930s or after. The mark, however, should never be confused as being a mark used by the first Limoges factory which was under the protection of the Comte d'Artois!

Overglaze decorating mark in gray-green, 1930s and after.

Créange, Henri

Créange was a negotiant for Limoges porcelain (Lesur and Tardy, p. 111). That is, he was an intermediary between factories and exporters. An Old Abbey trade mark was shown by Lesur and Tardy to have used by Créange ca. 1907. D'Albis and Romanet (p. 192), however, indicate that Latrille Frères used an Old Abbey mark and that the name actually refers to the factory which had been an abbey at one time. Examples with the Old Abbey mark shown by Lesur and Tardy often do have the white ware mark used by Latrille Frères (see Latrille Frères under Other Limoges Companies). Another version of an Old Abbey mark was found in conjunction with the "HC" monogram mark shown below for Créange. That mark of crossed swords was attributed to Créange in the first and second editions. Recently, however, examples of Granger's white ware mark and the crossed swords Old Abbey mark have been found. The Old Abbey mark shown by Lesur and Tardy for Créange was one I listed for Granger in the first edition, a banner type mark. But this mark was deleted for Granger in the second edition. To summarize, no Old Abbey mark is attributed to Créange. The Old Abbey banner mark is attributed to Latrille Frères, and the Old Abbey crossed swords mark is attributed to J. Granger (see J. Granger under Other Limoges Companies). Créange's monogram mark is considered an exporting mark, and thus may be found with perhaps either Old Abbey mark, although I have not seen any examples with the Créange monogram and the Old Abbey banner mark. Few examples of the Créange mark are seen.

Mark 1, underglaze white ware mark in green, ca. 1907 – 1914.

F & Co.

A mark incorporating these initials was found on a Bird of Paradise transfer patterned dinner ware.

Underglaze white ware mark in green with "L" over initials and "Made in France," ca. 1920 and after.

André François

This company was in business from about 1919 until the mid 1930s. Lack of examples indicates the factory evidently exported little, if any, porcelain to the United States.

Underglaze white ware mark in green, ca. after 1919 to mid 1930s.

G D with a Bee

These initials separated by a bee form an unidentified overglaze decorating mark.

Overglaze decorating mark in orange, early 1900s.

G. I. D. with Tower

The first letter of these initials could be an "S" rather than "G" because the letters are somewhat smudged. The mark is an unidentified underglaze white ware mark.

Underglaze white ware mark in green, ca. 1910 – 1930.

Gimbel Brothers

Like other American department stores, Gimbel Brothers, in New York City, imported Limoges porcelain. The mark shown includes "Limoges" as well as the store's name, indicating a special arrangement with some factory to imprint china with the Gimbel mark.

Overglaze importing mark in gray-green, ca. 1930s.

H & C

This underglaze white ware mark is unidentified. It is not a Haviland mark, and it does not seem to be associated with Hinrichs & Co., who were New York-based china importers.

Underglaze white ware mark in green with one line and "LIMOGES," (not a Haviland mark,) ca. 1880s – 1891.

Robert Haviland

Robert Haviland was the grandson of Charles Field Haviland. He established his own porcelain company around 1924. He was not connected with Haviland and Company or Theodore Haviland. He also did not become the successor to his grandfather's firm (see Charles Field Haviland under Major Limoges Companies). Robert Haviland did, however, purchase the Charles Field Haviland back mark from the Gérard and Abbot company (GDA) in 1941. That mark has been used by his company since that time. (See Gérard, Dufraisseix, and Abbot under Major Limoges Companies). Robert Haviland was associated with Le Tanneur until about 1948, and with C. Parlon from 1949. The company is currently in operation.

Mark 1, underglaze white ware mark in green or overglaze decorating mark, after 1924.

Mark 2, overglaze mark in brown, ca. late 1920s – 1948.

Mark 4, overglaze decorating mark, after 1949.

Mark 3, overglaze decorating mark in red, "CH. FIELD HAVILAND" in double circle, after 1941.

L. B.

These initials form an unidentified white ware mark. The mark was on an example with a Borgfeldt decorating mark.

Underglaze white ware mark in green, ca. 1910 – 1920s.

Raymond Laporte

Raymond Laporte was in business from about 1883 until 1897. Very few examples are found with the Laporte marks which were in the form of a butterfly. The marks seem to indicate the change in U. S. tariff laws of 1890 because Mark 1 does not include "France."

Mark 1, butterfly with initials "RL/L," ca. 1883 – 1890.

Mark 2, overglaze decorating mark in red, butterfly or insect with initials and "LIMOGES FRANCE," ca. 1891 – 1897.

F. Legrand

The Legrand company manufactured table wares during the 1920s, but eventually the factory diverted its production to industrial porcelain.

Underglaze white ware mark in green, star between two crescent shapes with "LIMOGES, FRANCE," ca. 1920s.

J. Mc. D. & S.

These initials are unidentified, but they are found as an exporting mark on china made by various companies in Europe and Japan during the latter part of the nineteenth century. Danckert (p. 242) shows these initials as an unidentified mark found on German china during the 1880s. The company either substituted its mark or had its mark added to china also made by Limoges factories. If there is a white ware mark, in addition to the J. Mc. D. & S. mark, the company which used the white ware mark probably also decorated the china. A new mark is shown in this edition of the J. Mc. D. & S. mark as part of a Tressemann & Vogt overglaze decorating mark (see Mark 3).

Mark 1, overglaze exporting mark in red, initials written in script form in an oval shape, 1880s – 1890s.

Mark 2, overglaze exporting mark in dark red, crown with initials and "Limoges," after 1890 – 1914.

Mark 3, overglaze exporting mark in purple in conjunction with the T. & V. bell mark, ca. 1891 – 1914.

A. Pillivuyt

A mark of "France Unique" with "AP & F" was used by the A. Pillivuyt factory. This Limoges company was in business from 1913 until 1936 (d'Albis and Romanet, p. 241).

Mark, ca. 1920s.

Pitkin & Brooks

This Chicago-based retailer was in business from 1872 until 1938. The company imported and decorated china. Their "P & B Limoges France" mark was applied to china made in Limoges and imported by the company. See an example made by Bawo & Dotter which also is stamped with the Pitkin & Brooks importing mark.

Overglaze importing mark in red, early 1900s to 1914.

Charles Serpaut

Before establishing his own company about 1920, Charles Serpaut worked for the Bernardaud factory (d'Albis and Romanet, p. 115). Serpaut's company was continued by his son until the late 1950s. The mark shown is circa 1920s – 1930s. After that time, an overglaze full name printed mark was used.

Underglaze white ware mark in green, ca. 1920s-1930s.

Teissonnière, Jules

White wares and decorative accessories were made by this factory from about 1908 until the 1940s.

Mark 1, initials in center of double circle with "PORCE- LAINES D'ART" printed inside circle, ca. 1908 – 1940s.

Mark 2, initials in shield, "PORCELAINES D'ART," "MADE IN LIMOGES FRANCE," ca. 1908 – 1940s.

Léon Téxeraud

Table china and decorative accessories were made by Téxeraud during the 1920s.

Mark 1, "EL TE" over "LIMOGES, FRANCE, UNIQUE," ca. 1920s.

Mark 2, "L. T." over "LIMOGES, FRANCE," ca. 1920s.

Union Limousine

This factory began operation about 1908, and it is still in business today. The mark shown here is from the 1930s – 1950s period.

Underglaze white ware mark in green, ca. 1930 – 1950s.

Noel Villegoureix & Cie.

Few examples are found with the Villegoureix mark. The company was in business from about 1919 until the mid 1920s.

Letter "V" in fancy shield, ca. 1920s.

Wanamaker's

An importing mark for the Philadelphia-based Wanamaker's department store is often found on china with other Limoges marks

Overglaze importing mark in green, early 1900s.

Miniatures in Limoges Porcelain

Limoges Miniatures

After my second edition was published in 1992, I began to receive inquiries about Limoges miniatures. Collectors wanted to know the history and value of these small items which include a variety of objects ranging from decorative plates to furniture, as well as small hinged boxes. I had not written about Limoges miniatures because they generally did not fall within the scope of my time frame, that is, the mid to late 1800s until 1930. I also considered miniatures to be a separate collecting category which I did not encounter frequently among collectors of Limoges porcelain. This stemmed from the age and nature of miniatures, generally mid 1900s, and often considered souvenir china.

Because of the numerous inquiries on the subject, I have decided to include a section on Limoges Miniatures in this edition. This section is not meant to be a thorough study of Limoges miniatures, but rather it is intended to answer some basic questions of collectors regarding Limoges miniatures, to show some examples of several types of Limoges miniatures, and to address another facet of Limoges porcelain collecting.

Miniatures have always fascinated collectors. They have been made throughout history, but their appeal is not confined to any one time. Miniatures are unique in that they re-create life-size objects in one to three inches, often with exquisite detail. They can be found in many mediums, including glass, wood, metals, and ceramics. These pieces also offer the collector the opportunity for a collection which does not take up a lot of space. Porcelain miniatures, and Limoges miniatures specifically, are made as both souvenir items and commemorative items as well as objects which reflect a collector's interest, such as dollhouse furniture.

Although some Limoges miniatures may have been made prior to World War II, most are from the 1950s and later. Strolling down the streets of Limoges, one can encounter numerous displays of a variety of miniatures which are currently being made. In the photographs that follow, three different types of miniatures are shown: hinged boxes, cobalt blue and gold miniatures, and polychrome miniatures which are commemorative of people, events, or works of art. The hinged boxes and cobalt blue pieces are modern, that is made during the 1980s and 1990s. Many of the polychrome pieces are earlier, circa 1940s – 1950s. Most Limoges miniatures do not have an identifiable factory mark. "Limoges, France," is often the only mark, sometimes accompanied by "peint a main" or "rehaussé a main" ("hand painted" or "embellished by hand"). Some of these marks are shown with the examples. Perhaps a more detailed study on Limoges miniatures can be made later, if collector interest warrants.

Limoges Boxes

The most interest today in Limoges miniatures centers around the small hinged boxes which are being made by numerous Limoges companies specifically for American importers. These boxes range in size from 1½" to 3". They are found in hundreds of shapes, from animals to hat boxes and shoes to fruit and vegetables, to mention just a few. Major department stores in the United States as well as countless mail order catalogs offer wide assortments of these modern boxes. Collectors can even join clubs devoted to the subject. Of course, today, one can access the Internet and find numerous offerings as well.

These new boxes began to be on the market during the mid 1980s, and today, one can rarely open a catalog without finding a large selection. The history of today's Limoges boxes can be traced to an American importer, Richard Sonking, who started a company in New York to import Limoges porcelain in the early 1970s. In the mid 1970s, having seen a collection of new snuff boxes made in Limoges which were based on eighteenth century boxes, Sonking was one of the first to import them to the United States, according to Furio's book, *The Limoges Porcelain Box,* 1998 (pp. 142, 143). The success of the boxes was increased by prestigious retailers, such as Gump's, offering them through their mail order catalog.

Although the history of small boxes can be traced back hundreds of years when they were used for snuff "tabatière", medicines "boîtes a pilules", and even beauty patches, and reflected tastes of that era in their decoration, today's Limoges boxes reflect modern life styles. They are made in an unending variety of shapes, and there is literally some offering to commemorate or celebrate almost anyone's vocation, hobby, special event or even favorite animal! The boxes are generally hand-painted and accented with gold. Hinged boxes are considered superior to those without hinges. The boxes vary widely in price, ranging from $30.00 – 40.00 to $200.00 – 300.00. The price differentials basically derive from the selling source. Those offered over the Internet may be quite inexpensive, while those from catalogs range from $150.00 – 200.00. Some department stores' selections and up-scale catalog prices are generally in the $200.00+ category.

I do not intend to offer a complete discussion of these modern boxes because there are too many to cover adequately in one section of this book. I would just like to make a few comments about these boxes so that basic questions of collectors about them can be addressed.

First, these boxes are not antique, although they can now be found at antique shops and antique shows. But many collectors, finding the boxes at those locations, write to find out the age and history of them. Today's boxes are collectible on their own merits because they reflect contemporary interests and life.

Second, Limoges boxes made during the 1980s and 1990s are too new to have acquired age value. To compute value based on scarcity or rarity of a box is not yet possible because those aspects have not been established. When it is possible to make a survey of the original prices of the boxes and the prices paid for the same box on the secondary market at a later time, then a value range can be made. The same is true for scarcity and rarity which cannot be established unless information is compiled from the manufacturers or importers documenting how many of a certain box were made. In the last several years, some advertisements do note "limited edition" in their advertisements. Knowing that only a few hundred boxes were made in a particular shape will be useful to determine the value for future collectors. But until those questions can be answered about the vast majority of other Limoges boxes, the value is essentially what one pays for a box at a department store or from a mail order outlet. If you purchase a box at an antique shop or show on the secondary market, then simply consult your current catalogs to find similar boxes and current prices.

Third, it is not possible to identify many of the manufacturers of the boxes, because, as was the custom historically, many small Limoges factories simply marked the china with "Limoges, France." While some catalogs mention specific Limoges factories, most do not. Any box that is not marked "Limoges, France" is not a Limoges box. The fake Limoges mark is also found on new boxes (see that mark in Chapter 1). Today, the market is also filled with unmarked boxes which are usually very inexpensive. Do not be misled by these other examples. You will find that the quality of porcelain and the workmanship is not on a par with true Limoges boxes.

Only a small selection of Limoges boxes, made basically in geometric shapes with floral decoration, are included here for the purpose of showing one category of Limoges miniatures. Marks are also shown for many of the examples. Boxes with the same marks are shown together. Most of the marks are unidentified. "Limoges, France," written in several different versions, is on all of the boxes. Some of the marks are stamps, and others are hand painted. One "Limoges, France" mark can be identified as a mark used by the Castel company. All of the marks are contemporary, from the 1980s and 1990s. The floral decorations and gold accents are hand painted. Individual price ranges are not quoted because prices are generally in the same category. The current prices for the boxes shown here range from **$150.00 – 175.00** for the floral decorated pieces and **$200.00 – 250.00** for those with figural decoration.

Plate 1090. Oblong box, 2⅜" l x ¾" w; pink floral design; marked "LIMOGES," printed in a crescent shape over "FRANCE," with "Peint Main," and artist's initials.

Mark, in green, on oblong floral decorated box.

Plate 1091. Rectangular box, 2" l x 1⅜" w; a yellow butterfly decorates lid; "LIMOGES FRANCE" mark, in green, with "Hand Painted by Paris Style."

Plate 1092. Fan-shaped box, 2⅝" l x 1⅛" h; marked similarly to preceding box, with "Porcelaine décorée à la main Paris Style," in gold, written in French.

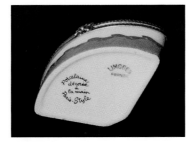

Mark on fan-shaped box.

Plate 1093. Square box, 1¾" sq.; red and yellow flowers; marked like preceding, without "Paris Style."

Mark on square box.

Plate 1094. Hexagon-shaped box, 2" d, 1½" h; marked with "LIMOGES" over "FRANCE," and the same "Paris Style" mark as on the fan-shaped box.

Mark on hexagon-shaped box.

Plate 1095. Box, 2½" l x 1½" w; transfer figural reserve on lid; deep rose-colored finish; marked, "PATE DE LIMOGES" (Paste of Limoges).

Mark on preceding box at left.

Plate 1096. Basket-shaped box, 1¼" h x 11¼" w; marked, "Limoges France peint main P.V."

Plate 1097. Rectangular box, 4" l x 2¾" d; butterflies and flowers; marked, "Dessiné et peint entièrement à la maion par Le Tallec à Paris France," with artist's initials and gold roses.

Mark on rectangular box.

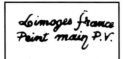

Mark on basket-shaped box.

Plate 1098. Heart-shaped box, 1⅝" l x 1¾ w; marked "Peint Main Limoges France."

Plate 1099. Oval box, 2⅛" l x 1½" w; hand-painted figure of a little girl wearing a hat and carrying a large ring or hoop; marked with "Hand Painted Rochard," and a mark for the factory, "Porcelaine Industrielle de Limousine."

Mark on oval box.

Mark on heart-shaped box.

Plate 1100. Pear-shaped box, 1⅜" d; marked on the interior base, "Limoges France Peint main ROCHARD" (mark not shown).

Plate 1101. Shell-shaped box, 1¾" d; red and green floral décor; marked, "CHAMART FRANCE," in a double circle with a *fleur-de-lis* in the center, and "LIMOGES" printed below mark.

Mark on shell-shaped box.

Plate 1102. Box, 4⅛" l x 1¼" w; gold diamond pattern; marked, "Limoges" over "FRANCE," with a star on either side of the mark. This is an underglaze mark, in green, used by the Castel company. "Sebering" is printed in gold, probably the mark of the exporter.

Castel underglaze mark on box at left.

Plate 1103. Square box, 1¾" sq.; gold and multi-colored flowers; Castel mark with the artist's initials.

Mark on square box.

Plate 1104. Serpentine-shaped box, 2" l; multi-colored floral decoration; marked "Limoges France," mark in green and artist signed in blue (mark not shown); trunk-shaped box, 2", marked "Made in France," with the same artist's initials as on square box at left (mark not shown).

Plate 1105. Rectangular box, 2⅛" l x 1½" w; transfer portrait of Madame Pompadour; Castel mark (see at top right).

Plate 1106. Serpentine-shaped box, 2" l x 1½" d; pink roses and gold scrolled designs; Castel mark with "LIMOGES" over "Made in France" in gold.

Mark on serpentine-shaped box at left.

Cobalt Blue Miniatures

The rich cobalt blue color has always been popular with porcelain collectors, and manufacturers of Limoges miniatures have taken that into account for their production. The examples here all have gold decoration, either in the form of flowers or figures. The decoration is generally of a decal or stenciled type. There is a wide variety of miniature objects in the following pictures. But you will notice that the decoration is not as varied. The same figural themes appear on many different items. Thus, in terms of collecting, one might concentrate on one type of figural decoration. Instead of dividing the china by type of object, I have grouped the pieces by figural or floral themes.

The cobalt blue pieces were made during the 1980s and after. A group of marks precedes the pictures, and the particular mark is noted in the caption for the object. Most of the marks are unidentified. The Castel company, however, is well represented in this section. Prices for cobalt blue miniatures range between $20.00 and $40.00, depending on the item and the decoration. Prices are quoted with the descriptions for the pieces. You will see that several boxes are also shown in this section because of their cobalt decoration. Since they are not hand-painted and also because they usually do not have hinged lids, their price is only a fraction of that of the boxes shown in the preceding section.

Marks on Cobalt Blue Miniatures

Mark A, monogram in a circle with "LIMOGES FRANCE" and "LIMOGES" over "FRANCE." This is a mark used by the Prevot company. This mark is also sometimes accompanied with "Limoges" over "France," printed in script form, see Mark C.

Mark B, "LIMOGES" over "FRANCE" with "Made in France."

Mark C, Prevot monogram mark with "Limoges" over "France."

Mark D, Castel mark, crown and house with "PORCE-LAINE LIMOGES CASTEL FRANCE."

Mark E, Castel mark, like Mark D, but without house.

Mark F, "LIMOGES FRANCE," printed within a double circle.

Mark G, "Porcelaine d'Art Limoges France," with "R" and "P" initials.

Mark H, "LIMOGES" over "France."

Mark I, "Limoges" over "France," printed in script form.

Mark J, "LIMOGES" printed over a line with "FRANCE," printed below the line.

Examples of Cobalt Blue Miniatures

"Stepping Out" decoration

A gentleman is taking the hand of the lady in this scene. She is holding a cane embellished with a ribbon.

Plate 1107. Vase, 1¾" h x 2" d; Mark G. **$20.00 – 25.00.**

Plate 1108. Shell dish, 2⅛" d; Mark B. **$20.00 – 25.00.**

Plate 1109. Stove, 2½" h; Mark F. **$28.00 – 32.00.**

Plate 1110. Swan, 2⅝" x 2¼"; Mark E. **$20.00 – 25.00.**

Plate 1111. Tea or coffee pot, 2½" h; Mark B. **$30.00 – 35.00.**

Plate 1112. Pitcher, 2" h; Mark E. **$18.00 – 22.00.**

Plate 1113. Oval box, 1½" x 1¼" x ¾", hinged lid; note that the scene is reversed on this piece, with the lady on the left. Mark J. **$25.00 – 35.00.**

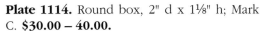

Plate 1114. Round box, 2" d x 1⅛" h; Mark C. **$30.00 – 40.00.**

"Proposal" Decoration 1

Popular decorations on the cobalt blue and gold miniatures are two proposal scenes. In this version, the gentleman is on his knee scene, proposing to the lady with the cane.

Plate 1115. Bell, ⅞" h x ⅞" d; Mark J. **$15.00 – 18.00.**

Plate 1116. Top hat, 1" h; Mark F. **$20.00 – 24.00.**

Plate 1117. Briefcase, 1⅜" w by 1¼" h; Mark J. **$28.00 – 32.00.**

Plate 1118. Television set, 3" h x 1½" w; Mark B. **$15.00 – 20.00.**

Plate 1119. Heart-shaped boxes, 2¼" d x 1⅜" h; this pair of boxes illustrates both the "Proposal 1" scene on the left and another "Stepping Out" scene on the right. In this second "Stepping Out" scene, the lady does not have a cane; perhaps she is the same as the lady in the second "Proposal" scene. Mark E. **$30.00 – 40.00 each**.

"Proposal" Decoration 2

In this proposal scene, the gentleman is on his knee, but the lady is holding a fan.

Plate 1120. Serpentine-shaped box, 2" l x 1⅜" d, hinged lid; Castel mark like Mark E, but without, "Porcelaine," and with "22 K Gold." **$45.00 – 55.00.**

Plate 1121. Square box, 1½" sq. x ¾" h, hinged lid; Mark J. **$30.00 – 40.00.**

Plate 1122. Round box, 1⅞" d x 1" h; Mark A. **$25.00 – 35.00.**

Plate 1123. Vase, 1⅝" h x 1¾" w, Mark B. **$20.00 – 25.00.**

Plate 1124. Vase, 2¾" h; a wide gold band and stenciled floral designs decorate neck; Mark A. **$20.00 – 25.00.**

Plate 1125. Bowl, 2½" d; Mark E. **$18.00 – 22.00.**

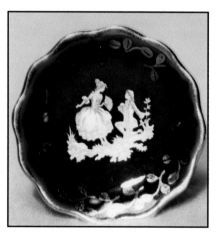

Plate 1126. Bowl, 2½" d; pattern accented with floral designs around inner border; Mark B. **$18.00 – 22.00.**

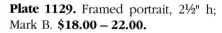

Plate 1127. Heart-shaped box, 2⅜" w x 1" h; Mark B. **$25.00 – 35.00.**

Plate 1128. Boot, 2½" h; mark B. **$10.00 – 12.00.**

Plate 1129. Framed portrait, 2½" h; Mark B. **$18.00 – 22.00.**

"Courting Scene"

Polychrome scenes can also be found on the cobalt blue and gold Limoges miniatures. Similar "courting" scenes, some based on the works of famous artists, like Boucher, are also shown in the following section of polychrome miniatures.

Plate 1130. Footstool-shaped box, 2⅜" d x 1½" h; Mark B. **$30.00 – 40.00.**

Floral and Other Decorations

Plate 1131. Set of furniture: 3 chairs, ⅞" h; table, ¾" x 1⅜" d; sofa, 1½" l; easy chair, ⅝" w; ottoman, ½" d x ⅜" h. Each piece marked "Limoges, France." **$90.00 – 100.00 set.**

Plate 1132. Pitcher, 2" h; Mark J. **$20.00 – 25.00.**

Plate 1133. "Lourdes" pitcher, 1¾" h; Mark A. **$15.00 – 20.00.**

Plate 1134. Slipper, 1⅝" l; Mark I. **$12.00 – 15.00.**

Plate 1135. High heel shoe, 1¾" l; Mark J. **$18.00 – 24.00.**

Plate 1136. Victorian style shoe, 1⅝" l; Mark J. **$18.00 – 24.00.**

Plate 1137. Cannon, 1" l; Mark F. **$15.00 – 18.00.**

Plate 1138. Scales, 2¼" w x 1⅝" h; Mark H. **$25.00 – 30.00.**

Plate 1139. Egg-shaped box, 2⅜" l x 1½" h; Mark E. **$40.00 – 50.00.**

Plate 1140. Boot, 2" h; Mark I. **$20.00 – 25.00.**

Plate 1141. Fish, 2" l; Mark F. **$20.00 – 25.00.**

Polychrome Limoges Miniatures

Compared to the cobalt blue miniatures, this group of miniatures has polychrome decoration, that is, a variety of colors. Polychrome miniatures can be found in a number of different objects like the cobalt blue miniatures. Table china items, such as pitchers, cups and saucers, and trays, as well as shoes, vases, and furniture were, and continue to be, made. Small plates, ranging in size from one to three inches, however, are the most representative of this category of miniatures, and the examples in this section are confined to the plates. You will see in the captions that some of these plates were actually designed as pins to wear. Slide fasteners were attached to the backs of the plates for this purpose.

Collectors are attracted to the miniature plates for several reasons. Size is, of course, the primary consideration. Among collectors of miniatures, the particular size which qualifies an object as "miniature" may vary. Miniatures are designed to replicate in a small size a normal size object. For china, the size is generally from one to three inches. Similar decorations, particularly on small plates, however, can be found in larger sizes, from four to six inches. Such pieces are often included in the collections of miniature plates because they are decorated similarly. I have limited the maximum size illustrated here, however, to three and one-half inches, with most examples being one to two inches in diameter. The first two photographs illustrate displays of some contributors' collections. It is obvious that a great many pieces can be enjoyed without using a lot of space.

The second point of interest for collectors is the particular decoration on the plates. The photographs are arranged according to decoration which spans a wide variety of themes. Romantic themes depicting couples in eighteenth century dress are very popular, as are portraits of historical figures. Miniature plates decorated with pastoral scenes, religious subjects, specific locations or structures, and designs to commemorate special events are also commonly found. Many of these colorful decorations were based on the original paintings of famous artists. Sometimes that artist's name is on the front of the piece. That "signature" is often incorrectly interpreted as the painter who decorated the porcelain. "Boucher," "Fragonard," "Lebrun," and "Watteau," famous eighteenth century artists, are just a few of the names encountered. Some of these names are visible on the pieces in the photographs. Copies of their paintings have historically been made into transfers or decals to decorate china. Such decorations continue to be used today. Although there are miniature paintings on porcelain which are truly hand painted, the decoration on Limoges polychrome miniatures is either a transfer or decal. Many of the transfers are highlighted with white enamel. When "hand painted" appears as a mark on the plate, it refers only to the enamel accents or gold embellishment.

The polychrome miniatures are also rarely marked with any stamp except "Limoges, France," printed in a number of different styles. A specific company cannot usually be linked to this type of mark. A few identified factory marks on the miniature plates shown here include "Porcelaine Artistique" marks used by Fontanille & Marraud and marks of Paul Pastaud (see the marks of these companies in Chapter 3); and marks of the Castel factory (see the Castel marks in this chapter under Cobalt Blue and Gold Miniatures). Marks for the miniature plates are not illustrated, but the mark on each piece is described in the caption of the photograph. Some of the "Limoges, France" marks are the same as or similar to the marks shown for the Cobalt Blue and Gold Miniatures. It is difficult to pinpoint specific dates or even time periods for the polychrome miniature plates. This type of miniature, however, generally pre-dates the cobalt blue and gold pieces and the Limoges boxes. The oldest examples shown here were made during the 1930s. Others are from the 1950s and after.

A third reason for the popularity of the miniature plates is cost. Prices, in general, have been quite reasonable, allowing collectors to amass a large number of decorative subjects for relatively small investments. A price range is not quoted for each individual plate, because to date there is no established secondary market price. Prices vary widely, according to source. Prices paid by collectors for the plates shown in the following photographs range on average from $20.00 to 60.00, with the higher prices paid for portraits of historical figures. But the same pieces are often priced considerably more if offered for sale at an antique show or shop. At those locations, the minimum price tag is $45.00 – 60.00 and can go well over $100.00. Collector interest, as with any antique, also influences the price. While collectors have paid $20.00 – 60.000 at one time for a certain decoration, they have also told me that they have purchased similar pieces at a later time for much higher prices, over $150.00. Other collectors have related purchasing these items for just a few dollars at yard sales and flea markets. Like the Limoges boxes, a thorough study regarding prices asked and paid for the miniature plates is necessary before usable value ranges can be established. That study must take into account such factors as popularity and rarity of decoration subject.

Examples of Polychrome Miniatures

Plate 1142. Showcase of miniatures

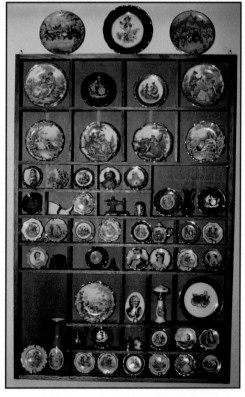

Plate 1143. Showcase of miniatures

Floral and Bird Themes

Plate 1144. Plate, 1" d; multi-colored flowers, framed by a dark wine-colored border; marked "Limoges, France," in gold, a modern mark.

Plate 1145. Plate, 2" d; red-orange flowers and green leaves on a white ground; marked "P. Pastaud LIMOGES (FRANCE)," in blue, after 1950.

Plate 1146. Plate 1¾" d; peacocks; marked "LIMOGES," over "FRANCE."

Cherubs and Classical Figures

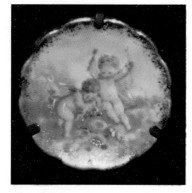

Plate 1147. Cherub plate, 1½" d; marked in green "MADE IN Limoges FRANCE"

Plate 1148. Cherub plate, 1½" d, marked like preceding examples.

Plate 1149. Classical figures, 2½" d, framed by a deep wine border; marked, "Porcelaine Artistique F. M. Limoges, France," in gold, a mark used by Fontanille & Marraud, after 1935.

Plate 1150. Classical figures, 2½" d; a child and two women; Fontanille & Marraud mark, after 1935.

Romantic Themes

Plate 1151. "The Progress of Love" scenes are shown on this and the following three plates. These decorations are transfers, based on the series by the artist Fragonard. He painted the four scenes for Madam Du Barry, the last mistress of Louis XV, but she refused the last two and had him removed from the Court. The originals are in the Frick Collection. Plate, 3¼" d; gentleman serenading a lady; all of the plates are marked in green "MADE IN Limoges FRANCE."

Plate 1152. Plate, 1½" d; couple walking in a garden.

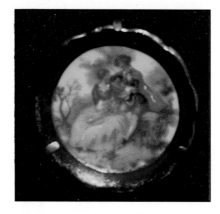

Plate 1153. Plate, 1½" d; couple seated in a garden.

Plate 1154. Plate, 1½" d; couple embracing by a river.

Plate 1155. Plate, 3½" d; couple in a field; the man is holding a shovel; artist signed "Paul" on front, marked in red, "Hand Painted," with an illegible symbol, ca. 1930s.

Plate 1156. Plate 3½" d; the decoration is similar to the preceding piece in color and theme, and the mark and signature are also the same; troubadour and lady.

Plate 1157. Plate, 3½" d; gentleman proposing to a lady (similar to the gold decoration found on the cobalt blue and gold miniatures); royal blue border. Fontanille & Marraud mark, after 1935.

Plate 1158. Plate, 3" d; seated couple, based on a painting by Watteau; marked in dark green "LIMOGES, FRANCE," and in light green "MADE IN Limoges FRANCE."

Plate 1159. Plate, 2¾" d; a gentleman and two ladies seated by a pond; marked "Limoges, France," in black and "Limoges," underlined with "FRANCE," printed below the line, in green.

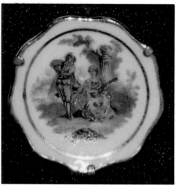

Plate 1160. Pin, 1½" d, with a slide fastener; courting scene portraying a lady strumming a mandolin while the gentleman stands beside her; marked "Limoges, France" in red, ca. 1930s – 1940s.

Plate 1161. Pin, 1½" d; gentleman plays the mandolin for the seated lady; marked "Limoges, FRANCE," in red.

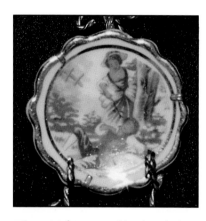

Plate 1162. Pin, 1½" d; a lady is trying to awaken the sleeping gentleman; impressed initials and numbers, "GL 43," in a circle with "MADE IN Limoges FRANCE" mark in green.

Plate 1163. Plate, 1¾" d; a lady leans against a tree with a goat by her side; the gentleman is strumming a musical instrument; marked "Limoges" over "FRANCE" in green.

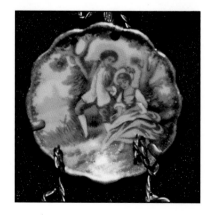

Plate 1164. Pin, 1½" d, with a slide fastener; a lady sits under a tree and a gentleman stands behind her; "MADE IN Limoges FRANCE mark in green.

Plate 1165. Plate, 1¾" d; a lady is serenaded by a gentleman dressed in green; marked "Limoges" over "FRANCE" in green.

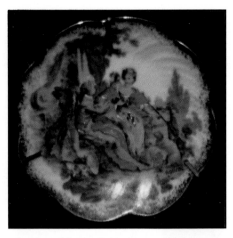

Plate 1166. Plate, 3" d; a pastoral courting scene with sheep in the foreground, based on an original painting by Watteau; marked "LIMOGES, FRANCE" in dark green, and "MADE IN Limoges FRANCE" in light green.

Plate 1167. Pin, 1½" d; a gentleman sits at a lady's feet, a scene based on a painting by Watteau; "MADE IN Limoges FRANCE" mark in green.

Plate 1168. Pin, 1½" d, another Watteau scene portraying a gentleman offering some flowers to the lady; marked the same as the Plate 1167 pin.

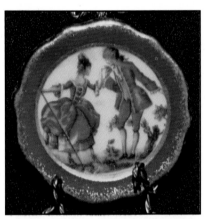

Plate 1169. Plate, 1¾" d; a gentleman is taking the hand of a lady holding a cane; this decoration is similar to the gold transfer, "Stepping Out," in the section on cobalt blue and gold miniatures; marked "LIMOGE FRANCE" (note lack of an "s" on Limoges).

Plate 1170. Plate 3⅜" d; couple in a garden by a fence; marked "P. Pastaud, Limoges France," in green.

Portraits of Historical Figures

Plate 1171. Plate, 1½" d; transfer portrait of "Josephine," marked "MADE IN Limoges FRANCE" in green.

Plate 1172. Plate, 2½" d; transfer portrait of "Josephine," marked with the impressed initials and numbers "GL 43," in a circle and "MADE IN LIMOGES FRANCE," printed in gold.

Plate 1173. Plate, 1½" d; transfer portrait of "Napoleon" marked the same as Plate 1172.

Plate 1175. Plate, 1½" d; transfer portrait of "Madame DuBarry," last mistress of King Louis XV; marked "MADE IN Limoges FRANCE."

Plate 1176. Plate, 3¼" d; transfer portrait of "Marie Antoinette," deep wine-colored border frames portrait; marked "Made in LIMOGES FRANCE" in green.

Plate 1174. Plate, 2½" d, "Napoleon" portrait surrounded by a bright pink border. Fontanille & Marraud scroll mark in gold.

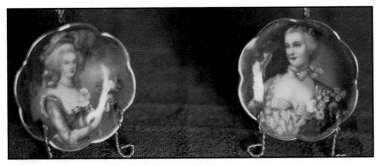

Plate 1177. Plates, 3" d; left: transfer portrait of "Marie Antoinette," based on the original painting by Madame Lebrun; right: transfer portrait of "Madame Pompadour," based on the original painting by Boucher; marked "MADE IN LIMOGES FRANCE" in light green, and "LIMOGES, FRANCE" in dark green.

Plate 1178. Plate, 3½" d; transfer portrait of "Marie Antoinette," marked "O.R." with "FRANCE," over initials, and "LIMOGES" below initials in gold.

Religious Themes

Plate 1179. Plate, 1½" d; transfer portrait of Christ wearing a crown of thorns; marked "MADE IN Limoges, FRANCE."

Plate 1180. Plate, 1½" d; "Fatima," scene commemorating apparitions of the Virgin Mary to shepherd children in Portugal, in 1917; marked "P. Pastaud Limoges France" in blue, and "Limoges" in black.

Plate 1181. Plate, 1½" d; "Sacred Heart Christ," marked "MADE IN Limoges FRANCE" in green.

Plate 1182. Plate 3½" d; "Madonna and Child," based on the original painting by Raffaello; marked "MADE IN LIMOGES FRANCE" in green.

Scenic Themes

Plate 1183. Plate, 1½" d; an autumn village scene; a winter church scene (not shown) is a companion to this piece; marked in green, "MADE IN LIMOGES FRANCE."

Plate 1184. Plate, 1¾" d; "The Gleaners," based on the original art by Millet; marked "LIMOGES FRANCE" within a circle, in green.

Plate 1185. Plate, 1¾" d; a man and woman are praying in a field; the transfer is based on "Angelus," an original painting by Millet; Castel mark in green, "Limoges," underlined, with "FRANCE," printed below the line and a star on either side of the line.

Plate 1186. Plate 1⅝" d; ship scene; cobalt blue border; marked "Limoges," underscored with "FRANCE" below the line.

Plate 1187. Pin, 1⅝" d; ships on the high sea; marked "LIMOGES," over "FRANCE" in red.

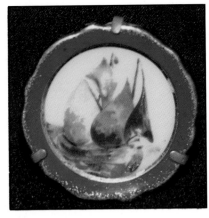

Plate 1188. Plate, 1¾" d; the same ship transfer is on this piece as on the preceding pin, but it is trimmed with a cobalt blue border; marked "Gsco" over "Limoges," over "France" in blue-green.

Plate 1189. Plate, 3¼" d; colorful horse and carriage scene; Fontanille & Marraud scroll mark in brown with "Label de Qualite," after 1935.

Plate 1190. Plate, 3¼" d; a companion scene to the piece in Plate 1189 and marked the same.

Plate 1191. Plate, 3½" d; horse and carriage scene, enameled over transfer, marked "MADE IN LIMOGES FRANCE" in green.

Plate 1192. Plate, 3¼" d; "Daimler 1886," is printed below this "horseless" carriage, probably a centennial souvenir plate; Fontanille and Marraud scroll mark.

Plate 1193. Plate, 1½" d; "Cries of London," based on the engravings by Frances Wheatley, for the Adams China Co., in England, in 1895. The series illustrates the hawkers and vendors selling their wares in the streets of London. "MADE IN Limoges FRANCE" mark in green.

Plate 1194. Plate 1½" d; windmill scene, marked "P. Pastaud, Limoges, France" in blue-green, and "Limoges, France" in black.

Plate 1195. Plate, 1½" d; souvenir for the French city, Cannes, famous for its film festivals which were instituted in 1946; "GL" over "43," impressed within a circle, and "Limoges" underscored with "FRANCE" printed under the line.

Bibliography

d'Albis, Jean. *Haviland.* Paris, Dessait et Tolra, 1988.

d'Albis, Jean and Céleste Romanet. La Porcelaine de Limoges. Paris: Editions Sous le Vent, 1980.

Alfassa, Paul et Jacques Guérin. *Porcelaine Française Du XVIIe Au Milieu Du XIXe Siècle.* Paris: Aux Editions Albert Levy, 1931.

Auscher, E. S. *Comment Reconnaitre Les Porcelaines et Les Faiences.* Paris: Librairie Garnier Press, 1914.

———. *A History and Description of French Porcelain.* Translated and edited by William Burton, F.C.S. London: Cassell and Company, Limited, 1905.

Barber, Edwin Atlee. *The Ceramic Collector's Glossary.* New York: The Walpole Society, 1914.

Blanc, Edmond. *Visite D'Une Fabrique De Porcelaine.* Paris: Imprimerie Charles-Lavauzelle & Cie, 1944.

Boger, Louise Ade. T*he Dictionary of World Pottery and Porcelain.* New York: Charles Scribner's Sons, 1971.

Brelingard, Desire. *Histoire Du Limousine.* Paris: Presses Universitaires De France, 1950.

Brunhammer, Yvonne, et. al. *Art Nouveau Belgium France: Catalog of an Exhibition Organized by the Institute for the Arts, Rice University, and the Art Institute of Chicago.* Rice University: Institute For the Arts, 1976.

Celebrating 150 Years of Haviland China 1842 – 1992, Villa Terrace Decorative Arts Museum, Milwaukee, Wisconsin, June 28-October 4, 1992. Haviland Collectors International Foundation, 1992.

Céramique Impressionniste: L'Atelier Haviland De Paris-Auteuil 1873-1882. Paris: Ancien Hotel Des Archevéques De Sens; Décembre 1974, Février 1975.

Chaffers, William. *Handbook of Marks and Monograms on Pottery and Porcelain.* Revised Edition. London: William Reeves, 1968.

———. *Marks & Monograms on Pottery and Porcelain.* Vol. 1. 15th Revised Edition. London: William Reeves, 1965.

Charles, Bernard H. *Pottery and Porcelain A Dictionary of Terms.* London-Vancouver: David & Charles, 1974.

Clark, Eleanor. *Plate Collecting.* Secaucus, New Jersey: Citadel Press, 1976.

Collard, Elizabeth. *Nineteenth-Century Pottery and Porcelain* in Canada. Montreal: McGill University Press, 1967.

Cox, W. E. *The Book of Pottery and Porcelain.* Vol. 1. New York: L. Lee Shepard Co., Inc., 1944.

Cushion, John Patrick (in collaboration with W. B. Honey). *Handbook of Pottery and Porcelain Marks.* London: Faber & Faber, 1956.

———. *Pocketbook of French and Italian Ceramic Marks.* London: Faber & Faber, 1965.

Danckert, Ludwig. *Handbuch des Europäischen Porzellans.* Munchen: Prestel-Verlag, 1954.

———. *Handbuch des Europäischen Porzellans.* Munchen: Prestel Verlag, 1984.

Eberlein, Harold Donaldson and Roger Wearne Ramsdell. *The Practical Book of Chinaware.* Philadelphia and New York: J. B. Lippincott Company, 1925 and 1948.

Ernould-Gandouet, Marielle. *La Céramique en France au XIXe Siècle.* Paris: Gründ, 1969.

Fontaine, Georges. *La Céramique Française.* Paris: Presses Universitaires De France, 1965.

Furio, Joanne. *The Limoges Porcelain Box.* Lake Warren Press, 1998.

Gaston, Mary Frank. *The Collector's Encyclopedia of Limoges Porcelain.* Paducah, Kentucky: Collector Books, 1980; Revised Prices, 1984.

———. *The Collector's Encyclopedia of Limoges Porcelain, Second Edition.* Paducah, Kentucky: Collector Books, 1992.

———. *Haviland Collectibles and Objects of Art.* Paducah, Kentucky: Collector Books, 1984.

———. "Limoges Porcelain: French and American Decoration." *The Antique Trader Weekly,* July 3, 1985.

———. "Limoges Porcelain." *The Antique Trader Price Guide To Antiques,* April, 1986.

Gérard, Dufraisseix & Cie. Catalog. *The Ch. Field Haviland Limoges China,* n. d. (circa 1890s).

Grollier, Charles de. *Manuel de L'Amateur De Porcelaines.* Paris: Auguste Piccard Ed., 1922.

Haggar, Reginald G. *The Concise Encyclopedia of Continental Pottery and Porcelain.* New York: Hawthorne Books, Inc., 1960.

Hamer, Frank. *The Potter's Dictionary of Materials and Techniques.* London: Pitman Publishing; New York: Watson-Guptill Publications, 1975.

Head, Margaret G. *Charles Field Haviland China Identification Guide,* Book 1. Monroe, Michigan: E. C. Kraus Printing, 1982.

Hillier, Bevis. *Pottery and Porcelain 1700-1914.* New York: Meredith Press, 1968.

Honey, W. B. *European Ceramic Art.* Faber & Faber, 1952.

———. *French Porcelain of the 18th Century.* London: Faber & Faber, 1950.

How Things Work. Vol. II. Geneva: Bibliographisches Institut and Simon and Schuster Inc., American Edition, n. d.

Jacobsen, Gertrude Tatnall. *Haviland China: Volume One.* Des Moines, Iowa: Wallace-Homestead, 1979.

Jamreau, Guillaume. *Les Arts Du Feu.* Paris: Presses Universitaires, 1948.

Jenkins, Dorothy H. *A Fortune in the Junk Pile.* New York: Crown Publishers, Inc., 1963.

Klapthor, Margaret Brown. *Official White House China.* Washington, Smithsonian Press, 1975.

Kovel, Ralph M. and Terry H. Kovel. *Dictionary of Marks: Pottery and Porcelain.* New York: Crown Publishers, Inc., 1953 and 1972.

———. *Know Your Antiques.* New York: Crown Publishers. Inc., 1967 and 1973.

———. *Kovel's New Dictionary of Marks.* New York: Crown Publishers, Inc., 1986.

Landais, Hubert. *La Porcelaine Française XVIIIe Siècle.* Paris: La Librairie Hachette, 1963.

Le Duc, Geneviève et Henri Curtil. *Marques Et Signatures De La Porçelaine Française.* Paris: Editions Charles Massin, 1970.

Les Porcelaines Françaises. Avant-propos de Mm. Marc H. Gobert et M. Leyendecker. Paris: Tardy, 1950.

Lesur, Adrien and Tardy. *Les Porcelaines Françaises.* Paris: Tardy, 1967.

"Limoges ou Deux Siècles de Porcelaine." Pp. 87-103 in *Revue des Industries d'art Offrir.* August, 1978.

Limoges, Raymonde. *American Limoges.* Paducah, Kentucky: Collector Books, 1996.

"Limoges, Une vie de porcelaine," Comité National d'Expansion de la Porcelaine de Limoges, n.d.

Mackay, James. *Dictionary of Turn of the Century Antiques.* London: Ward Lock Limited, 1974.

Mésière, Ernest (ed.). *Porcelaine Theodore Haviland.* Paris: Haviland Company, 1912.

Meslin-Perrier, Chantal. "Pouyat 1835 – 1912," Exposition Musée National Adrien Dubouche, Limoges, 24 Juin-30 Septembre, 1994.

O'Gorman, Joseph H. *Limoges – Its People – Its China.* Prepared by the editor of the B. & D. Bulletin. New York: Bawo & Dotter, 1900.

Penkala, Maria. *European Porcelain A Handbook for the Collector.* Second

Edition. Rutland, Vermont: Charles E. Tuttle, 1968.

Platt, Dorothy Pickard. *The Story of Pickard China.* Hanover, Pennsylvania: Everybody's Press, Inc., 1970.

Poche, Emanuel. *Porcelain Marks of the World.* New York: Arco Publishing Co., Inc., 1974.

Reed, Alan B. Collector's *Encyclopedia of Pickard China.* Paducah, Kentucky: Collector Books 1995.

Rhodes, Daniel. *Stoneware and Porcelain: The Art of High-Fired Pottery.* Philadelphia: Chilton Company, 1959.

Robert, Maurice. *Les Poteries Populaires Et Les Potiers Du Limousin Et De La Marche (du XVIIIe siècle a nos jours).* Paris: Editions F. E. R. N., 1972.

Röntgen, Robert E. *Marks on German, Bohemian and Austrian Porcelain 1710 to the Present.* Exton, Pennsylvania: Schiffer Publishing Co., 1981.

Rothenberg, Polly. *The Complete Book of Ceramic Art.* New York: Crown Publishers, 1972.

Savage, George. *Ceramics For The Collector An Introduction to Pottery and Porcelain.* New York: The Macmillan Company, 1949.

————. *Seventeenth and Eighteenth Century French Porcelain.* New York: Macmillan Company, 1960.

Savage, George and Harold Neuman. *An Illustrated Dictionary of Ceramics.* New York: Van Nostrand Reinhold Company, 1974.

Schleiger, Arlene. *Two Hundred Patterns of Haviland China,* Books I, II, III, IV. Omaha, Nebraska: Arlene Schleiger, 1973, 1970, 1969, 1968.

Thorn, C. Jordan. *Handbook of Old Pottery & Porcelain Marks.* New York: Tudor Publishing Company, 1947.

Tilmans, Emile. *Porcelaines De France.* Paris: Editions Mondes, 1953.

Van Patten, Joan F. *The Collector's Encyclopedia of Nippon Porcelain.* Paducah, Kentucky: Collector Books, 1979.

Weiss, Gustav. *Book of Porcelain.* Translated by Janet Seligman. New York: Praeger Publishers, Inc., 1971.

Wood, Serry. *Haviland, Limoges.* Watkins-Glen, New York: Century House, 1951.

Wynter, Harriet. *An Introduction to European Porcelain.* London: Arlington Books, 1971.

Young, Harriet. *Grandmother's Haviland.* Second Revised Edition. Des Moines, Iowa: Wallace-Homestead Book Co., 1970.

Index and Cross Reference
to Companies, Initials, and Symbols

Italic plate numbers after company names identify examples; page numbers at end of each entry show histories and marks.

Index To Limoges Artists
Numbers refer to Plate numbers.

A number of artists' names are found on factory and studio decorated Limoges porcelain. Some are seen more than others, such as *Dubois, Duval, Luc, Max, Muville,* and *René.* Unfortunately, we have no specific information about these artists. We do not know if they worked primarily for one factory or studio. Because the same names are found on china made by different companies, it seems that some may have moved from one factory or studio to another, or even worked independently.

The signatures are not always clear. The names were usually written with quite a flourish, and it is easy to misinterpret the letters. For example a "y" on the end of a name may look like a "t" or vice versa. In general, French signatures consist of just one name. An initial rarely precedes the artist's name. The signatures appear on the front of pieces 99 percent of the time. Occasionally, an artist's initials may be on the back of a piece. A list of Limoges artists with examples in this edition are listed below with reference to the plate numbers that exhibit their work; the themes of decoration and the Limoges companies with examples by that artist follow in parentheses. This type of listing may help individualize the painter, especially those artists with more than one example.

It was common practice, at factories and art studios, for individuals to specialize in a particular form of decoration. For decorators with several examples, only one decorative theme may be associated with the name. For others, a variety of subjects are found. Remember, many of the artist signed pieces are not completely hand painted. Rather, they are part transfer and part hand colored or touched up with enamel, the *mixtion* decorating method. This practice explains the multiple versions of the same cavalier, cherubs, flowers, and figural scenes.

Some pieces of china are discovered which have a recognized signature of a Limoges artist, but there is no factory mark on the china, or the factory mark is not visible. Two such pieces which fall into this category are shown on the following page. The signatures on these objects are familiar and recognizable ones found on many pieces of Limoges porcelain. Because we do not know the factory mark, the pieces could not be placed with the other photographs under a specific Limoges company or maker. These examples are too unusual however, not to include, and they seem to be a fitting end for this edition!

Plate 1196. Lamp, 24" h; red and yellow roses painted on a light gray-green ground; handles and trim heavily gilded; artist signed, "René." $2,200.00 – 2,400.00.

Plate 1197. Urn, 7" h; dragon shaped handles and other fittings are gilded brass; courtship scene and flowers decorate reserved on front framed with gold scroll designs; artist signed, "Luc." $1,400.00 –1,600.00.